ICSA Study Text

Certificate in Corporate Governance

ICSA Study Text

Certificate in Corporate Governance

Paul Moxey

icsa

The Governance
Institute

First published 2018
Published by ICSA Publishing Ltd
Saffron House
6–10 Kirby Street
London EC1N 8TS

© ICSA Publishing Ltd, 2018

Typeset by Frances Rooney.

British Cataloguing in Publication Data
A catalogue record for this book is available from the British Library.

ISBN   9781860727252

Contents

How to use this study text — ix

Syllabus outline — xi

Acronyms and abbreviations — xiv

About the author — xvi

Acknowledgements — xvii

Part one:
General principles of corporate governance — 1

1 Introducing corporate governance — 3

1. Introduction — 3

2. Overview of corporate governance — 3

3. Principles, codes and provisions — 15

2 Corporate governance development in the UK — 24

1. Introduction — 24

2. Corporate governance development for UK listed companies — 24

3. Approaches in different sectors — 35

3   Corporate governance development around the world   **45**

1.   Introduction   45

2.   Governance code development around the world   45

3.   G20/OECD Principles of Corporate Governance   46

4.   The European approach   47

5.   The South African approach   50

6.   The Mauritian approach   50

7.   The US approach   51

4   Current corporate governance issues and likely developments   **58**

1.   Introduction   58

2.   Overview of issues in corporate governance   58

3.   Ethics, values, culture and behaviour   67

4.   Value creation and corporate or organisational purpose   71

5.   Sustainability and corporate social responsibility (CSR)   75

Part two:
The board, shareholders and corporate reporting   **81**

5   The board   **83**

1.   Introduction   83

2.   The role of boards   83

3.   The structure and composition of boards and the roles of different directors   86

4.   Board committees   92

5.   Directors' remuneration   94

6   Shareholders   **100**

1.   Introduction   100

2.   Engaging with shareholders   100

3.   Shareholder rights   102

4.   Shareholder responsibilities   103

5.   The complex investor chain linking providers of capital with companies   105

6.   Problem areas   109

7   Corporate reporting   **117**

1.   Introduction   117

2.   Overview of corporate reporting   117

3.   The contents of the annual report   122

4.   Practical issues   128

Part three:
Board procedure and governance administration   **131**

8   Good meeting practice   **133**

1.   Introduction   133

2.   Overview of good board meeting practice   133

3.   Key documents that should be available to boards   138

4.   Running the meeting   144

9   Board effectiveness   **149**

1.   Introduction   149

2.   The company secretary   149

3.   Board effectiveness evaluation   153

4.   Problem areas for directors and boards in effective decision making   159

Part four:
Risk governance   **165**

10   Board oversight of risk   **167**

1.   Introduction   167

2.   What is risk?   168

3.   Important risk terms   169

4.   What is the board's role in relation to risk?   173

11   Sources of risk   **184**

1.   Introduction   184

2.   Categories of risk   184

3.   Learning from the 2008 financial crisis and corporate failures   189

4.   Boards as a source of risk   194

12   Practical issues in the management of risk   **199**

1.   Introduction   199

2.   Managing risk   199

3.   Dealing with malpractice   209

4.   Assurance on risk management   217

     Test yourself answers   223

     Glossary   234

     Index   238

How to use this study text

This study text has been developed to support ICSA's Level 4 Certificate in Corporate Governance and includes a range of navigational, self-testing and illustrative features to help you get the most out of the support materials.

The text is divided into three main sections:

◆ introductory material
◆ the text itself
◆ reference material.

The sections below show you how to find your way around the text and make the most of its features.

Introductory material

The introductory section includes a full contents list and the aims and learning outcomes of the qualification, as well as a list of acronyms and abbreviations.

The text itself

Each part opens with a list of the chapters to follow, an overview of what will be covered and learning outcomes for the part.

Every chapter opens with a list of the topics covered and an introduction specific to that chapter.

Chapters are structured to allow students to break the content down into manageable sections for study. Each chapter ends with a summary of key content to reinforce understanding.

Features

The text is enhanced by a range of illustrative and self-testing features to assist understanding and to help you prepare for the examination. You will find answers to the 'Test Yourself' questions towards the end of this text. Each feature is presented in a standard format, so that you will become familiar with how to use them in your study.

These features are identified by a series of icons.

The text also includes tables, figures and other illustrations as relevant.

Reference material

The text contains a range of additional guidance and reference material, including a glossary of key terms, footnotes and a comprehensive index.

Stop and think

Test yourself

Making it work

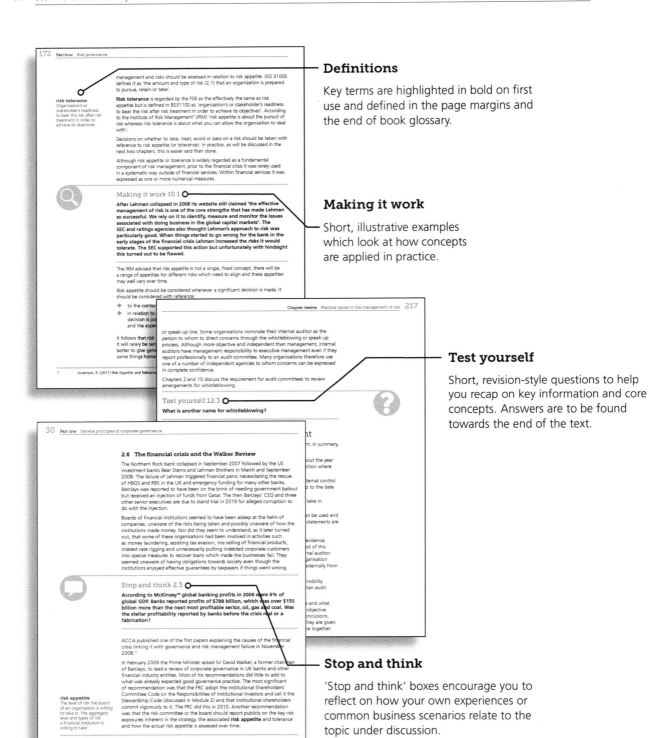

Definitions

Key terms are highlighted in bold on first use and defined in the page margins and the end of book glossary.

Making it work

Short, illustrative examples which look at how concepts are applied in practice.

Test yourself

Short, revision-style questions to help you recap on key information and core concepts. Answers are to be found towards the end of the text.

Stop and think

'Stop and think' boxes encourage you to reflect on how your own experiences or common business scenarios relate to the topic under discussion.

Syllabus outline

Qualification outline and aims

The Level 4 Certificate in Corporate Governance has been designed to help students develop a strong core knowledge of corporate governance principles which can be applied across the private and other sectors. The course focuses on the roles and responsibilities of the board and company secretary and introduces students to other key features of corporate governance including risk management and corporate reporting. On completion of the course students will be qualified to support their organisation in dealing with legal, financial and regulatory issues.

Part one: General principles of corporate governance — 27.5%

Overview

The module introduces the general principles of corporate governance including what corporate governance is, its purpose, scope, history and why it is important. It also looks at how different countries have approached corporate governance, including the use of non-statutory governance codes and where it fits in a country's regulatory framework.

Learning outcomes

In this module you will:

1. Understand how corporate governance principles and provisions are developed and their importance in the global economy.
2. Know the main features of key corporate governance codes nationally and internationally.
3. Be able to evaluate different approaches to corporate governance.
4. Understand key issues and developments in corporate governance.

Part two: The board, shareholders and corporate reporting – 25%

Overview

This module explains the two key groups of actors in corporate governance: boards of directors and shareholders and what they do.

The module explores the roles of the board, the different types of director and the main board sub-committees. It will examine the different types of shareholder and some of the complexities of the share ownership chain. It also gives an introduction to corporate reporting, including its purpose and content.

Learning outcomes

In this module you will:

1. Understand the roles and responsibilities of boards, board members and board committees.
2. Know about the role of shareholders in the corporate governance system.
3. Understand key aspects of corporate reporting.

Part three: Board procedure and governance administration – 20%

Overview

This module explains what should make good board and sub-committee meeting procedure and the governance administration to enable it.

The module outlines what happens in board and sub-committee meetings, the information needed to enable good meetings, the timetable, key board documents and the pivotal role of the company secretary.

Learning outcomes

In this module you will:

1. Understand aspects of good meeting practice and the key documents required.
2. Understand the role and responsibilities of the company secretary.
3. Know the principles of board evaluation.

Part four: Risk governance – 27.5%

Overview

The module explains the role of the board in relation to ensuring the resilience of the organisation and its strategy in the face of risk. It considers the main aspects of risk management including risk appetite, identification, assessment and treatment or transfer.

Learning outcomes

In this module you will:

1. Understand key risk concepts, categories and sources of risk.
2. Understand the role of the board and sub-committees in relation to risk.
3. Know about key practical issues affecting boards and challenges to having effective risk management.

Acronyms and abbreviations

ACCA	Association of Chartered Certified Accountants
AIM	Alternative Investment Market
BIS	Department for Business, Innovation and Skills
BOFI	Banks and Other Financial Institutions
BSI	British Standards Institute
CA2006	Companies Act 2006
CBI	Confederation of British Industry
CCG	Clinical commissioning group
CDO	Collateralised debt obligation
CEO	Chief Executive Officer
CFO	Chief Financial Officer
CIPFA	Chartered Institute of Public Finance Accountants
COSO	Committee of Sponsoring Organizations of the Treadway Commission
CSR	Corporate Social Responsibility
DB	Defined benefit (pension)
DC	Defined contribution (pension)
EC	European Commission
ECGI	European Corporate Governance Institute
ESG	Environmental, Social and Governance
EU	European Union
FCA	Financial Conduct Authority
FRC	Financial Reporting Council
FSA	Financial Services Authority (replaced in 2013 by the Prudential Regulation Authority and the Financial Conduct Authority)
FSB	Financial Stability Board

G20	Group of Twenty
GAAP	Generally Accepted Accounting Principles (US) Practices (UK)
GRI	Global Reporting Initiative
HMRC	Her Majesty's Revenue and Customs
IIA	Institute of Internal Auditors
IAASB	International Auditing and Assurance Standards Board
IAS	International Accounting Standards
IASB	International Accounting Standards Board
IBE	Institute of Business Ethics
IFAC	International Federation of Accountants
IFC	International Finance Corporation
IFRS	International Financial Reporting Standards
IPR	Intellectual Property Rights
IRM	Institute of Risk Management
ISA	International Standards on Auditing
LSE	London Stock Exchange
LTCM	Long term capital management
LTIPs	Long Term Incentive Plans
NED	Non-executive director
OECD	Organisation for Economic Cooperation and Development
OEIC	Open-ended investment company
PCT	Primary care trust
PRA	Prudential Regulation Authority
ROA	Return on assets
ROE	Return on equity
SFIs	Standing Financial Instructions
SIFI	Systemically Important Financial Institutions
SME	Small or medium enterprise
SOs	Standing orders
SSAP	Statement of Standard Accounting Practice
TI	Transparency International
UNEP	United Nations Environmental Programme

About the author

Paul Moxey is visiting professor of Corporate Governance at London South Bank University, a fellow of scenario and futures consultants SAMI Consulting, co-chairman of the CRSA Forum, a network of practitioners established in 1994 interested in the behavioural and cultural aspects of risk, governance and organisational performance, an editorial board member of Governance and a trustee of a sailing club.

He is an acknowledged expert in corporate governance and risk management and for 13 years led the Association of Chartered Certified Accountants' (ACCA) global thought leadership on these subjects. He now writes and works with boards and executive teams in assessing and improving their culture and governance and risk management practices to improve organisational performance and resilience.

Paul is also a chartered accountant and a chartered secretary and earlier in his career was a company secretary and CFO of a UK plc. He has also been chairman of a small housing charity, and has founded and sold a successful small retail and printing business.

Other publications include:

- Incentivising Ethics
- Capitalism and the Concept of the 'Public Good'
- Culture and Channelling Corporate Behaviour Summary of Findings.
- Creating Value Through Governance: Towards a New Accountability.
- Risk and Reward Tempering the Pursuit of Profit.
- Corporate Governance and the Credit Crunch

Acknowledgements

I would like to thank in particular Professor Andrew Chambers for his support, wisdom, friendship and encouragement over the last 20 years, the late Sir Adrian Cadbury for his guidance and the following for their inspiration, the knowledge they shared and the many discussions we enjoyed which enabled me to write this book:

Roger Adams, Prof Jill Atkins, Roger Barker, Adrian Berendt, Peter Bonisch, Peter Brown. John Bruce, Peter Butler, Mark Cardale, Julia Casson, Prof. Colin Coulson Thomas, Alan Craft, Steve Connor, Tim Crowley, Frank Curtiss, Brandon Davies, John Davies, Prof Ken d'Silva, Neville De Spretter, Jeff Earl, Sam Eastwood, Gillian Fawcett, Philippa Foster Back, Jane Fuller, Prof Bob Garratt, Seamus Gillen, Jason Gold, Pam Gordon, Jonathan Hayward, Garry Honey, Catherine Howarth, Jonathan Hunt, David Jackson, Rachel Jackson, Prof. Mike Jones, Prof. Guy Jubb, Paul Johnson, Con Keating, Judge Mervyn King, Dan Konigsberg, Tim Leech, Malcolm Lewis, Astrid Lovelace, Bob May, Prof. Michael Mainelli, Paul Makosz, Prof. Terry McNulty, David Meggitt, Caroline Oliver, Michael Parker, Spencer Pickett, Chris Pierce, Sallie Pilot, Sarah Pumfrett, Jenny Rayner, Val Richardson, Prof. Jeff Ridley, Gill Ringland, Dan Roberts, Ian Rusby, Ken Rushton, Marc Schelhase, Pauline Schu, Saskia Slomp, Anita Skipper, Ruth Steinholtz, Dan Swanson, Aziz Tayyebi, Bernard Taylor, Lorraine Thomas, Vincent Tophoff, Sean Tulley, Shann Turnbull, Jorgen Walter Hansen, John Watts, Mark Wearden, Mike Weaver, Simon Webley, Stephen White, Carolyn Williams, Graham Wilson, Sarah Wilson, Phil Winrow and John Yarnold.

Finally I should like to thank my wife, Hilary, and family for their enthusiasm throughout.

The King IV Report on Corporate Governance for South Africa 2016, Copyright and trade marks are owned by the Institute of Directors in Southern Africa, and the IoDSA website link is: http://www.iodsa.co.za/?page=AboutKingIV

The 7 principles of public life on p.36-37 contains public sector information licensed under the Open Government Licence v3.0.

Corporate Governance Guidance and Principles for Unlisted Companies in the UK on p.40-43 © 2018 Institute of Directors. All rights reserved. https://www.iod.com/

The company mission of Panasonic on p.73-74 © Panasonic Corporation http://panasonic.com/global/home.html

The Principles for Responsible Investment on p.76 © PRI Association. For more information, visit: www.unpri.org

Figure 4.1 on p.79 Copyright © December 2013 by the International Integrated Reporting Council ('the IIRC'). All rights reserved. Used with permission of the IIRC. Contact the IIRC (info@theiirc.org) for permission to reproduce, store, transmit or make other uses of this document.

The failure of HBOS plc (HBOS) on p.155-156 © https://www.bankofengland.co.uk

Every effort has been made to locate and acknowledge sources and holders of copyright material in this text. In the event that any have been inadvertently overlooked, please contact the publisher.

Part one

Chapter one
Introducing
corporate
governance

Chapter two
Corporate
governance
development in the
UK

Chapter three
Corporate
governance
development
around the world

Chapter four
Current corporate
governance
issues and likely
developments

General principles of corporate governance

Overview

This part, the first of four, introduces the general principles of corporate governance, including what corporate governance is, its purpose, its scope, why it is important and its history. It also looks at how different countries have approached corporate governance, including the use of non-statutory governance codes and where it fits into a country's regulatory framework.

Chapter 1 provides an overview of the subject, explains the difference between principles and provisions and introduces some key governance theories. Chapter 2 considers how corporate governance has developed in the UK, first for companies listed on the London Stock Exchange and then in other sectors.

Chapter 3 explains how governance has developed globally. Finally, Chapter 4 covers some of the current key issues in governance and likely developments, including the influence of recent scandals, the importance of ethics, values and corporate culture, what organisations exist to do and their place in society and corporate social responsibility.

Learning outcomes

At the end of this part, students will be able to:

◆ understand what corporate governance is, its purpose and its importance in the global economy;

◆ appreciate the key generally accepted principles of corporate governance;

◆ understand how regulators use codes, principles and provisions to ensure good corporate governance;

◆ appreciate key corporate governance theories;

◆ understand how corporate governance has evolved in the UK, in different sectors and globally;

◆ consider the main features of key corporate governance codes nationally and internationally;

◆ demonstrate an ability to evaluate different approaches to corporate governance;

◆ identify the key issues and developments in corporate governance;

◆ demonstrate an understanding of ethical theories and the importance of ethics in corporate governance;

◆ understand the main aspects of corporate social responsibility;

◆ appreciate the role of corporate governance in value creation; and

◆ identify some of the limitations of corporate governance.

Chapter one
Introducing corporate governance

CONTENTS

1. Introduction
2. Overview of corporate governance
3. Principles, codes and provisions

1. Introduction

This chapter introduces **corporate governance** and key terms. It provides an overview of corporate governance, explains the difference between principles and provisions and introduces some key governance theories.

corporate governance
The system by which organisations are directed and controlled.

2. Overview of corporate governance

2.1 The origins of corporate governance

Corporate governance is about the way corporate organisations are directed, controlled and accountable. It is a relatively new term, seldom used before 1990, although the need for it is old, going back to when people first organised themselves into groups to perform a task on behalf of others and the owners of assets entrusted those assets to others. Today, good corporate governance is seen as essential to ensuring organisations have the right strategy, are not risk prone, manage their assets and protect them from loss, behave ethically, do not have excessive executive pay and prepare **financial statements** which present the organisation's financial position to its owners fairly, truly and understandably. For companies the owners are **shareholders**. While governance is principally about how **boards** of corporate organisations operate as they direct and control them, corporate governance is also seen as important to ensuring that owners of organisations hold those running them to account.

financial statements
A financial report by an organisation prepared for an external audience complying with applicable law and standards setting out its financial position at a particular date, its income and expenditure and movements of funds for a particular period.

shareholder
Real and legal person who holds shares in a company, and generally whose name would appear on the company share register.

board
The governing body of a company and many other organisations whose members are directors.

2.2 Definitions of corporate governance

Probably the most widely used definition of corporate governance is 'the system by which companies are directed and controlled'. This is the definition given in the 1992 'Report of The Committee on the Financial Aspects of Corporate

Cadbury Report
The 1992 Report of The Committee on the Financial Aspects of Corporate Governance.

Governance'.[1] The report, widely known as the **Cadbury Report** after its chairman, was the response to the collapses of Coloroll and BCCI in 1990. Coloroll was a company that grew rapidly as an acquirer of other companies and used creative accounting to give, falsely, the impression of healthy profit. BCCI (Bank of Credit and Commerce International) revealed massive losses following financial crimes.

Cadbury Committee
The Committee on the Financial Aspects of Corporate Governance.

While this committee (the **Cadbury Committee**) was working, the Daily Mirror boss Robert Maxwell was found to have stolen from the Mirror pension fund and the fruit trading company turned conglomerate Polly Peck also collapsed with debts of £1.3 billion. There was much concern about the state of UK plc so the Cadbury Report in 1992 attracted much interest.

The Cadbury Committee, chaired by the late Sir Adrian Cadbury[2], gave birth to modern corporate governance and was a voluntary initiative by the Financial Reporting Council, the London Stock Exchange and the accountancy profession. The most influential part of the report was the two-page Code of Best Practice, widely referred to as the Cadbury Code. It was the first corporate governance code and, although not part of this syllabus, is well worth reading and is still relevant.

Another influential interpretation of corporate governance comes from the Group of Twenty (G20)/Organisation of Economic Cooperation and Development (OECD) Principles of Corporate Governance 2015[3], which explains it 'involves a set of relationships between a company's management, its board, its shareholders and other stakeholders' and 'provides the structure through which the objectives of the company are set, and the means of attaining those objectives and monitoring performance are determined'.

accountability
The quality or state of being accountable meaning an obligation or willingness to accept responsibility and to give account for actions and omissions.

The British Standard Institute (BSI), in its Governance Standard[4], emphasises **accountability**, saying it is the 'system by which the whole organization is directed, controlled and held accountable to achieve its core purpose over the long term'. The most recent definition from what is likely to be a highly influential source comes from the the King IV Report on Corporate Governance™ for South Africa 2016[5], which says corporate governance 'is the exercise of ethical and effective leadership by the governing body towards the achievement of the following governance outcomes: an ethical culture, good performance, effective control and legitimacy'.

1   1992 Report of 'The Committee on the Financial Aspects of Corporate Governance', Gee and Co. Ltd London (widely known as the Cadbury Report), www.ecgi.org/codes/documents/cadbury.pdf

2   Sir Adrian Cadbury at the time was the chairman of Cadbury Schweppes. In addition to the Financial Reporting Council, the London Stock Exchange and representatives from the accountancy profession the committee's other members included representatives from the CBI (Confederation of British Industry), the Bank of England, the Hundred Group of Finance Directors, the Institutional Shareholders' Committee, the Law Society, the Institute of Directors and academia.

3   OECD (2015) G20/OECD Principles of Corporate Governance, www.oecd.org/daf/ca/Corporate-Governance-Principles-ENG.pdf

4   British Standards Institution (2013) *Code of practice for delivering effective governance of organizations*, BSI Standards Limited.

5   The King IV Report on Corporate Governance for South Africa 2016, copyright and trade marks are owned by the Institute of Directors in Southern Africa, http://www.iodsa.co.za/?page=AboutKingIV

Stop and think 1.1

We have seen a number of definitions of corporate governance. Which is most relevant for you in your organisation? Would you define it differently?

2.3 The purpose of corporate governance

As corporate governance developed in the 1990s and 2000s, there continued to be some diversity of opinion about its purpose. Broadly the question was whether corporate governance is about compliance or about performance. An example of thinking that it is primarily about compliance is to be found in the introduction of the 2015 Finnish Code of Corporate Governance[6].

Stop and think 1.2

The Finnish Code of Corporate Governance states: 'The purpose of the Corporate Governance Code is to harmonise the procedures of listed companies and to promote openness with regard to corporate governance and remuneration. From the perspective of a shareholder and an investor, the Corporate Governance Code increases the transparency of corporate governance and the ability of shareholders and investors to evaluate the practices applied by individual companies. The Corporate Governance Code also provides investors with an overview of the kinds of corporate governance practices that are acceptable for Finnish listed companies.'

Does this make governance an end in itself? What is the value for organisations of having good corporate governance if corporate governance does not help make them perform better in the medium to long term?

In the UK none of the codes before 2010 stated the purpose of corporate governance. During the 1990s and 2000s there was concern in many circles that corporate governance was mostly about compliance with **provisions** in governance codes and that such compliance was divorced from the important business of running a successful organisation. The seventh version of the UK governance code in 2010, published by the Financial Reporting Council (FRC), corrected this and made it clear that the purpose was about more than compliance: 'The purpose of corporate governance is to facilitate effective, entrepreneurial and prudent management that can deliver the long-term success of the company.'

provisions
More prescriptive elements of a code, other guidance, law or regulation requiring adherence.

Despite this clarity, comments in the media, surveys and research which focuses on compliance and the engagement of some investors, suggest that many still,

6   Securities Market Association Finnish Corporate Governance Code 2015, https://cgfinland.fi/wp-content/uploads/sites/39/2018/04/hallinnointikoodi-2015eng.pdf

value
A person, team or organisation's judgement of what is important in work and/or in life.

sustainable value
Value which is created which is sustainable, and unlikely to be eroded, over many years.

management
The planning, execution and monitoring of the activities of an organisation in order to achieve objectives.

executive
A senior manager with delegated authority and accountability for one or more functions who may also be a director.

director
A formally appointed member of a board.

mistakenly, perceive corporate governance to be a box-ticking exercise and not really relevant to ensuring that organisations create sustainable **value**. The failure in January 2018 of Carillion plc, a UK FTSE 250 construction company, was a salutary reminder that compliance with the UK Corporate Governance Code is no guarantee for shareholders, or any other stakeholder, about the company's health. It is governance performance that matters but assessing performance is not easy. This study text aims to explain how good governance will facilitate effective, entrepreneurial and prudent management that can deliver long-term **sustainable value** and accountability.

2.4 The distinction between corporate governance and management

The Cadbury Report definition could be confused with a definition of **management** and for many people the difference between corporate governance and management may not be obvious. The differences will be explained in subsequent chapters but for now it is important to recognise that corporate governance is essentially about what boards of directors and shareholders do and don't do. Management is about what executives and managers do. Boards generally make decisions as a collective body whereas managers will generally act individually in accordance with what has been delegated by the board. Where an **executive** is also a member of the board of **directors** it can be helpful to think of them having two hats, one for acting as a board member and one for acting as a manager and only one hat can be worn at any one time. When wearing the board member hat the executive is functioning as part of the board, when wearing the manager hat they are acting as a manager.

Test yourself 1.1

What do the definitions of corporate governance and views on its purpose have in common? Do you see any contradictions?

Come back to this question when you reach the middle and end of the text.

2.5 Corporate governance scandals and regulatory responses

In the UK, and to a lesser extent in other countries, corporate governance practices and views on corporate governance have developed in response to various corporate and organisational scandals. As explained above, UK scandals around 1990 led to the first governance code. Since then, further scandals led to new versions of governance codes in the UK and elsewhere intended to address perceived shortfalls in the versions which were current at the time. These scandals and the code changes they brought about are discussed later in the book.

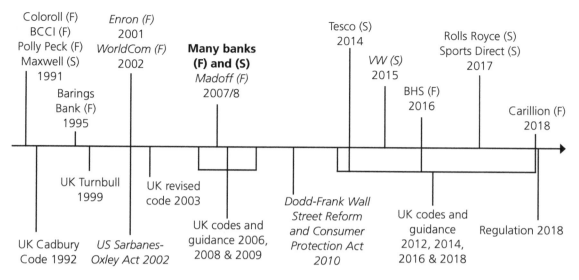

Figure 1.1: Significant corporate failures (f) and scandals (s) and regulatory responses.

2.6 The evolving regulatory background including the company law framework

UK companies are incorporated under the **Companies Act 2006**, which regulates how they are formed, controlled and can be wound up. Other types of organisation also owe their existence to some form of legal framework.

Most large charities are also companies and are subject to the Companies Act and charity law. Public sector organisations such as NHS foundation trusts are established as Public Benefit Corporations under the Health and Social Care (Community Health and Standards) Act 2003 and each trust is established under a separate Establishment Order which is statutory instrument. Local authorities are statutory corporations created under an Act of Parliament. Older universities are corporations established under Royal Charter and newer ones are companies limited by guarantee or Higher Education Corporations under the 1988 Education Reform Act. More detailed consideration of the legal form of these organisations is outside the scope of this text.

All organisations have to operate within the law and, in addition to the legislation which gives them their existence, are subject to other laws and **regulations** such as concerning health and safety, employment and environmental protection, money laundering, commercial contracts, consumer protection and the preparation of financial statements. Companies providing financial services are also subject to financial services legislation and regulation. Public companies listed on the main market of the London Stock Exchange are also subject to the UK Listing Authority **Listing Rules**,[7] **Disclosure and**

Companies Act 2006
An Act of Parliament which consolidated and updated previous companies acts. It is the primary source of company law in the UK and the longest piece of legislation in the history of Parliament.

regulation
A rule or directive made and maintained by the government or other authority.

Listing Rules
These are the obligations issued by the FCA that companies with a listing on the London Stock Exchange have to meet and are based on the minimum EU directive standards.

---

7   FSA (2002) The Listing Rules, The Financial Services Authority, London. https://www.handbook.fca.org.uk/handbook/LR.pdf

Disclosure and Transparency Rules
These are rules of the Financial Conduct Authority (FCA) to implement the EU Transparency Directive and to make other rules to ensure there is adequate transparency of and access to information in the UK financial markets. The Rules apply to companies whose shares have a Premium listing on the London Stock Exchange.

Premium listing
The Listing Rules allow for three types of listing on the London stock Exchange Main Market: Premium, Standard and High Growth Segment. The rules for a Standard listing comply with EU requirements. The rules for a Premium listing are higher than required by the EU. Most UK companies with a listing have a Premium listing for their ordinary shares. The UK Code of Corporate Governance applies to these companies.

principles
The fundamental and foundational high level elements of a code or other guidance.

company law
The set of laws that control how businesses are formed, controlled and wound up.

Transparency Rules in the FCA Handbook and the Takeover Code. Much of UK law, regulations and codes have been influenced by EU directives and recommendations. One of the Listing Rules is a requirement for the large companies with a **Premium listing** (see Chapter 2) to state how they apply the main **principles** in the UK Corporate Governance Code and a statement on whether all the Code provisions have been complied with and, if any have not been complied with, the reasons for non-compliance.

The Companies Act 2006[8] is effectively the foundation on which the UK corporate governance system and its voluntary code of corporate governance is laid. Similarly in other countries, the **company law** framework provides a foundation for their corporate governance codes. The 2006 Act replaced previous Companies Acts and since coming into force has been subject to amendment such as to enact EU Directives. Previous UK codes of governance have not repeated what is contained in the Companies Act or other regulation, and provisions are removed from the Code if legislation is passed. Versions of the UK Code before 2003 included requirements for disclosure of director remuneration but these were removed from the 2003 and subsequent versions following the enactment of the Directors' Remuneration Report Regulations 2002 on disclosure of director remuneration in listed companies. The 2018 Code, however, in Provision 5 paraphrases some of the requirements introduced in the Companies (Miscellaneous Reporting) Regulations 2018[9] which requires companies to report how the directors have had regard for various stakeholder matters in accordance with their duty under s. 172 of the Companies Act 2006 from January 2019.

The UK Companies Act 2006 codified seven duties for directors of companies. These duties are owed by directors to the company rather than anyone else including shareholders. The duties which apply to all directors whether they are executive, non-executive or the chairman are based on, and should be interpreted and applied as, common law rules and equitable principles. A director is a person formally appointed as a director but may also include a person who is a 'shadow director' meaning a person in accordance with whose directions or instructions the directors of the company are accustomed to act (Section 251).

The following is a summary of directors' main duties under the Companies Act. More detailed guidance is available in the ICSA Guidance Note on Directors general duties.[10]

1.   Section 171: to act within their powers in accordance with the company's constitution. A company's constitution is its articles of association. They set out, amongst other things, the powers of directors and directors must only use these powers for the purpose intended. So for, example, the directors

---

8   The Companies Act 2006, www.legislation.gov.uk/ukpga/2006/46/contents

9   The Companies (Miscellaneous Reporting) Regulations 2018, www.legislation.gov.uk/ukdsi/2018/9780111170298

10   ICSA (2015) Guidance Note on Directors general duties, https://www.icsa.org.uk/assets/files/free-guidance-notes/directors-general-duties(1).pdf

should not issue new shares with the intention of frustrating a takeover bid and company funds should only be used for the commercial purpose of the company. Formal procedures should always be followed when a meeting of the board is held.

2. Section 172: to promote the success of the company.
   This is a key section and is discussed in more detail later in this chapter and in Chapter 4.

3. Section 173: to exercise independent judgement.

   Directors must always exercise independent judgement uninfluenced by a director's personal interests, the influence of other directors or the influence of particular shareholders including when they might have been appointing by a particular shareholder or group of shareholders.

   This duty does not apply where a director is acting in accordance with a resolution passed by shareholders in a general meeting or if the director was acting in accordance with the company's constitution. Nor would it prevent a director from acting in accordance with a previous collective board decision.

4. Section 174: to exercise reasonable care, skill and diligence to be exercised to the standard expected of:

   - someone with the general knowledge, skill and experience reasonably expected of a person carrying out the functions of the director; and

   - the actual knowledge, skill and experience of that particular director.

   The standard expected in these two tests is what would be exercised of a reasonably diligent person. The standard that would be expected of a professional, such as an accountant in relation to financial matters, would be higher than that of a lay person.[11]

   This is an important and complex area of law. There are few decided legal cases to assist but the decision in the failure of the merchant bank Barings plc in 1995 is relevant: three directors were disqualified. The Court of Appeal confirmed the High Court judgment[12] in the disqualification case determined:

   - 'Directors have, both collectively and individually, a continuing duty to acquire and maintain a sufficient knowledge and understanding of the company's business to enable them properly to discharge their duties as directors.

   - Whilst directors are entitled (subject to the articles of association of the company) to delegate particular functions to those below them in the management chain, and to trust their competence and integrity to a reasonable extent, the exercise of the power of delegation does not absolve a director from the duty to supervise the discharge of the delegated functions.

---

11   *Dorchester Finance Co v Stebbing* [1989] BCLC 498.

12   *Re Barings Plc, Secretary of State for Trade and Industry v Baker* [1998] BCC 583 at 586 and (No 5) (2000) CA [60].

- No rule of universal application can be formulated as to the duty referred to in (ii) above. The extent of the duty, and the question whether it has been discharged, must depend on the facts of each particular case, including the director's role in the management of the company.'

- The higher the level of remuneration the greater the level of responsibilities which might reasonably be expected (prima facie, at least) to go with it.[13]

5. Section 175 to avoid conflicts of interest.

A director must avoid situations in which s/he has, or can have, a direct or indirect interest or conflict of duties that conflicts, or possibly may conflict, with the interests of the company. This applies in particular to the exploitation of any property, information or opportunity. It is immaterial whether the company could take advantage of the property, information or opportunity.

This duty does not apply to a conflict of interest arising in relation to a transaction or arrangement with the company.

Nor is it infringed if the situation cannot reasonably be regarded as likely to give rise to a conflict of interest or if the matter has been authorised by the directors in accordance with the constitution. Such authorisation is effective only if any requirement as to the quorum at the meeting at which the matter is considered is met without counting the director in question or any other interested director, and the matter was agreed to without their voting or would have been agreed to if their votes had not been counted.

6. Section 176 not to accept benefits from third parties.

This is an extension of the duty to avoid conflicts of interest. This duty is not infringed if the acceptance of the benefit cannot reasonably be regarded as likely to give rise to a conflict of interest. Nor are benefits received by a director from a person by whom his/her services (as a director or otherwise) are provided to the company.

A director of a company must not accept a benefit from a third party conferred by reason of his/her being a director, or doing (or not doing) anything as director. 'Third party' means a legal person other than the company.

In practice, organisations should have detailed policies and procedures covering what directors and other employees may and may not accept from third parties, for example regarding the giving or receiving of hospitality. It is good practice to maintain a register of benefits received and offered.

---

13   Courtney. T.B (2016) The Law of Companies (4th edn) Bloomsbury Professional, Great Britain.

7. Section 177: to declare an interest in a proposed transaction with the company.

   This is a further requirement regarding conflicts of interest. If a director is in any way, directly or indirectly, interested in a proposed transaction or arrangement with the company, he must declare the nature and extent of that interest to the other directors. The declaration may be made at a meeting of the directors, or by notice to the directors in writing before the company enters into the transaction or arrangement.

   A director is treated, by company law, as being aware of matters of which he ought reasonably to be aware.

   A director need not declare an interest if it cannot reasonably be regarded as likely to give rise to a conflict of interest or the other directors are already aware or ought reasonably to be aware of it; or if it concerns terms of his/her service contract.

   The requirement does not apply to transactions buying or selling shares in a company. The duty may apply, however, to transactions involving the director's spouse. It is good practice for a director not to take part in a board meeting where s/he has an interest in a proposed transaction.

2.7 Accountability

Accountability is a key aspect of corporate governance. A person, team, board, or organisation is accountable if they can be held to account for their action (or lack of it) or are required to give an account of their action (or lack of it). Staff, including executives, in organisations should be accountable to boards and boards should be accountable to their owners, which for a company will be its shareholders and for a public body the government. In some cases account will need to be given to other stakeholders.

The Companies (Miscellaneous Reporting) Regulations 2018 require most companies to give account in the annual report for how the directors have had regard for various stakeholder matters in performing their duty under s. 172.

Those to whom a person, team or organisation is accountable should have the power to hold them to account. In practice this is where problems often arise. As discussed later, examples of governance failure are frequently also examples of accountability failure, where shareholders have not held boards to account or boards have not held executives to account to prevent something going wrong or afterwards.

2.8 Recurring themes such as ethics and values

Each successive corporate governance scandal highlights the importance of companies and their staff having good values and **ethics**. Ethical lapse can lead to prosecution, damaged reputation and occasionally corporate failure such as was the case with accounting firm Arthur Andersen in 2002. Most codes refer to ethics and/or values but usually not in a way which seems to have had much useful impact. Having previously been a rarely discussed subject, the importance of culture has now reached centre stage in code development

ethics
Moral principles that govern a person's or an organisation's behaviour or conduct.

in a number of countries. The 2016 South African King IV Code stands out among governance codes around the world for placing ethics at the heart of governance. In the UK, the FRC embarked on the culture coalition project to gain a better understanding of how boards are currently addressing culture, to encourage discussion and debate, and to identify and share good practice to help companies. This led to the publication of 'Corporate Culture and the Role of Boards' in 2016 and in July 2018, a new Corporate Governance Code[14] which for the first time included culture in the principles and provisions.

Making it work 1.1

In 2000 Arthur Andersen was one of the Big Five global professional accounting firms. Headquartered in the US its partners and staff, sometimes known as Androids, prided themselves on being the best and most highly paid in the business. At one time the firm enjoyed a high reputation for quality, professionalism and ethics. Its roots lay in providing accounting and auditing services and associated tax compliance work. In the late 1980s it had developed a highly successful, lucrative and rapidly growing consulting side providing consulting services mainly to its audit clients on tax, corporate finance and computer services.

Audit partners were expected to help facilitate the selling of consulting services to their clients. It was not uncommon for the five biggest accounting firms to have more revenue from consulting services than audit which generated relatively higher profit so that most of the profits of Andersen would have come from consultancy. This created an obvious conflict of interest for an auditor.

In the late 1980s and early 1990s the firm, and Andersen's Houston office in particular, had the misfortune to be the auditor of a number of companies linked with accounting scandal. The best known of these scandals was Enron. While in 2001 Enron fell into insolvency the Andersen partners and staff responsible for Enron decided to shred the audit working papers, which was both highly unprofessional and no doubt intended to thwart any attempts by regulators to investigate their work. The US Securities & Exchange Commission (SEC) was already annoyed by Andersen's association with a number of other scandals and pushed for Andersen to be held to account. In 2002 Andersen was found guilty of obstructing justice in the Enron scandal. Under SEC rules Andersen could no longer carry out audit, which meant the firm could no longer remain in business. The conviction was later overturned but it was too late for Andersen. It seemed that the act of shredding in one office destroyed a global firm employing tens of thousands of professionals.

14   FRC (2018) the UK Corporate Governance Code, The Financial Reporting Council, www.frc.org.uk/directors/corporate-governance-and-stewardship/uk-corporate-governance-code

What was once the most global and integrated of the Big Five fell apart almost overnight. Andersen Consulting, the consulting arm of Andersen had already separated itself from the firm and later rebranded itself Accenture. Those left at Andersen lost their jobs, although few were unemployed for long as Andersen's national practices around the world were taken over by what had been rival Big Five firms.

Andersen's full role in the demise of Enron will never be fully known. The episode led, however, to massive reform of the regulation of the accounting and auditing professions around the world and US legislation in the form of the US Sarbanes-Oxley Act 2002[15].

2.9   Consequences of governance failure

The consequences of governance failure can be severe. When Enron collapsed, its staff lost their jobs and many of them also saw their pensions all but wiped out. Investors lost money and suppliers lost custom. It also led to widespread mistrust of corporate financial statements and the auditing profession and directly led to additional regulation in the form of the Sarbanes-Oxley Act 2002, which created a considerable regulatory burden and additional expense for companies with shares listed in the US and their suppliers. Governance failure may not usually lead to the collapse of an organisation but could result in significant financial loss in terms of profits and share price, wasted resources and reputational damage for organisations. There can be knock-on damage to organisational sectors and even countries. Reputational damage erodes trust, which is vital to a healthy economy. Governments know that a reputation for poor governance will make it harder for business to raise finance and to invest.

Sarbanes-Oxley Act 2002
An Act passed by US Congress to protect investors from fraudulent accounting by companies, improve disclosure and controls, including accountability over corporate reporting. It was a response to accounting scandals such as at Enron, WorldCom and Tyco.

2.10 The importance of corporate governance to the global economy

It follows that good governance is very important to companies and countries. Companies with good governance are likely to enjoy a higher share price, lower cost of capital, easier access to finance and may find it easier to recruit good staff, win and retain customers and secure favourable terms with suppliers. Countries whose companies generally enjoy a good reputation for governance are more likely to have thriving stock markets with higher asset prices, better liquidity and lower spreads between buy and sell prices. Such countries will also be more attractive for inward foreign investment. While there may be a degree of complacency in some developed countries about governance, demonstrating good governance is seen as particularly important in developing countries.

2.11 Difficulties of linking good governance with corporate performance

Establishing a causal link between good governance and corporate performance is perhaps the holy grail of corporate governance. There have been studies which have found correlation between criteria that could be indicative of good

---

15   Sarbanes–Oxley Act (2002), also known as the 'Public Company Accounting Reform and Investor Protection Act', USA.

governance and aspects of performance but no clear causal link has yet been established and there is other evidence linking some governance indicators with poorer performance. There are many different measures for performance but no truly reliable indicators of good governance. It is possible to identify various structural elements of what are generally accepted as necessary for good governance, such as having a balanced board and having the roles of **chief executive** and chairman fulfilled by different people. While such elements may be necessary for good governance they are by no means sufficient so correlations between such elements and performance do not reveal a clear causal link. Good governance is more about what people do than whether these basic elements are in place.

chief executive
The most senior executive or manager in an organisation and usually a executive director. They will normally have delegated authority from the board for running the organisation.

Test yourself 1.2

One of the studies which found a correlation between governance and performance was by Shaukat and Trojanowski (2014).[16] They found a strong positive association between a board governance index they constructed from the UK Code requirements and operating performance in listed companies. They also found that investors seemed not to price governance indicators into share price. Investors seemed surprised by stronger corporate performance in terms of ROA, ROE and ROIC in one year and Shaukat and Trojanowski argued that such financial better performance could have been predicted and so should have been priced into the share price in the previous year.

ROA, ROE and ROIC
Financial performance ratios – return on assets, return on equity and return on invested capital.

What would you include in a board governance index?

2.12 Difficulties of recognising 'good governance'

It follows that it is difficult to recognise good governance. Poor governance can often only be recognised after something has gone wrong. Companies whose governance was later found to be wanting often appeared previously to be well governed, meeting most of the generally recognised criteria for good governance. Enron was one example. Another was Barclays, which in the late 2000s was assessed by staff at the Financial Services Agency (FSA) as having governance which was best in class at about the same time the FSA Chairman had serious concerns about the culture and tone at the top. The FSA chairman wrote in April 2012 to the then Barclays chairman about what the FSA saw as behaviour at 'the aggressive end of interpretation of the relevant rules and regulations' and about the bank's 'tendency to seek advantage from complex structures or favourable regulatory interpretations'.[17] The staff who assessed Barclay's governance as best in class would probably have seen that Barclays appeared to have the right governance structures and procedures in place but they failed to identify that they were not working as they should.

16   Shaukat and Trojanowski (2014) Board Governance and Corporate Performance in the UK, Open Research Exeter.

17   House of Commons Treasury Committee (2013) Fixing LIBOR: some preliminary findings Second Report of Session 2012–13, https://publications.parliament.uk/pa/cm201213/cmselect/cmtreasy/481/481.pdf

More recently, the 2016 Annual Report of Carillion plc, published in March 2017, stated that it fully complied with the 2014 Corporate Governance Code. The detailed disclosures on corporate governance gave the impression of a company with good governance and a board which took governance seriously. The financial statements in the annual report suggested a profitable company in reasonable financial health and there was a clean (unqualified) audit report. Nevertheless the company failed in January 2018. The subsequent Parliamentary Inquiry was highly critical of certain directors and the auditors. Although the board seemed to go through the motions of good governance, good governance was actually lacking.

At the time of writing there are no reliable comprehensive tests of good governance and this seems likely to remain the case for some time. One reason is that good governance ultimately depends on having 'good' people running an organisation who do the 'right' things. Good means good in terms of character, honesty, judgement, knowledge, skill and experience. Right things means that these people can work well together in successfully and ethically running an organisation so that any individual's weaknesses are countered and their strengths reinforced.

3. Principles, codes and provisions

3.1 Generally accepted corporate governance principles

Although it is difficult to recognise 'good' governance because what is 'good' depends on people and what they do there are nevertheless a number of principles which over time have become generally accepted as fundamental. These can be regarded as necessary but not necessarily sufficient as good governance depends on how well the principles are applied.

At a broad high level generally accepted principles include that:

◆ boards should be balanced with a suitable mix of executive and independent non-executive directors;

◆ the roles of chairman and chief executive should be fulfilled by different people;

◆ boards should be effective and the effectiveness of the board should be evaluated periodically;

◆ owners and, in appropriate circumstances other significant stakeholders, can and do hold boards to account; and

◆ organisations should report in a fair and balanced way to shareholders or other key stakeholders on their performance.

The last principle is perhaps the most important. Most codes are voluntary and rely on disclosure and transparency so that shareholders and other stakeholders can know what is going on and influence organisations if practices are felt to be wanting.

A fifth principle is also important if not universally agreed on. This is that executives are held to account by their boards and boards are held to account by shareholders. Unfortunately, as will be discussed later, such accountability does not work as well as it should.

Making it work 1.2

Opinions have changed over the years on what is necessary for good governance. In 2000 McKinsey[18] carried out a survey of the opinions of institutional investors on whether they would pay more for a company with good board governance practices. They contrasted six 'poor' practices with six 'good' practices. Over 80% of the respondents said that they would pay more with a premium ranging from 18% for a UK company and 22% for an Italian one to 27% for companies in Venezuela and Indonesia. One of the 'poor' practices was that directors are compensated only in cash and one of the 'good' practices was that a large part of director pay is in stock or options.

Since 2000, however, there have been many instances of directors using dubious – and sometimes fraudulent – accounting practices to make the financial results look better than they were in order to trigger bonuses in the form of shares, options or payments and of directors cashing in their options and selling their stock shortly before company bad news. Enron is a classic example. Therefore while it is generally agreed that, where possible, directors' financial interests should be linked to shareholders' interests it has been found to be very difficult to achieve in practice. Many now argue that compensation with cash is preferable to compensation with shares and options and variable pay based on organisational performance is now seen as poor practice. The 2018 UK Code says that any remuneration other than a fee could impair the independence of a non-executive director.

In July 2018 the FRC published a revised code. This text assumes readers will study the new Code and become familiar with it. This text, therefore, does not discuss the Code in detail except where required by the context to explain particular issues. The new Code puts greater emphasis than before on the application of principles.

internal control
A process effected by an entity's board of directors, management, and other personnel, designed to provide reasonable assurance regarding the achievement of objectives relating to operations, reporting, and compliance. (COSO) or simply the means by which an organisation achieves its objectives.

The Code can be used as a framework and benchmark to enable you to compare earlier versions and other codes. The principles cover board leadership and company purpose; division of responsibilities (within the board); (board) composition, succession and evaluation; audit, risk and **internal control**; and (board) remuneration. The FCA's Listing Rules as they apply to premium listed companies require such companies to state in a corporate governance statement forming part of their Annual Report how they have 'applied' the Principles – in other words, such companies are expected to behave in accordance with the

18   McKinsey (2000) Investor Opinion Survey on Corporate Governance, McKinsey & Company, London, www.oecd.org/daf/ca/corporategovernanceprinciples/1922101.pdf

Principles and state how they have done so. The Listing Rules further require premium listed companies to state whether or not they have complied with the Provisions of the Code, and if they have not to explain why they have not and further detail the circumstances. This latter requirement is known as 'comply or explain'. This 'comply or explain' approach has, with some notable exceptions, such as in South Africa (see Chapter 3), been adopted in most governance codes around the world.

The principles could therefore be said to be mandatory but how they are applied is discretionary, as is whether or not to comply with the provisions. The principles and provisions are intended to be a complete set of requirements and if a company applies the principles and complies with the provisions or gives proper reason for any non-compliance then a company would be regarded by most people as having good governance. It is not a guarantee however.

Making it work 1.3

The Royal Bank of Scotland (RBS) failed in October 2008, requiring injection of £45.5 billion of government capital. RBS's annual reports in 2008 and 2009[19] said the RBS complied with all of the provisions of the FRC Combined Code issued (2006) except in relation to the provision that the Remuneration Committee should have delegated responsibility for setting remuneration for the Chairman and executive directors. The reasonable explanation given was that the company 'considers that this is a matter which should rightly be reserved for the Board'.

In December 2010 the FSA concluded its first inquiry into the failure of RBS.[20] The report said the FSA did not identify any instance of 'failure of governance on the part of the Board'. Many found this surprising and the FSA was told to think again. A year later the FSA concluded 'RBS's failure amid the systemic crisis resulted from poor decisions by its management and Board'.[21]

The change of view reflects that there are varying opinions on what corporate governance is. The first review seems to have taken a narrow view, looking at compliance with the governance code and, in the absence of any evidence of dishonesty, did not regard poor decision making by the board as a failure of governance. Most governance experts and regulators would now agree that poor decision making by

---

19   RBS (2008) Annual Report and Accounts 2008, http://investors.rbs.com/~/media/Files/R/RBS-IR/annual-reports/rbs-group-accounts-2008.pdf
         RBS (2009) Annual Report and Accounts 2009, http://investors.rbs.com/~/media/Files/R/RBS-IR/annual-reports/rbs-group-accounts-2009.pdf

20   FSA (2010) FSA closes supervisory investigation of RBS, The Financial Services Authority, London, www.fsa.gov.uk/library/communication/statements/2010/investigation_rbs.shtml

21   FSA (2010) FSA closes supervisory investigation of RBS, The Financial Services Authority, London, www.fsa.gov.uk/library/communication/statements/2010/investigation_rbs.shtml

a board is very much a governance issue. Good governance should help ensure good board decisions.

The principles and provisions in the 2018 Code have evolved since the 2003 version and many governance codes around the world have adopted similar principles.

Stop and think 1.3

In South Africa greater emphasis on ethics has been given in each of the four versions of its governance code than in the UK. The 2016 UK Code did not contain any principles or provisions referring to ethics, and 'values' is mentioned in just one supporting principle. The 2018 Code still makes no mention of ethics although culture, values and integrity are now mentioned in the principles and provisions. The South African King 4 Code (2016) does, however. The first three King principles put ethics centre stage. It says the governing body should:

1. **'Lead ethically and effectively.'**

2. **'Govern the ethics of the organisation in a way that supports the establishment of an ethical culture.'**

3. **'Ensure that the organisation is and is seen to be a responsible corporate citizen.'**

What do you consider to be the most important governance principles for your organisation and business sector?

3.2 How regulators seek to ensure good governance through principles, provisions and rules

In the UK, corporate governance has evolved on top of an existing foundation comprising the company law framework, financial reporting and auditing standards, institutions such as the stock exchange and professional bodies, investors who were able and willing to use their shareholdings to influence company boards and boards of directors who, in the main, want to do a good job. The Cadbury Committee, which produced the world's first governance code in 1992, comprised representatives from these institutions and was a voluntary initiative and remained so until 2003 when, following the collapse of Enron and other US corporate failures, the FRC, which is an independent regulator, took on responsibility for the Combined Code.

The UK approach in the listed company sector has been to create a series of voluntary codes of corporate governance based initially on principles and then a combination of principles and provisions coupled with disclosure. As explained in 1.6 the Listing Rules make it mandatory for Premium listed companies to comply with the Code but is up to companies to decide and explain how they do so. It is up to shareholders, however, rather than regulators to apply pressure on companies to ensure they comply with the Code.

The benefits of such a voluntary approach are seen as giving greater flexibility for regulators, companies and shareholders, both in setting the code requirements and then interpreting and applying them. It is also argued that good governance practice is not easily reduced to a set of legally enforceable rules.

Making it work 1.4

Sir Adrian Cadbury explained in his book, Corporate Governance and Chairmanship,[22] the advantage for good corporate governance in having a principle-based code rather than detailed legal requirements. This is illustrated, as stated above, in the generally accepted principle that the roles of the chairman and chief executive should be held by different people. The aim is that there should be a clear division of responsibilities between the person who runs the board, normally the chairman, and the person who runs the company, normally the chief executive. If there was only a legal requirement to have both a chairman and a chief executive the law could be complied with by appointing two people but where one of them acts as a 'puppet' on the instructions of the other so that effectively just one person has full control. The letter of the law would be complied with but the purpose frustrated. There would be little opportunity for shareholders or anyone else to tackle the company as it could claim it has acted within the law. A code requiring companies to explain how they apply the principle would make it possible for shareholders to intervene if a puppet is appointed.

The key point here is that a code facilitates shareholders in being involved in ensuring good governance whereas a legal requirement would not and would need enforcement by a supervisory authority.

The 2018 Code retains this concept of separation in both a principle and a provision.

Principle G:

'The board should include an appropriate combination of executive and non-executive (and, in particular, independent non-executive) directors, such that no one individual or small group of individuals dominates the board's decision making. There should be a clear division of responsibilities between the leadership of the board and the executive leadership of the company's business.'

Provision 9 (part):

'The roles of chair and chief executive should not be exercised by the same individual.'

---

22   Cadbury, A. (2002) Corporate Governance and Chairmanship, Oxford University Press, Oxford.

3.3 Evaluating governance – conforming and performing

As stated in section 2.12 it is difficult both to recognise good governance and to evaluate whether an organisation has good governance. In the 1990s and early 2000s it was generally, but not universally, considered reasonable to equate good governance with good compliance with the relevant code. So, for example, a company that seemed to comply or conform fully with the UK Code stating how it applied all the code principles and complied with its provisions was seen as well governed. Certainly the FSA seemed to take this view (as shown in the Royal Bank of Scotland inquiry, discussed above). The financial crisis highlighted the error in equating good governance with governance compliance or conformance. It is now more widely accepted that governance performance matters more and that governance compliance at best may be a necessary condition of good governance. Performance is about what boards and others do and that is strongly influenced by corporate culture and the board's and company's values and attitudes.

Test yourself 1.3

How would you evaluate corporate governance in an organisation?

3.4 Corporate governance theories

Numerous theories have evolved in academic study of corporate governance. This text is intended to be practically, rather than academically, based so does not cover the theories in detail but some theories are particularly important to the understanding and evaluation of corporate governance practice. These are:

◆   agency theory;
◆   stewardship theory;
◆   stakeholder theory; and
◆   enlightened shareholder theory.

Agency theory
Agency theory is about the relationship between principals and their agents and the separation of ownership and control. In a modern corporate setting the principals are the owners of an organisation, for example shareholders, and the agents are boards of directors that control organisations. These principals and agents have different financial interests and motivations. According to agency theory the agents will pursue actions that maximise their personal benefit at the expense of the principals. The principals want to preserve and grow the value of what they own. The agents want to be paid for running the organisation. To some extent there is a mutual interest – neither the board nor the owners want the organisation to fail but boards are likely to want a larger share of a company's assets than its owners would like.

The board, or perhaps usually the executive element of it however, is more likely to be interested in short-term rewards in the form of salary, bonuses and share-based remuneration such as gifts of shares or grants of options to buy shares at a favourable price. This tension has resulted in some egregious results such as where executives falsified financial statements to trigger bonuses and share options, after which the company collapsed. In other cases executives have taken advantage of opportunities to engage in risky trading practices where they can gain personally with the shareholders bearing the risk.

Stewardship theory

Like agency theory, stewardship theory is about the relationship between the owners of assets and the board of directors. In stewardship theory the directors are appointed by the owners who act as stewards on behalf of the owners, understanding and acting in their interests. The directors have a **fiduciary duty** to act in the owners' interests rather than their own. So the essential difference is that under agency theory the directors are likely to act in their own interest and under stewardship theory they will act in the owners' interest. Under both theories boards are accountable to owners and, as discussed in Chapter 7, the accounting profession's origins stem from a steward's responsibility to give account to an owner for his/her stewardship of their assets.

fiduciary duty
Where one person or group is in a position of trust and has a legal or ethical obligation to act for the benefit or best interests of another person or group.

It would seem that stewardship theory more accurately defines the relationship between most boards and owners most of the time but the motivation for directors to act in their own interest is always potentially present and board and executive culture and ethics are particularly important. Agency theory tends to explain matters better when they go wrong. The UK Code of Corporate Governance and most other codes are based on the concept of stewardship while aiming to address some of the implications of agency theory such as to ensure that no single individual dominates board decision making.

The concept of stewardship is also now used to define the responsibilities of institutional shareholders to the ultimate providers of capital such as pension funds, insurance companies, investment trusts and individuals saving for a pension. The FRC Stewardship Code[23] sets out how these responsibilities should be discharged (see Chapter 5).

Stakeholder theory

Under stakeholder theory an organisation and its directors have a broader responsibility and accountability going beyond just the organisation's owners. This reflects the fact that organisations have a licence from society to operate. This confers obligations on the organisation to behave in a way which is socially and environmentally responsible and has regard for all its stakeholders such as employees, the public, customers, suppliers, taxpayers and the environment. The South African King IV Code on Corporate Governance reflects stakeholder theory but most codes, including the UK Code until 2018, do not. Critics of stakeholder theory argue that it does not reflect the legal reality that a director's duty is to the company and its shareholders rather than other stakeholders.

---

23   FRC (2012) The UK Stewardship Code, The Financial Reporting Council UK, www.frc.org.uk/Our-Work/Publications/Corporate-Governance/UK-Stewardship-Code-September-2012.pdf

Enlightened shareholder theory

Enlightened shareholder theory blends stewardship theory with stakeholder theory and has a firm foundation in s. 172 of the UK Companies Act 2006 (reproduced below) which says that directors must act in a way that promotes the success of the company for the benefit of its members (shareholders), having regard to a number of matters which include stakeholder interests.

'S. 172 Duty to promote the success of the company – directors must act in the way they consider, in good faith, would be most likely to promote the success of the company for the benefit of its members as a whole, and in doing so have regard (amongst other matters) to—

1. the likely consequences of any decision in the long term,
2. the interests of the company's employees,
3. the need to foster the company's business relationships with suppliers, customers and others,
4. the impact of the company's operations on the community and the environment,
5. the desirability of the company maintaining a reputation for high standards of business conduct, and
6. the need to act fairly as between members of the company.'

The theory is that having regard for the matters listed in s. 172 will mean that the company will create more value for its members over the long term than would be the case if the directors only had regard for the company and its shareholders. Critics, however, argue that s. 172 is just empty wordage which makes little difference in practice and does not set out how directors should have regard for these matters. There have been no legal cases to test this piece of law which perhaps demonstrates ineffectiveness.

Section 172 has generated considerable discussion and some controversy as it is perceived to create an ambiguity around whether a director's duty is ultimately to the company or to its shareholders. The prevailing view of many directors is that their duty is to shareholders so that in practice they consider their duty is to maximise share price. This could mean they agree to a takeover bid if that will mean shareholders receive a premium over the extant share price but the company disappears. The concern is that this can lead boards to prioritise short-term profit over long-term value creation and to approve takeover bids which do not benefit the company or its stakeholders.

The Companies (Miscellaneous Reporting) Regulations 2018 require, from January 2019, all companies of significant size (private as well as public) to explain how their directors have had regard for matters one to five of s. 172 in performing their duty under s. 172 to promote the success of the company. This will apply to all companies that meet two out of three requirements: a turnover greater than £36 million; a balance sheet total of more than £18 million or more than 250 employees.

Chapter summary

◆ Corporate governance is a new term, coming to prominence in the UK in the 1990s, although the issues it addresses are old.

◆ The first widely used definition of corporate governance came from the Cadbury Report in 1992: the system by which companies are directed and controlled.

◆ The purpose of corporate governance, according to the UK Code of Corporate Governance, is to facilitate effective, entrepreneurial and prudent management that can deliver the long-term success of the company.

◆ Corporate governance practices and regulation have evolved in response to corporate scandals.

◆ Practices and regulation have evolved on top of the existing company law framework.

◆ Section 172 of the UK Companies Act lists seven directors' duties.

◆ Accountability, ethics and culture are key aspects of corporate governance.

◆ Good corporate governance should mean better organisations and better economies but it is difficult to prove a link and recognise good governance.

◆ Key governance theories include agency and stewardship.

◆ There are a number of widely accepted governance principles found in many governance codes.

◆ Voluntary principle-based codes are generally thought to be better than prescriptive regulation and legislation.

Chapter two

Corporate governance development in the UK

CONTENTS

1. Introduction
2. Corporate governance development for UK listed companies
3. Approaches in different sectors

1. Introduction

This chapter considers corporate governance in the UK. It begins with corporate governance development for companies listed on the London Stock Exchange and then considers how it has developed in other sectors.

2. Corporate governance development for UK listed companies

Listed companies
Companies listed on a recognised stock exchange.

This section outlines how corporate governance has developed in the UK in the **listed** company sector. Listed refers to a listing on the London Stock Exchange (LSE). The LSE has three markets: the main market, AIM (previously called the Alternative Investment Market), and the Professional Securities Market.

The main market has four segments: Premium, Standard, specialist fund and high growth. The Listing Rules require companies with a Premium listing only to comply with the UK Code. There are around 1,400 such companies, of which nearly 900 are investment companies. Only around 520 of the Premium listed companies are what the LSE terms premium equity commercial companies. These companies are of enormous importance to the UK economy and include the largest UK companies employing millions of staff.

Stop and think 2.1

One of the first British examples of corporate governance failure was the South Sea Company.[1] It was formed in 1711 and given a monopoly of trade with the South American Spanish colonies in return for assuming interest bearing government debts.

The directors issued misleading news of trading prospects driving up the share price. New issues of shares took place and paper fortunes were made. The reality was that the share price was not reflected by its corporate performance: it was not profitable nor did it have good prospects which should have meant the shares were only worth the value of any saleable assets of the company less its liabilities. The directors, knowing this, sold their shares triggering panic selling by other shareholders. The share price crashed and many people, including Sir Isaac Newton, lost fortunes. A Parliamentary investigation revealed fraud and corruption by the South Sea Company directors and members of the government.

The story came to be known as the South Sea Bubble. These bubble events happen from time to time. Others include the Dutch Tulip Bulb Bubble 80 years earlier, the dot.com boom of the late 1990s to 2001 and the US property boom of the mid 2000s.

Adam Smith's 'Wealth of Nations'[2] in 1776 later highlighted the agency problem of company directors managing other people's money, saying that it cannot be expected that they should watch over it with the same 'anxious vigilance' they would if the money was their own.

What lessons for the present can be learned from the South Sea Company?

Two corporate failures led to first developments in what we now call corporate governance. In 1990, Coloroll collapsed and then the Polly Peck International scandal in 1991. Coloroll was a wallpaper manufacturer which expanded rapidly through acquiring other businesses. It reported steadily rising profits but this was a result not of actual profit growth but of aggressive use of accounting techniques which made the company appear more profitable than it was. Rising reported profits were used to support a series of refinancing measures but in 1990 the company had debts of £350 million and inadequate real profits to support such debt. Attempts to refinance the group failed and receivers were called in. Banks were owed c.£200 million, of which only half was recovered. The managing director of Coloroll went on to become chairman of Carillion, which failed in January 2018 in circumstances resembling that of Coloroll in several ways including debt-funded growth and aggressive accounting.

1   Balen, M. (2002) A Very English Deceit: The secret history of the South Sea Bubble and the first great financial scandal, Fourth Estate, London.

2   Smith. A (1838) (1998) Wealth of Nations, Oxford University Press, Oxford.

Polly Peck had been a fast growing global trading conglomerate posting rising profits. Its share price had risen steeply. Financial results reported for the six months to 30 June 1990 showed record profits and assets of £933 million, including £403 million cash at banks. In autumn 1990 its premises were raided by the Serious Fraud Office and its shares were suspended on the London Stock Exchange. Investigations revealed a deficit of £551 million – a difference of nearly £1.5 billion. Its boss, Asil Nadir, kept the board in the dark about what was going on and was eventually found guilty of stealing £29 million from the company.

2.1 The Cadbury Report[3]

As the published financial statements of both companies gave little indication of any looming financial problem prior to their failure, concerns were raised about whether UK company accounting and auditing practices could be relied on. The Cadbury Committee was set up to address the financial aspects of corporate governance.

Making it work 2.1

While the committee was working two more corporate scandals occurred, adding to its importance. BCCI, a British registered bank, went into liquidation owing £10 billion to creditors. It was found that the bank had been involved in money laundering and fraudulent loans. The external auditors were later fined over £100 million.

The other scandal concerned Robert Maxwell and the Daily Mirror Group. Maxwell who had been criticised in a Department of Trade and Industry investigation in 1970 as 'not a person who can be relied upon to exercise proper stewardship of a publicly quoted company' acquired a number of publishing companies including Mirror Group Newspapers (MGN). Over a five-year period more than £100 million belonging to the MGN pension fund was lent to his personal companies, mostly without the knowledge of the majority of the pension fund trustees. Maxwell died mysteriously in 1991 and his business empire collapsed with liquidity problems. The auditor was subsequently fined more than £3 million.

The problems revealed by these scandals included:

◆ dominant chief executives running the company who were not held to account by the board;

◆ other directors who did not know what was going on and did not challenge the chief executive;

◆ theft, fraud and unauthorised lending;

3 Report of the Committee on The Financial Aspects of Corporate Governance (1992)

◆ aggressive, creative and fraudulent accounting used to create the misleading impression of profitability and financial stability;

◆ high-growth strategies supported by debt which ultimately were not sustainable; and

◆ audits which failed to highlight accounting impropriety.

The Cadbury Committee issued its report in 1992. Its full title was 'Report of The Committee on the Financial Aspects of Corporate Governance' but it became widely known as the Cadbury Report. The 90-page report was a thorough analysis of the issues and the heart of its recommendations was a Code of Best Practice intended to achieve high standards of corporate behaviour for all UK listed companies. Companies were to be required to state whether they had complied with the Code and give reasons for any non-compliance. The idea was that the information disclosed would enable shareholders to judge whether companies had good governance. The Code of Practice was short, just two pages, and covered the role of the board, the role of executive and non-executive directors and reporting and controls.

The Cadbury Code was the first code of corporate governance anywhere in the world. It makes interesting comparison with later, much longer, codes. The Report and the Code were written with the belief and expectation that most directors want to do a good job and be seen to do so and that what was needed was some encouragement. On the whole this worked and the Code became widely accepted.

It was fortunate that in 1992 UK insurance and pension funds held over 50% of the UK stock market by value compared with less than 9% in 2014. This meant that in 1992 UK institutional shareholders could exert more pressure on UK companies than is the case today. This is considered in more detail in Chapter 6.

2.2   The Greenbury Report and executive pay

In 1994 a major corporate concern was executive pay, particularly with pay increases for chief executives of then recently privatised public utilities such as British Gas. Sir Richard Greenbury was asked by the Confederation of British Industry (CBI) to lead a study group on directors' remuneration. Their report noted large pay increases and gains from share options in the privatised utilities which sometimes coincided with staff reductions and pay restraint for other staff. There were further concerns about compensation paid to departing directors and the accountability of directors.

Greenbury's solution was a code on executive pay. Executive pay would be determined by remuneration committees comprising independent non-executive directors. This committee would report to shareholders each year explaining the approach to executive pay and detailing the elements in the remuneration of individual directors. It was somewhat naively felt that the key to encouraging enhanced director performance lay in having remuneration packages which linked pay to individual and corporate performance as this would align the interests of directors and shareholders. Consistent with the Cadbury Code approach of encouraging shareholders to apply pressure for good governance it would be up to shareholders to intervene if they disapproved of executive pay practices.

Although the Greenbury Report[4] said that 'companies should not pay above average levels regardless of performance' this is precisely what happened. No board wanted to consider their chief executive was mediocre and for him/her to be paid an average rate, nor obviously did chief executives. Remuneration consultants compared pay levels with other chief executives and successfully argued that their chief executive was better than average and should be paid accordingly.

2.3   Hampel and the Combined Code

In 1995 the FRC established a Committee on Corporate Governance with support from other stakeholder institutions such as the Stock Exchange, CBI, the professions and investor bodies, chaired by Sir Ronald Hampel, to review the governance recommendations at the time, identify any new issues and bring them together.

The Committee reported in early 1998 and the Combined Code (combining the Cadbury and Greenbury codes) of Corporate Governance was published later in the year as part of the Listing Rules. The Hampel report[5] suggested that companies believed that the Cadbury and Greenbury codes were being treated as sets of prescriptive rules. The report said that 'good corporate governance was not just a matter of prescribing particular corporate structures and complying with a number of hard and fast rules; there is a need for broad principles'. The Combined Code[6] attempted to address this by splitting governance recommendations into principles and provisions. Companies were required to report how they applied each of the principles and confirm whether they complied with the provisions and if not provide an explanation. It was for shareholders to evaluate such explanations.

2.4   The Higgs and Smith reports

The collapse of Enron in 2001 and the ensuing scandal, together with other US corporate scandals such as WorldCom at around the same time, once again called into question the reliability of financial statements and external auditors' opinions on them. They also prompted people to ask what boards and non-executive directors had been doing and why they seemed ineffective in preventing accounting fraud.[7] This triggered considerable activity by regulators, policy makers and the accounting and auditing professional bodies in the USA,

---

4   Greenbury, R. (1995) Directors' remuneration: Report of a study group chaired by Sir Richard Greenbury Gee, www.ecgi.org/codes/documents/greenbury.pdf

5   Committee on corporate governance (1998) Final report, Gee Publishing, London, www.ecgi.org/codes/documents/hampel.pdf

6   Committee on Corporate Governance (1998) Combined Code Principles Of Good Governance And Code Of Best Practice, www.ecgi.org/codes/documents/combined_code.pdf

7   A comprehensive coverage of accounting fraud is given in Jones, M (2011) Creative Accounting, Fraud and International Accounting Scandals, John Wiley and Sons, Chichester.

the UK and the EU.

In the UK the Department of Trade and Industry initiated a review, led by Sir Derek Higgs, of the role and effectiveness of non-executive directors and the FRC asked Sir Robert Smith for additional guidance on audit committees. The FRC also looked at the regulation of the accounting and auditing professions and the reporting and auditing standards they used.

Both reports were issued in January 2003. The Smith Report[8] recommended audit committees should review arrangements for whistleblowing and review the independence, objectivity and effectiveness of the external auditor and recommend a policy for the board on fees paid to the auditor for services other than audit.

The Higgs report[9] was more controversial. His 120-page report, after evidence gathering and consultation, included a proposed revised governance code. His ground-breaking proposal was that boards should evaluate their own performance; this was not popular at the time but is now widely accepted. Higgs also proposed that boards should consist of at least 50% independent non-executive directors, whereas previously three non-executive directors (NEDs) were considered sufficient.

Stop and think 2.2

Why do you think Higgs felt there should be a high proportion of independent NEDs?

2.5   The 2003 Combined Code

Higgs' proposed code was regarded by companies as going too far. In 2003 the FRC issued a revised Combined Code that reflected the Higgs and Smith reports and included requirements for a board effectiveness review and for boards to have at least 50% independent non-executive directors. Instead of the very detailed new provisions proposed by Higgs there came a new set of supporting principles to support the principles that were renamed 'main principles'. Companies were required to state how they applied both the main and the supporting principles and whether they complied with the provisions and if not why not.

The Code was revised in 2006 and 2008 with minor changes. The 2008 Code quietly dropped the requirement for boards to report on how they applied the supporting principles in the Code. For some this reinforced the view that most people were uninterested in the principles and bothered only with compliance with provisions, perpetuating concerns that governance was overly concerned with compliance at the expense of corporate performance.

---

8   FRC (2003) Audit committees combined code guidance: A report and proposed guidance by an FRC-appointed group chaired by Sir Robert Smith Financial Reporting Council London, www.ecgi.org/codes/documents/ac_report.pdf

9   Higgs, D. (2003) Review of the Role and Effectiveness of Non-executive Directors, The Department of Trade and Industry, London.

2.6   The financial crisis and the Walker Review

The Northern Rock bank collapsed in September 2007 followed by the US investment banks Bear Sterns and Lehman Brothers in March and September 2008. The failure of Lehman triggered financial panic necessitating the rescue of HBOS and RBS in the UK and emergency funding for many other banks. Barclays was reported to have been on the brink of needing government bailout but received an injection of funds from Qatar. The then Barclays' CEO and three other senior executives are due to stand trial in 2019 for alleged corruption to do with the injection.

Boards of financial institutions seemed to have been asleep at the helm of companies, unaware of the risks being taken and possibly unaware of how the institutions made money. Nor did they seem to understand, as it later turned out, that some of these organisations had been involved in activities such as money laundering, assisting tax evasion, mis-selling of financial products, interest rate rigging and unnecessarily putting indebted corporate customers into special measures to recover loans which made the businesses fail. They seemed unaware of having obligations towards society even though the institutions enjoyed effective guarantees by taxpayers if things went wrong.

Stop and think 2.3

According to McKinsey[10] global banking profits in 2006 were 6% of global GDP. Banks reported profits of $788 billion, which was over $150 billion more than the next most profitable sector, oil, gas and coal. Was the stellar profitability reported by banks before the crisis real or a fabrication?

ACCA published one of the first papers explaining the causes of the financial crisis linking it with governance and risk management failure in November 2008.[11]

In February 2009 the Prime Minister asked Sir David Walker, a former chairman of Barclays, to lead a review of corporate governance in UK banks and other financial institution entities. Most of his recommendations did little to add to what was already expected good governance practice. The most significant of recommendation was that the FRC adopt the Institutional Shareholders' Committee Code on the Responsibilities of Institutional Investors and call it the Stewardship Code (discussed in Module 2) and that institutional shareholders commit vigorously to it. The FRC did this in 2010. Another recommendation was that the risk committee or the board should report publicly on the key risk exposures inherent in the strategy, the associated **risk appetite** and tolerance and how the actual risk appetite is assessed over time.

risk appetite
The level of risk the board of an organisation is willing to take or 'the aggregate level and types of risk a financial institution is willing to take'.

10   McKinsey Quarterly (2008) What's in Store for Global Banking? January 2008.

11   Moxey, P. and Berendt, A. (2008) Corporate Governance and the Credit Crunch ACCA Discussion Paper, ACCA London, www. accaglobal.com/content/dam/acca/global/PDF-technical/corporate-governance/cg_cc.pdf

2.7 The UK Corporate Governance Code 2010

The Walker Review[12] was just one of several reviews by regulators. The FRC consulted in 2009 on what changes were needed, including changes to reflect the Walker recommendations. The name Combined Code was dropped and the Code became the UK Corporate Governance Code. The changes were evolution rather than revolution, with new principles and provisions calling for boards to do what they should have been doing already. For example, one new principle was 'the board is responsible for determining the nature and extent of the significant risks it is willing to take in achieving its strategic objectives'. This was to implement the Walker recommendation on risk appetite and tolerance. A new principle B3 was added: 'All directors should be able to allocate sufficient time to the company to discharge their responsibilities effectively', which is really a statement of the obvious.

The Code also introduced a requirement for boards to explain their **business model** and made another obvious point that performance-related pay should be aligned to companies' long-term interests and their risk policies and systems.

business model
A description or representation of how a business makes its money and/or creates value.

Test yourself 2.1

What is a business model?

The FRC recognised that the cognitive bias '**groupthink**' could have been a factor in the financial crisis with individual directors not being willing to voice concerns about what was going on or planned. To address this the FRC added new principles on the composition and selection of the board, appointing members on merit against objective criteria, and with due regard for the benefits of diversity.

groupthink
Occurs when a group of people with a desire for harmony or conformity in the group does not question or challenge leading to dysfunctional decision making.

2.8 The UK Corporate Governance Codes 2012, 2014, 2016

The FRC continued to fine-tune the Code, which gradually got longer. In 2012 changes included a provision requiring description of boards' policies on diversity, including gender, and any measurable objectives set for implementing the policy, and progress on achieving the objectives initiated.

One apparently minor change was to add the word 'fair' to principle C1: 'The board should present a fair, balanced and understandable assessment of the company's position and prospects.' Another change was that FTSE350 companies should put their external audit contract to tender at least every ten years.

The financial crisis revealed that banks, which in February 2008 had appeared financially solid, and received clean audit reports, could a few months later

---

12   Walker, D. (2009) A review of corporate governance in UK banks and other financial industry entities, July, The Walker Review, Secretariat, London, www.ecgi.org/codes/documents/walker_review_consultation_16july2009.pdf
      Walker, D. (2009) A review of corporate governance in UK banks and other financial industry entities: Final recommendations, November, The Walker Review, Secretariat, London, www.ecgi.org/codes/documents/walker_review_261109.pdf

accounts
The term accounts may also be used for financial statements used within an organisation for management and control purposes.

need government rescue. This called into question the reliability of external audit once again and whether it was correct to prepare **accounts** using the **going concern** basis of accounting. The going concern basis of accounting is the basis used for all organisations expecting to remain in business. The 2014 Code introduced a provision that directors should state whether they considered it appropriate to adopt the going concern basis of accounting and identify any material uncertainties that could change this in the next 12 months. The alternative accounting basis is to value assets at the price they could fetch if the organisation was being broken up.

The 2014 Code also included changes requiring boards to consider and report on the risks which could threaten the business model and ability to remain in business. Amendments were made to the principles and provisions on remuneration.

The 2016 update of the Code was driven by the changes required from the implementation of the European Union's Audit Regulation and Directive.

going concern
The accounting basis used for all organisations expecting to remain in business. The alternative basis is to value assets at what price they could fetch if the organisation was being broken up. In the general sense it means an organisation is viable, is able to meet its financial obligations and will remain in business over the medium to long term.

Test yourself 2.2

1. **When was the requirement to have independent NEDs make up at least 50% of the board introduced?**

2. **When was the Stewardship Code introduced?**

3. **When was a requirement for companies to disclose their business model introduced?**

4. **When was a provision requiring disclosure of the board's policy on diversity introduced?**

2.9 Recent developments

Changes to the UK Code had been incremental for many years but when Theresa May launched her campaign in July 2016 to be the new leader of the Conservatives and prime minister, she announced her intention to make sweeping changes to the corporate governance of listed and large companies. The Department for Business, Innovation and Skills (BIS) launched an inquiry in September 2016 and two months later the new Department for Business Energy and Industrial Strategy (BEIS) launched consultation Green Paper 'Review of Corporate Governance and the Purpose of the Corporation'. Notable among the responses to the Green paper was that of The House of Commons Work and Pensions Committee in February 2017,[13] which made recommendations including:

◆   the application of the UK Code of Governance should extend to large private companies which have over 5,000 members of a defined benefit pension scheme; and

---

13   House of Commons (2017) Work and Pensions Committee Response to the Government's consultation on corporate governance reform, 6 February, https://publications.parliament.uk/pa/cm201617/cmselect/cmworpen/995/995.pdf

◆ the interests of pension scheme trustees should be added to the list in s. 172 of the Companies Act 2006 (CA2006) of matters to whom directors should have regard when making decisions.

The FRC,[14] acknowledging the need for reform, undertook the most fundamental review of the UK Corporate Governance Code since the Higgs Review. The House of Commons BEIS Committee[15] issued its final report in April 2017 and the Government issued a response in August 2017.[16] The BEIS Committee published comments on the Government's response in September 2017.[17] These are considered in Chapter 4.

The FRC issued a new consultation in December 2017,[18] which included a proposed revised Corporate Governance Code and proposed revised guidance on board effectiveness and issued both in final form in July 2018. The FRC said that starting points for the review were the 1992 Cadbury Code and whether the aims of the first Code were still relevant.

The new Code is shorter and gives more emphasis to applying the Code principles and giving informative disclosure on how they have been applied. Some of the detailed provisions have been shortened and some have been moved to the separate Guidance on Board Effectiveness.[19] The new Code also has a new emphasis on directors acting with integrity, corporate culture and values. It tries to encourage governance policies and practices that both generate value for shareholders and aim to benefit society. This is the first time that stakeholder issues have been included in the UK Code, which was arguably overdue. These new concepts link the UK Code with directors' duties under UK Companies Act 2006 s. 172.

The first, second, fourth and fifth principles (A), (B), (D) and (E) are worth highlighting:

A. A successful company is led by an effective and entrepreneurial board, whose function is to promote the long-term sustainable success of the company, generate value for shareholders and contribute to wider society.

---

14   FRC (2017) Response to BEIS Corporate Governance Reform Green Paper, 17 February The Financial Reporting Council, www.frc.org.uk/Our-Work/Publications/Corporate-Governance/FRC-Response-to-BEIS-Green-Paper-consultation-on-C.pdf

15   House of Commons Business, Energy and Industrial Strategy Committee (2017) Corporate Governance: Third Report of Session 2016–17, 5 April, https://publications.parliament.uk/pa/cm201617/cmselect/cmbeis/702/702.pdf

16   Department for Business, Energy and Industrial Strategy (2017) Corporate Governance Reform, The Government response to the green paper consultation, www.gov.uk/government/uploads/system/uploads/attachment_data/file/640631/corporate-governance-reform-government-response.pdf

17   House of Commons Business, Energy and Industrial Strategy Committee (2017) Corporate governance: Government Response to the Committee's Third Report of Session 2016–17, 12 September, https://publications.parliament.uk/pa/cm201719/cmselect/cmbeis/338/338.pdf

18   FRC (2017) Proposed Revisions to the UK Corporate Governance Code, the Financial Reporting Council, www.frc.org.uk/consultation-list/2017/consulting-on-a-revised-uk-corporate-governance-co

19   FRC (2018) Guidance on Board Effectiveness The Financial Reporting Council, www.frc.org.uk/getattachment/61232f60-a338-471b-ba5a-bfed25219147/2018-Guidance-on-Board-Effectiveness-FINAL.PDF

B. The board should establish the company's purpose, strategy and values, and satisfy itself that these and its culture are aligned. All directors must act with integrity, lead by example and promote the desired culture.

D. In order for the company to meet its responsibilities to shareholders and stakeholders, the board should ensure effective engagement with, and encourage participation from, these parties.

E. The board should ensure that workforce policies and practices are consistent with the company's values and support its long-term sustainable success. The workforce should be able to raise any matters of concern.

The second, fifth and sixth new provisions are also significant:

2. The board should assess and monitor culture. Where it is not satisfied that policy, practices or behaviour throughout the business are aligned with the company's purpose, values and strategy, it should seek assurance that management has taken corrective action. The annual report should explain the board's activities and any action taken. In addition, it should include an explanation of the company's approach to investing in and rewarding its workforce.

5. The board should understand the views of the company's other key stakeholders and describe in the annual report how their interests and the matters set out in section 172 of the Companies Act 2006 have been considered in board discussions and decision-making. The board should keep engagement mechanisms under review so that they remain effective.

   For engagement with the workforce, one or a combination of the following methods should be used:

   ◆ a director appointed from the workforce;
   ◆ a formal workforce advisory panel;
   ◆ a designated non-executive director.

   If the board has not chosen one or more of these methods, it should explain what alternative arrangements are in place and why it considers that they are effective.

6. There should be a means for the workforce to raise concerns in confidence and – if they wish – anonymously. The board should routinely review this and the reports arising from its operation. It should ensure that arrangements are in place for the proportionate and independent investigation of such matters and for follow-up action.

These principles and provisions will challenge some boards, although it is arguable that good boards should be doing what is required already. A particular issue will be how best to monitor and assess culture: this will be a new area for many companies. Done well, it will be time consuming but could have considerable benefits. Done superficially, boards will be able to say they have fulfilled the requirement but are unlikely to learn anything useful.

The 2018 Code seems in most respects to be a significant improvement on earlier codes, being both shorter and addressing important issues thrown up in recent years. The failure of Carillion, however, may have implications for governance not currently addressed in the Code once all the investigations have been completed and the full facts are known.

3. Approaches in different sectors

There is general agreement that the governance principles – but not necessarily the provisions – in the UK Code are applicable to other types of organisation. It is therefore not surprising that the Code has been influential in other sectors. This section looks at the financial sector, the National Health Service (NHS), the not-for-profit sector including charities and companies without a listing on the Main Market of the London Stock Exchange such as smaller quoted companies, publicly held companies without a main listing including companies on the AIM and private companies including small and medium enterprises (SMEs).

3.1 The financial sector

Before the financial crisis the financial sector was already highly regulated and it was generally felt that the UK Code was applicable with no additional governance requirements needed. As already mentioned, things changed after the crisis. The sector is now more highly regulated than before with new areas of regulation such as the Senior Managers' Regime, which potentially makes individual directors and executives performing 'senior management functions' personally responsible for matters under their control. The Financial Conduct Authority (FCA) and Prudential Regulation Authority (PRA) have set a list of functional responsibilities which must be allocated to named individual managers. In addition financial institutions must list key activities, business areas and functions and allocate responsibility for these to one or more senior managers. The senior managers concerned will be accountable and will also be required to take reasonable steps to prevent regulatory breach in their area.

The FCA also requires pre-approval of board members and people responsible for a list of functions such as heads of finance, compliance, internal audit and risk. It will make a Fit and Proper Assessment of individuals who will need to show that they possess the necessary level of competence, knowledge and experience, requisite qualifications and demonstrate integrity.

The Swiss-based Bank for International Settlements (BIS), owned by 60 central banks, issued corporate governance principles for banks in 2015.[20] These are detailed guidelines for individual banks which use the word 'should' throughout, setting out what boards, senior management and supervisors should do. The 13 principles include three on the board but otherwise emphasise different matters from that covered by the new and previous UK Codes. These include three principles on risk and principles on senior management, group structure, compliance, internal audit, compensation and disclosure. The last principle is on the role of bank supervisors. BIS says that national jurisdictions should apply the principles as they see fit. It remains to be seen what impact they will have.

---

20   Bank for International Settlements (2015) Corporate Governance Principles for Banks, www.bis.org/bcbs/publ/d328.pdf

Test yourself 2.3

What is the Senior Managers' Regime?

3.2   The National Health Service

The NHS took close interest during the 1990s in the development of corporate governance in the private sector. This was partly because the NHS had had its own governance scandals in the early 1990s involving a costly and failed computer procurement at Wessex Regional Health Authority (RHA) and a series of financial scandals at West Midlands RHA. In 1994 the NHS Executive issued Codes of Conduct and Accountability in one document, followed in 1995 by a Code of Practice on Openness. The Code of Conduct set out three public service values: accountability, probity and openness and set out general principles for openness and public responsibilities, public business and private gain, expenditure, staff and suppliers. The Code of Accountability explained the statutory accountability of NHS organisations to the Secretary of State and Parliament along with the roles of the board, the chairman, non-executive directors and requirements for audit and remuneration committees, reporting and controls, declaration of interests and employee relations. The document was short with just 12 pages but the NHS Executive later published further detailed guidance and requirements.

The three NHS public services values above were replaced by the Seven Principles of Public Life, commonly known as the Nolan Principles[21] issued by the Government in 1995 for:

- ◆   the civil service;
- ◆   local government;
- ◆   the police;
- ◆   the courts and probation services;
- ◆   non-departmental public bodies; and
- ◆   health, education, social and care services.

The seven Nolan principles are:

1.   Selflessness: Holders of public office should act solely in terms of the public interest. They should not do so in order to gain financial or other benefits for themselves, their family or their friends.

2.   Integrity: Holders of public office should not place themselves under any financial or other obligation to outside individuals or organisations that might seek to influence them in the performance of their official duties.

3.   Objectivity: In carrying out public business, including making public appointments, awarding contracts, or recommending individuals for

---

21   Nolan, A. (1995) The Seven Principles of Public Life, Committee on Standards in Public Life, www.gov.uk/government/publications/the-7-principles-of-public-life

rewards and benefits, holders of public office should make choices on merit.

4.   Accountability: Holders of public office are accountable for their decisions and actions to the public and must submit themselves to whatever scrutiny is appropriate to their office.

5.   Openness: Holders of public office should be as open as possible about all the decisions and actions they take. They should give reasons for their decisions and restrict information only when the wider public interest clearly demands.

6.   Honesty: Holders of public office have a duty to declare any private interests relating to their public duties and to take steps to resolve any conflicts arising in a way that protects the public interest.

7.   Leadership: Holders of public office should promote and support these principles by leadership and example.

The Nolan principles are still relevant and provide a blueprint for establishing the values and culture of every NHS, and any public sector, organisation. The Nolan principles' importance was reaffirmed by HM Treasury in 2015 in 'Managing Public Money'.[22] Additionally, since 2010 all NHS bodies have been required to have regard to the NHS Constitution for England[23] in all their decisions and actions. The Constitution lists principles, values and rights and responsibilities of patients, the public and staff. Since the 1980s the NHS has seen many changes in its organisational structure and in the way health services are commissioned and provided.

In summary, hospital care was once managed by area health authorities reporting to regional health authorities (RHAs). Area health authorities were abolished in the 1980s and replaced by district health authorities. The first NHS trusts were created in 1990, responsible for providing healthcare commissioned by district health authorities, which reported to RHAs, which reported to the NHS Executive. The larger, more financially successful NHS trusts became NHS foundation trusts, which were subject to looser control from the NHS. District health authorities, the NHS Executive and RHAs were abolished in the early 2000s and replaced by primary care trusts (PCTs), strategic health authorities and regional outposts of the Department of Health. Strategic health authorities, PCTs and the outposts were abolished and replaced by clinical commissioning groups (CCGs) in 2012 under the control of the NHS Commissioning Board while most of the remaining NHS trusts became foundation trusts.

Shortcomings in governance in the NHS have come to light in recent years not from financial impropriety but from systemic failures in care such as exemplified by the deaths resulting from deficient care at Mid Staffordshire NHS Foundation

---

22   HM Treasury (2015) Managing Public Money, www.gov.uk/government/uploads/system/uploads/attachment_data/file/454191/ Managing_Public_Money_AA_v2_-jan15.pdf

23   HM Government 2015 NHS Constitution for England, www.gov.uk/government/publications/the-nhs-constitution-for-england/ the-nhs-constitution-for-england

Trust. The independent Francis Report[24] found deficiencies in staffing and governance where board members should have been more aware of the problems which persisted for years and had not been addressed and too much attention had been given to data rather than patient care and concerns raised by staff, patients and relatives. Further major changes to the NHS took place in 2013. In summary, the present configuration of the NHS is as follows:

The government decides how much money the NHS receives and set priorities. The Secretary of State for Health is in charge of the Department of Health, which passes money on to a range of different organisations. Most of it goes to NHS England, created in 2013 and taking over from the NHS Commissioning Board established a year earlier, which is responsible for overseeing the commissioning, planning and buying of the range of NHS services.

NHS England also in effect sets strategy and behaves like an NHS headquarters.[25] NHS England commissions some services directly but passes on most of its money to the circa 200 clinical commissioning groups (CCGs) around the country, which identify local health needs and plan and buy care for the local area. CCGs buy healthcare from a variety of organisations, including NHS trusts which run hospital and community services, charities, GPs, local authorities and the private sector. NHS England also funds the two main regulators: NHS Improvement and the Care Quality Commission. NHS Improvement is responsible for the financial regulation, performance management and governance of NHS trusts and foundation trusts. The Care Quality Commission, an independent regulator, inspects the quality of care provided.

As the NHS organisations changed, arrangements for governance and accountability have also changed. Most NHS organisations, however, are still run by a board or governing body which is required to have structures and processes very similar to listed company boards. A key difference however is that whereas in the listed company sector shareholders are expected to hold boards to account, there is no equivalent mechanism in the NHS. Instead foundation trust boards theoretically report to a council of governors appointed by its members who are patients and members of the public who volunteer for the role.

Foundation trusts have four types of governor: public elected by the members; staff elected from the staff body; appointed from bodies, such as a local authority, the police or a charity, entitled to appoint a governor and in an optional category patient, carer or service user. Foundation trusts have some discretion on the make-up of the governing body but there must be more public governors than the total of all the other governors and there must be at least three staff governors. All governors have the same statutory role and responsibility.

---

24   Mid Staffordshire NHS Foundation Trust Public Inquiry (2013) The Francis Inquiry into Mid-Staffordshire NHS Foundation Trust (the Francis Report), London: The Stationery Office, http://webarchive.nationalarchives.gov. uk/20150407084003/http://www.midstaffspublicinquiry.com/

25   King's Fund, www.kingsfund.org.uk/audio-video/how-does-nhs-in-england-work

CCGs, which are also accountable to NHS Improvement, are led by clinicians and have a governing body consisting of executive officers, GPs, clinicians and lay members. The governing body is expected to operate in much the same way as other boards but one of their key roles is to ensure the inherent conflict of interest where GP CCG members can both commission services and provide them themselves is managed.

While these NHS bodies all have a governing body, they also all have an **'accountable officer'** or 'accounting officer' (both terms are currently used) who is accountable to the Accounting Officer of NHS England, who in turn is accountable to parliament for the quality of the administration that he or she leads. This officer will be the chief executive so, while the governing body as a whole has an accountability to NHS Improvement, the chief executive has a separate accountability to the NHS England chief executive and to parliament. The accountability of a trust or CCG chief executive is set out in various documents such as an Accountable Officer Memorandum for chief executives issued by the Accounting Officer;[26] NHS Foundation Trust Accounting Officer Memorandum[27] and Clinical commissioning group guidance on senior appointments, including accountable officer.[28] Chief executives, inter alia, are required to make an annual governance statement.[29] NHS trusts which are not foundation trusts must make a governance statement drawing on best practice available including those aspects of the UK Governance Code considered to be relevant to the NHS trust. Foundation trusts are expected to comply with the NHS Foundation Trust Code of Governance[30] and CCGs with the Corporate Governance Framework issued by the NHS Commissioning Board.[31]

accountable officer
A term used in the public sector for the head of an organisation accountable to the next higher level in the bureaucracy and ultimately to a Secretary of State and then Parliament. Under the Public Finance and Accountability (Scotland) Act 2000 accountable officers have a personal responsibility for the propriety and regularity of the public finances for the body for which you are answerable and ensuring that the resources of the body are used economically, efficiently and effectively.

Test yourself 2.4

How is governance enforced in NHS foundation trusts?

3.3   The not-for-profit sector

This sector includes charities and organisations such as housing associations and universities. Large charities are usually companies and housing associations and universities may also be charities and companies. If companies they may,

---

26   See, for example, Accountable officer memorandum for chief executives of NHS trusts, www.info.doh.gov.uk/doh/finman.nsf/0 72561aa006322660725618c006b09a0/3bf24de22efb45cd802568f70038d723?OpenDocument

27   Monitor (2015) NHS Foundation Trust Accounting Officer Memorandum, www.gov.uk/government/uploads/system/uploads/attachment_data/file/451565/NHS_Foundation_Trust_Accounting_Officer_Memorandum.pdf

28   NHS England (2015) Clinical commissioning group guidance on senior appointments, including accountable officer, www.england.nhs.uk/wp-content/uploads/2015/10/ccg-snr-appt-guidance.pdf

29   NHS Improvement (2017) NHS trusts: annual governance statement requirements and update on going concern, www.gov.uk/.../nhs-foundation-trusts-accounting-officers-responsibilities

30   Monitor (2014) The NHS Foundation Trust Code of Governance, Updated July 2014.

31   NHS Commissioning Board 2013 Corporate governance framework.

under the Companies Act, be limited by guarantee rather than by shares. The main differences are that companies limited by guarantee have guarantors for a fixed amount of money rather than shares and – obviously perhaps – may not distribute profits to shareholders. Instead, any surplus funds must be used for the purpose of the company.

A considerable amount of guidance has been written for this sector, including the Charity Governance Code.[32] Its third and latest edition was published in 2017. There are two versions: one for smaller and one, a little more detailed, for larger charities.

Charities should apply seven principles:

- organisational purpose;
- leadership;
- integrity;
- decision-making, risk and control;
- board effectiveness;
- diversity; and
- openness and accountability.

These are supported by 'outcomes' and 'recommended practices'. The Code is voluntary and based on 'apply and explain' rather than comply or explain. Charities are encouraged to apply the practices or explain what they have done instead or why they have not applied it and publish a brief statement in their annual reports explaining their use of the code.

Other codes in this sector include the Housing Federation Code of Governance (2015)[33] and the Higher Education Code of Governance[34] by the Committee of University Chairs (2014).

3.4 Other and smaller companies

Guidance and principles for unlisted companies
There are about 25 privately owned companies that employ more than 10,000 staff. The largest is the Swire group, headquartered in London with 130,000 employees worldwide, and John Lewis Partnership, owned by its employees, with 90,000 staff. Another well-known group is Virgin. At present there are no governance requirements for such companies although some choose to follow the UK Code.

---

32   Charity Governance Code Steering Group 2017 Charity Governance Code for larger charities (and smaller charities), www.charitygovernancecode.org/en

33   Housing Federation 2015, Code of Governance, www.ccha.biz/wp-content/uploads/2016/08/NHF-Code-of-Governance-2015.pdf

34   Committee of University Chairs (2014) Higher Education Code of Governance.

There are 2.6 million registered UK companies, compared to 1,400 with a Premium listing. The Institute of Directors issued Corporate Governance Guidance and Principles for Unlisted Companies in the UK[35] in 2010. The guidance is detailed but phased so that it has a section of nine principles which should apply to all unlisted companies regardless of size and five more applicable only to large and/or more complex companies. They summarise the essence of generally accepted good governance practice and so are reproduced below:

Phase 1 principles: Corporate governance principles applicable to all unlisted companies

1. Shareholders should establish an appropriate constitutional and governance framework for the company.

2. Every company should strive to establish an effective board, which is collectively responsible for the long-term success of the company, including the definition of the corporate strategy. However, an interim step on the road to an effective (and independent) board may be the creation of an advisory board.

3. The size and composition of the board should reflect the scale and complexity of the company's activities.

4. The board should meet sufficiently regularly to discharge its duties, and be supplied in a timely manner with appropriate information.

5. Levels of remuneration should be sufficient to attract, retain and motivate executives and non-executives of the quality required to run the company successfully.

6. The board is responsible for risk oversight and should maintain a sound system of internal control to safeguard shareholders' investment and the company's assets.

7. There should be a dialogue between the board and the shareholders based on a mutual understanding of objectives. The board as a whole has responsibility for ensuring that a satisfactory dialogue with shareholders takes place. The board should not forget that all shareholders have to be treated equally.

8. All directors should receive induction on joining the board and should regularly update and refresh their skills and knowledge.

9. Family-controlled companies should establish family governance mechanisms that promote coordination and mutual understanding among family members, as well as organise the relationship between family governance and corporate governance.

---

35   Institute of Directors (2010) Corporate Governance Guidance and Principles for Unlisted Companies in the UK, www. iod.com/Portals/0/PDFs/Campaigns%20and%20Reports/Corporate%20Governance/Governance%20code%20for%20 unlisted%20companies.pdf?ver=2016-11-29-134715-607

Phase 2 principles: Corporate governance principles applicable to large and/or more complex unlisted companies

1. There should be a clear division of responsibilities at the head of the company between the running of the board and the running of the company's business. No one individual should have unfettered powers of decision.

2. All boards should contain directors with a sufficient mix of competencies and experiences. No single person (or small group of individuals) should dominate the board's decision-making.

3. The board should establish appropriate board committees in order to allow a more effective discharge of its duties.

4. The board should undertake a periodic appraisal of its own performance and that of each individual director.

5. The board should present a balanced and understandable assessment of the company's position and prospects for external stakeholders, and establish a suitable programme of stakeholder engagement.

One could take slight issue, however, with phase 1 principle 5, which seems to presuppose that boards are primarily interested and motivated by money. There is a wide body of evidence suggesting that what motivates people is more complex and remuneration is just one of many motivators.

The Companies (Miscellaneous Reporting) Regulations 2018
In August 2017 the UK government invited[36] the FRC to work with others to create a voluntary set of corporate governance principles for large private companies. The government also announced its intention to introduce secondary legislation to require companies of a significant size to disclose their corporate governance arrangements in their directors' report and on their website.

In June 2018 the FRC published a consultation document on the corporate governance principles for large private companies developed by a coalition group chaired by James Wates.[37] Large private companies will be encouraged to follow six principles to inform and develop their corporate governance practices and adopt them on an 'apply and explain' basis. Unlike the UK Code for premium listed companies there are no provisions to accompany the principles. Instead there is guidance for companies to consider in applying the principles.

This Companies (Miscellaneous Reporting) Regulations 2018 will, after January 2019, require directors' reports in the annual reports of large private companies (having either more than 2,000 employees or a turnover of at least £200 million and a balance sheet total of more than £2 billion) to include a statement of

---

36   ibid. Corporate Governance Reform: The Government response to the green paper consultation.

37   FRC (2018) Consultation on the Wates Corporate Governance Principles for Large Private Companies Financial Reporting Council, www.frc.org.uk/getattachment/48653f86-92c3-4cd6-8465-da4b7cac0034/;.aspx

corporate governance arrangements which discloses:

(a) which corporate governance code, if any, the company applied;

(b) how the company applied (the) corporate governance code; and

(c) if the company departed from (the) corporate governance code, the respects in which and reasons why it did so.

It is therefore up to companies to choose which corporate governance code to use.

AIM Rules

Around 1,000 companies are listed on AIM (formerly called the Alternative Investment Market). They were not required under the AIM Rules to adhere to the provisions of the UK Code but were encouraged to develop strong governance procedures and aspire to achieve the key elements set out in the Code as they grow. They were encouraged by the London Stock Exchange[38] in 2012 to adhere to the Quoted Companies Alliance (QCA) Guidelines, which are based on the Code but tailored to the needs of growth companies and their investors. These guidelines were superseded by the QCA Corporate Governance Code for Small and Mid-Size Quoted Companies 2013[39] and replaced in April 2018 by the QCA Corporate Governance Code which is intended to be a practical, outcome-orientated approach tailored for small and mid-size companies.

AIM companies will have a nominated adviser (Nomad) approved by the Stock Exchange who will help bring them to the market and who would be expected to assist the company in introducing appropriate corporate governance standards. AIM companies are required to have in place sufficient procedures, resources and controls in the context of the responsibility of a company's Nomad to assess the ongoing suitability of their AIM company clients.

The voluntary recommendation was replaced with a requirement in March 2018 when the London Stock Exchange issued AIM Rules for Companies.[40] These require, from 28 September 2018, each AIM company to disclose details of a recognised corporate governance code that the board of directors has decided to apply, how the company complies with that code, and where it departs from its chosen corporate governance code an explanation of the reasons for doing. This information should be reviewed annually and companies' websites should include the date on which this information was last reviewed.

---

38   London Stock Exchange plc (2010) Corporate Governance for Main Market and AIM Companies White Page Ltd, www.londonstockexchange.com/companies-and-advisors/aim/publications/documents/corpgov.pdf

39   Quoted Companies Alliance (2013) Corporate Governance Code for Small and Mid-Size Quoted Companies 2013, www.theqca.com/shop/guides/70707/corporate-governance-code-for-small-and-midsize-quoted-companies-2013.thtml

40   London Stock Exchange 2018 (2018) AIM Rules for Companies, www.londonstockexchange.com/companies-and-advisors/aim/advisers/aim-notices/aim-rules-for-companies-march-2018-clean.pdf

It is for each AIM company board to decide which governance code to use. AIM companies incorporated in the UK are likely to use either the QCA Corporate Governance Code or the UK Corporate Governance Code.

Chapter summary

◆ One of the first corporate governance scandals was the South Sea Company.

◆ Modern UK corporate governance began following the failure of Coloroll and Polly Peck.

◆ These and subsequent scandals had a number of problems in common, including dominant CEOs, other directors who were supine, theft and/ or fraud, aggressive or fraudulent accounting, high growth strategies and audits which found nothing wrong.

◆ These scandals resulted in the Cadbury Code in 1992 for listed companies, the first governance code in the world.

◆ Since 1992 there have been more scandals, including those associated with the financial crisis which triggered a series of changes to the Code now called the UK Corporate Governance Code.

◆ The Prime Minister in 2016 triggered consultations on governance, which led to legislative changes and changes to the UK Code.

◆ The governance system for listed companies has been influential in other sectors which have their own codes.

◆ A key difference for organisations without shareholders is that some other body or group is needed to hold their boards to account.

Chapter three
Corporate governance development around the world

CONTENTS

1. Introduction
2. Governance code development around the world
3. G20/OECD Principles of Corporate Governance
4. The European approach
5. The South African approach
6. The Mauritian approach
7. The US approach

1. Introduction

This chapter looks at how corporate governance has spread around the world over the last 25 years or so. Most parts of the world have largely followed the UK approach, with voluntary codes theoretically enforced by shareholders. The notable exception is the United States, where regulators have been more prescriptive.

2. Governance code development around the world

Corporate governance since the Cadbury Code in 1992 has become a global phenomenon. The **International Finance Corporation (IFC)** states that governance codes can be found in 120 countries. The **European Corporate Governance Institute (ECGI)** maintains web links for most of the governance codes in the world, listing past and current codes and related guidance for 99 countries, with many countries having several listed. The UK has the most entries with 37, which includes superseded main codes, related guidance such as on audit committees and internal control and private sector guidelines such as the Hermes Principles; it does not list any of the public or voluntary sector codes. The ECGI also lists regional and international codes such as the G20/OECD Principles of Corporate Governance, UN Guidance on Good Practices in Corporate Governance Disclosure 2006, various pan-European guidelines

International Finance Corporation (IFC)
A member of the World Bank Group, the IFC is the largest global development institution focused on the private sector in developing countries. It assists in areas such as finance, infrastructure, employee skills, and regulatory environment.

European Corporate Governance Institute (ECGI)
A European based international scientific non-profit association that provides a forum for debate and dialogue between academics, legislators and practitioners, focusing on major corporate governance issues and best practice. Its primary role is to undertake, commission and disseminate leading research on corporate governance.

and European Bank for Reconstruction and Development, Commonwealth and international comparative studies.

The UK voluntary code approach has been adopted in many countries but whether or not such an approach will work depends on the authority of the institutions which support it. Cadbury makes the point that the 1992 Code would not have worked without the backing of the London Stock Exchange. Nor should we take for granted the importance to the effectiveness of the UK Code of UK established practices, structures and mechanisms such as well-developed company law, accounting and auditing frameworks. The IFC has issued toolkits for countries wanting to improve governance.

Test yourself 3.1

Where can you find a resource giving access to most of the world's corporate governance codes?

3. G20/OECD Principles of Corporate Governance

Organisation for Economic Co-operation and Development (OECD)
The OECD is an international organisation based in Paris with 35 member countries. OECD helps governments foster prosperity and fight poverty through economic growth and financial stability. It also helps to ensure governments take into account environmental implications of economic and social development.

The **Organisation for Economic Co-operation and Development (OECD)** issued Principles of Corporate Governance[1] (the Principles) in 1999 and revised versions in 2004 and 2015. The latest revision was carried out under the auspices of the OECD Corporate Governance Committee with all G20 countries invited to participate with the 35 OECD Member countries.

Unlike national governance codes the Principles are aimed at national policy makers to help them 'evaluate and improve the legal, regulatory, and institutional framework for corporate governance, with a view to support economic efficiency, sustainable growth and financial stability'. The first four are about establishing an appropriate environment for good governance such as company law, ownership rights, functioning capital markets and recognising the rights of stakeholders. The last two are the most relevant to companies: the fifth principle is about company disclosures and the sixth is about the responsibilities of the board.

The OECD has also issued Guidelines for Corporate Governance of State-owned Enterprises[2], the most recent version in 2015, and a large number of reports on such matters as governance in particular countries and regions, supervision and enforcement on corporate governance and a Corporate Governance Factbook[3]

1   G20/OECD (2015) Principles of Corporate Governance, www.oecd-ilibrary.org/docserver/9789264236882-en.pdf?expires=153 2518109&id=id&accname=guest&checksum=149D664F21B6F106F6CF4B4430F2140B

2   OECD (2015) OECD Guidelines on Corporate Governance of State-Owned Enterprises, Paris, http://mof.gov.il/gca/about/ documents/oecd-guidelines-corporate-governance-soes-2015.pdf

3   OECD (2017) OECD Corporate Governance Factbook 2017, www.oecd.org/daf/ca/Corporate-Governance-Factbook.pdf

comparing governance requirements and structures in different countries. The OECD has also issued extensive guidance on corporate responsibility, including government-backed guidelines for multinational enterprises.

4. The European approach

Following the US scandals at Enron and WorldCom in 2001, the European Commission (EC) convened a high level group of company law experts led by the Dutch corporate lawyer Jaap Winter. At the time there was concern among governance specialists in the UK and several other EU countries that a US-style legislative response, like the Sarbanes-Oxley Act, would be recommended.

The EC might have taken little notice of the subsequent Winter report[4] but for a major scandal at the Italian company Parmalat.

Making it work 3.1

Parmalat

Founded in 1961, Parmalat became a major international group with multiple interconnected subsidiaries largely controlled by the Tanzi family. Parmalat defaulted on a €150 million bond in 2003 and was declared insolvent. It later turned out that Parmalat had been technically insolvent since listing on the Milan Stock Exchange in 1990 but this was hidden by deliberate misstatement through falsification of financial statements which included fictitious transactions, invented assets, overstated earnings and understated debts by around €14.5 billion. A Cayman Islands subsidiary was used as an accounting dump to hide liabilities. The fraud was extensive, sophisticated and complex, taking place over many years. In many ways it was like another Enron.

In the subsequent enquiries questions were raised about the influence of the Tanzi family, the role of the board, board committees such as the audit committee and management, along with the gate keepers involved such as internal audit and the firms of external auditors. Questions were also raised about Italian accounting and auditing standards and why investors and financial analysts failed to spot anything was wrong.

Parmalat meant the EC took the 140-page Winter report on 'a modern regulatory framework for company law in Europe' seriously. It was thorough and laid the way for governance to evolve in EU countries. Winter rejected ideas of a US legislative approach and of a single European governance code but said companies should include in their annual report and accounts a coherent and descriptive statement covering the key elements of the corporate governance

---

4   High Level Group of Company Law Experts (2002) Report of the High Level Group of Company Law experts on a modern
        regulatory framework for company law in Europe, www.ecgi.org/publications/documents/report_en.pdf

rules and practices they apply. He recommended the EC issue a framework directive setting out the principles for such disclosure. He advocated countries develop their own codes, reflecting their own requirements but having regard to the framework directive.

The EU approach, on the whole, has been strongly influenced by the UK approach. The approach has worked and has continued to allow member countries to keep their own corporate laws and corporate structures: for example, several countries, such as Germany, allow two-tier boards with a supervisory and a management board as well as the Anglo-Saxon single board. EU directives have resulted in little new governance legislation in the UK but directives on the content of company annual reports and external auditing, including a requirement on audit committees, have been brought into UK law.

The Netherlands is an interesting example, where enthusiasm for corporate governance may be even stronger than in the UK. Like the UK, the Netherlands has a more dispersed ownership structure than most other EU countries. The first Dutch code was issued in 2003 and the latest in December 2016. Most Dutch companies, like German ones, have two-tier boards with management and supervision divided between the management and supervisory boards. The Dutch code places greater emphasis than UK Codes on long-term value creation, culture, risk management and reporting misconduct. The previous Dutch code was perhaps ahead of its time and based on a principle of 'apply or explain' but the current version is based on 'comply or explain'.

In September 2017 a voluntary group of pension funds, insurers and asset managers led by Eumedion issued a draft stewardship code for consultation. Eumedion is a members' association of c.70 institutional investors dedicated to enhancing the corporate governance, environmental and social performance and strategy of listed companies. The new code was published in July 2018[5] and will come into force as of 1 January 2019.

Stop and think 3.1

The Dutch have also taken the financial crisis very seriously. The Dutch banking Association Code[6] requires bank employees to swear a bankers' oath:

'Bankers' Oath: I swear/promise within the limits of my role that I perform at any moment in the banking sector:

that I will perform my duties with integrity and care;

that I will carefully consider all the interests involved in company, i.e. those of the clients, the shareholders, the employees and the society in

---

5   Eumedion (2018) Dutch Stewardship Code, www.eumedion.nl/nl/public/kennisbank/best-practices/2018-07-nederlandse-stewardship-code.pdf

6   Nederlandse Vereniging van Banken (Dutch banking Association) (2014) Future-oriented Banking Social Charter Banking Code Rules of Conduct, www.nvb.nl/english/2273/future-oriented-banking-toekomstgericht-bankieren.html

which the company operates;

that in this consideration, I will give paramount importance to the client's interests;

that I will comply with the laws, regulations and codes of conduct applicable to me;

that I will observe confidentiality in respect of matters entrusted to me;

that I will not abuse my knowledge;

that I will act in an open and assessable manner and I know my responsibility towards society;

that I will endeavour to maintain and promote confidence in the financial sector.

So help me God/This I declare and promise.

Name [signature]'

Should a similar oath be adopted in the UK?

A possible weakness of the EU approach is that by following the UK approach – where governance practice is supposed to be enforced by active institutional investors – most other EU countries, with the exception of the Netherlands, have investors who are less active and less likely to try to enforce good governance. The UK has the greatest dispersion of shareholdings in the EU with no major shareholder owning 25% or more in about 90% of companies listed on the LSE. This compares with Italy, where about two-thirds of listed companies are controlled by a single shareholder and other countries such as France where some shares have higher voting rights – meaning fewer shares are needed to have effective control[7]. Furthermore, large institutional investors are less likely to want to invest at all in companies listed on the smaller stock exchanges.

The **European Bank for Reconstruction and Development** produced in 2010 a set of 'Core Principles of a Corporate Governance Framework (CGF)'.[8] It provides a succinct two-page set of ten principles, which could be useful for UK readers who may take our highly developed legal framework for granted – to remind them that good governance depends on legal issues such as shareholder rights and not just codes – and to readers from developing countries as a brief summary of governance.

European Bank for Reconstruction and Development
Established to help build market-oriented economies and promote private and entrepreneurial initiative in Central and Eastern Europe in 1991. It has since expanded and is owned by 66 countries from five continents, as well as the European Union and the European Investment Bank.

Test yourself 3.2

Who is the intended audience of the G20/OECD Principles of corporate governance?

7   See OECD Factbook, ibid.

8   The European Bank for Reconstruction and Development (2010) Core Principles of a Corporate Governance Framework (CGF), www.ecgi.org/codes/documents/ebrd_cgprin_2010.pdf

5. The South African approach

South Africa has some large companies listed on the Johannesburg Stock Exchange, such as Anheuser-Busch Inbev SA/NV, Old Mutual and British American Tobacco, but the majority of South African listed companies are smaller and have a controlling owner or group of shareholders.

South Africa has been a leader in governance since the first King Report in 1994. The King Code is now in its fourth edition and each code has stood out in its time for the way it emphasises ethics, values, stakeholder inclusivity, integrated reporting, and corporate citizenship and responsibility. Like the previous Dutch Code, King III was based on 'apply or explain' but King IV[9] is based on 'apply and explain' so organisations should both apply, and state how they apply, corporate governance principles. This requirement is the same as the UK requirement regarding principles but the UK Code has provisions with which companies must comply or explain.

King IV is intended to apply to all types of organisation regardless of legal form. King IV's objectives are to:

◆ promote good governance as integral to running an organisation and delivering governance outcomes such as an ethical culture, good performance, effective control and legitimacy;

◆ broaden its acceptance making it fit for implementation across a variety of sectors and organisational types;

◆ reinforce corporate governance as a holistic and interrelated set of arrangements to be understood and implemented in an integrated manner;

◆ encourage transparent and meaningful reporting to stakeholders; and

◆ present corporate governance as concerned with not only structure and process, but also with an ethical consciousness and conduct and outcomes.

You are encouraged to download and read the King IV Report.

6. The Mauritian approach

The 2016 version of the 'The national code of corporate governance for Mauritius'[10] is an interesting development. It consists of a reduced set of eight principles on just two pages and, like King IV, the 'apply and explain' approach. Public interest and public sector entities required to report on governance must state how they apply the principles and external auditors should assess non-compliance. Other types of organisation are encouraged to use the code. Using external auditors to assess compliance can be a good way

9 Institute of Directors Southern Africa (2016) King IV Report on Corporate Governance for South Africa, www.adamsadams.com/wp-content/uploads/2016/11/King-IV-Report.pdf

10 Ministry of Financial Services (Mauritius) (2016) The national code of corporate governance for Mauritius, www.nccg.mu/sites/default/files/files/the-national-code-of-corporate-governance-for-mauritius_2016.pdf

for countries to improve corporate governance where investors are less likely to apply the necessary pressure on companies. The report also gives useful guidance in applying each of the principles although companies are not required to report on whether they follow the guidance. There are separate sections for different sectors: banks, stock exchange listed companies, statutory bodies, groups and subsidiaries, family companies, holders of a 'category 1' global business licence and management companies. The appendices give examples of board documents such as a board charter and a directors' code of ethics. The Code should be a very useful document, not just in Mauritius but elsewhere too.

Test yourself 3.3

How can corporate governance be enforced?

---

7. The US approach

It is sometimes said that the UK has a principles-driven approach to accounting and governance, whereas the US has a rules-driven approach, but this may be an oversimplification. In the US there is no voluntary national code of principles equivalent to the UK Corporate Governance Code. Instead, the US has a system of federal and state legislation, plus rules administered by the Securities and Exchange Commission (SEC) and stock exchanges. The federal government has passed two major pieces of legislation: the Sarbanes-Oxley Act 2002, introduced after a series of corporate scandals including Enron and WorldCom, and the Dodd-Frank Act (Dodd-Frank Wall Street Reform and Consumer Protection Act 2010) after the financial crisis. The Dodd-Frank Act created financial regulatory processes to limit **risk** by enforcing transparency and accountability. Although the US approach is often characterised as 'regulator led' compared with approaches in the UK and most other countries which are termed 'shareholder led'[11], such distinctions are also an oversimplification. US public companies generally have dispersed shareholdings and unitary boards.

It is more common in the US for the chairman and CEO to be the same person; in the early 2000s, outside directors tended to be friends of the CEO/chairman. Listed companies are rarely under the control of a major shareholder and, certainly in the recent past, many could be described as 'ownerless corporations'[12] controlled by the executives without shareholders or outside directors holding them to account.

risk
The 'effect of uncertainty on objectives' or something which might happen which would have a dangerous, unpleasant or costly outcome or doing, or exposing someone to, something which might have a dangerous, unpleasant or costly outcome.

---

11   See speech by Ethiopis Tafara, Director, Office of International Affairs Director, Office of International Affairs U.S. Securities and Exchange Commission given in Madrid and London on 8–9 February 2007, www.sec.gov/news/speech/2007/spch020807et.htm

12   See for example 'Who owns a company?' – speech by Andrew Haldane, Chief Economist and Executive Director, Monetary Analysis & Statistics Bank of England, 28 July 2015. Given at the University of Edinburgh Corporate Finance Conference on 22 May 2015, www.bankofengland.co.uk/publications/Pages/speeches/2015/833.aspx

Making it work 3.2

Enron was a small energy company formed in 1985 with the merger of a natural gas company and a pipeline company. It grew rapidly in energy trading, taking advantage of deregulation and employing Wall Street corporate finance methods. It reported revenue in 2000[13] of $101 billion and assets of $65 billion. It was widely regarded as one of the most admired and innovative companies in the world. Some people though had trouble understanding the business model and how Enron made money. Analysts who questioned Enron's success were ridiculed by the company as being too stupid to understand. No one would accuse Enron's senior executives of lacking originality. In the 1990s, banks were making increasing use of structured finance vehicles, including special purpose entities (SPEs), to create new financial products. Enron used the same concepts to create new markets such as in gas contracts. It both ran those markets and participated in them. Being both a trader and a market maker gave Enron considerable commercial advantage.

It was a profitable business but not profitable enough to support the stellar stock rating or the credit rating which Enron needed to stay within its borrowing conditions. To boost profits Enron created SPEs (also called Structured Finance Vehicles or Special Purpose Vehicles) and valued them using 'mark to market' accounting which allowed Enron to use values derived from a model of its own construction to create false profits, overstate assets and understate liabilities. The problem with using models is that the model may bear little relation to a market; the model can be gamed (manipulated) allowing modelers to get any answer they want from it, which is exactly what Enron did.

There were many practices which were on the borderline of fraud and legality. A few months before Enron failed, a company vice president tried to blow the whistle over some of the transactions involving other SPEs created by the Enron chief financial officer (CFO) to hide what was really happening and create false profits. Enron booked false profits on transactions with its SPEs matched by the false assets in the form of amounts owed to Enron by the SPEs. The SPE accounts would have shown liabilities and losses but Enron relied on a US accounting technicality, and the opinion of its auditor Arthur Andersen, which allowed Enron to exclude these SPE liabilities from its group balance sheet while Enron group accounts showed the profits and assets.

UK accounting standards and the tests for what results to consolidate were different. It is likely that if Enron had been a UK company it would have had to consolidate the SPEs into its group accounts so that the group accounts would not have shown such profits or assets. In the UK a company's results must be consolidated into the consolidated results of the holding company if the holding company has effective control over

---

13   Enron (2000) Enron Annual Report 2000, http://picker.uchicago.edu/Enron/EnronAnnualReport2000.pdf

the company. Enron relied on a rule which said that if another person owned 3% or more of a company it would not have to be consolidated. Theoretically there was a similar control test in the US but for some reason the auditors allowed Enron not to consolidate the SPE's results.

When Enron collapsed in 2001 it was the largest corporate bankruptcy in US history. Staff lost their jobs and pensions and some of the executives went to jail. Enron was originally described as an accounting and audit failure. It was, but it was also a systems failure where conflicts of interest triumphed over inappropriate regulation. De-regulation of the energy markets enabled Enron to grow and flawed accounting rules allowed ambitious people to report assets and profits which did not exist and make liabilities which did exist disappear yet stay within the letter of the accounting rules.

Enron's 2000 annual report claimed its cultural values included:

◆   'Respect: We treat others as we would like to be treated ourselves. We do not tolerate abusive or disrespectful treatment.

◆   Integrity: We work with customers and prospects openly, honestly and sincerely. When we say we will do something, we will do it; when we say we cannot or will not do something, then we won't do it.'

This was not really true. The business culture meant that many managers, directors, banks, auditors and lawyers either knew or guessed that seriously unethical practices were taking place yet turned a blind eye, presumably because they were all getting rich.

The directors confessed they 'had no inkling that Enron was in troubled waters until mid-October 2001' after its problems had been reported in the newspapers.

What should Enron teach us?

A number of important corporate governance problems are exemplified by Enron. US financial reporting standards allowed accounts which complied with the letter of a standard while ignoring its intention. The board relied on advice by the auditor and their lawyer in creating corporate structures which complied with the letter of rules rather than their principles. The US board structure did not control the many conflicts of interest between executives.

The chief executive of Enron, Jeffrey Skilling, needed the auditor Arthur Andersen to accept mark to market accounting as Enron's trading strategy depended upon it. Strangely, Skilling took part in an Enron internal video where he parodied himself suggesting that he had come up with a new form of accounting known as 'hypothetical future-value' accounting, which would boost Enron's profits even higher – very close to what happened. The curious thing about mark to model accounting is that the two sides to a transaction can both appear to create a profit. This is in effect what Enron's CFO, Andrew Fastow, engaged in so creatively. He could not have done so without involvement from many major banks. People working for major banks such as Citigroup and JP Morgan Chase were actively involved. Although no liability was admitted, in 2003 these two banks agreed to pay $300 million in fines and over $4 billion in settlements to former Enron shareholders three years later. Other banks were involved too and legal proceedings continue and settlements so far amount to around $7 billion.

Banks provided finance to Enron's special purpose entities with which it and others could trade. Raptor and LGM were two such SPEs. Bullet points from a sales presentation given by Enron's CFO to a number of banks described Raptor as 'a structured finance vehicle capitalized with an Enron stock derivative and LJM equity, that will enter into derivative transactions with Enron related investments in Enron's merchant investment portfolio.' In further bullet points, Fastow said 'Raptor helps Enron manage the impact of the price volatility of its merchant investment portfolio on its income statement.' He projected a rate of return of 84%, which should have seemed too good to be true and raised suspicion, and said LGM was used for 'speed, flexibility, complexity of transaction and confidentiality'. 'Complexity' should certainly not be seen as a virtue. Later banks tried to sue Enron for being misled about what they were financing.

The auditor, Arthur Andersen, either looked the other way or actively aided Enron in its deception. We cannot know for sure as Andersen shredded the working papers before itself collapsing.

There a number of similarities between circumstances surrounding Enron and the financial crisis:

◆   Enron had a complex business model which few, if anyone, outside the organisation fully understood. Questions about the model or detail were met from Enron with comments along the lines of: 'if you do not understand you are too stupid for us to explain it to you.' Analysts and others learned that to question the wonder story of Enron could cost them their job.

◆   The directors of Enron did not really understand the business model – at least that is what they told the courts. Banks also have a complex business model, which the financial crisis revealed few understood.

◆   Enron and counter parties were booking profits on the same transactions, e.g. A has a deal with B and both A and B report a profit on the same deal.

◆   Enron and its special purpose entities entered into large transactions with banks. Banks also use special purpose entities. Many trading transactions entered into by banks are with other banks. It is not clear how much of banks' reported profits in the years leading up to the financial crisis came from trading with other banks.

◆ **Enron special purpose entities were used to hide liabilities and create artificial profits.**

◆ **Enron's ability to create new markets owed significantly to deregulation of markets. Banks also benefited from a period of deregulation in the 1980s and 90s and light touch regulation thereafter until the financial crisis.**

◆ **Enron lobbied politicians and made friends with them; this helped Enron get deregulation in their markets which increased the opportunity for real and fictitious profits. Banks are also active lobbiers.**

◆ **Enron's auditors, lawyers and bankers benefited financially from their involvement. Much attention focused on possible conflicts of interest of the auditors when they perform significant consulting work.**

◆ **After the bankruptcy most Enron executives were able to keep the proceeds of Enron stock they had sold although a few went to jail.**

◆ **Credit rating companies failed to predict Enron's problems. Nor did they detect the problems that led to the financial crisis.**

Enron was an immensely complicated deception. The deception at WorldCom, a telecommunications company, was more straightforward. Operating expenses to do with maintaining phone lines was reclassified by late journal adjustments as additions to fixed assets which boosted both profits and assets. WorldCom filed for bankruptcy in 2002 and the CEO was found guilty of financial fraud. Like Enron, WorldCom was audited by Andersen. Some auditors were incredulous that Andersen had not found these adjustments.

The very detailed provisions of the Sarbanes-Oxley Act 2002 seemed to address each of the issues identified at Enron and WorldCom one by one, treating the symptoms of the problem rather than the causes. Some of the main provisions are:

Section 302, which inter alia required:

◆ the CEO and CFO to certify that the annual report does not contain any material untrue statement;

◆ the financial statements fairly presents the company's financial condition; and

◆ the signing officers have reviewed internal controls over financial reporting.

Section 402 requires certification that having assessed internal controls they are effective and the auditor must attest this assessment.

Section 404 requires public companies' annual reports to include the company's own assessment of internal control over financial reporting, and an auditor's attestation.

Section 409 requires companies to disclose urgently information on any material changes to the financial condition or operations.

Section 806 protects whistleblowers.

Section 902 and 6 enables penalties of up to 20 years in prison for altering, concealing or destroying records and 10 years for not maintaining audit papers.

These rules have generated considerable extra work for companies, external auditors and consultants. If people thought Sarbanes-Oxley would prevent financial manipulation, fictitious profits and wrongdoing in the USA they were in for a nasty surprise with the financial crisis. According to McKinsey, global banking profits in 2006 were $788 billion, making it by a margin of over $150 billion the most profitable sector. Global banking revenues were 6% of global GDP and its profits per employee were 26 times higher than the average of other industries. By late 2008 it was clear that this profitability and implied stability of banks was a mirage.

The Dodd-Frank Act is intended to prevent reoccurrence and is more about financial markets regulation than corporate governance, although there is one key set of provisions which are key to governance. The Act requires the SEC to adopt rules requiring companies to disclose the ratio of CEO annual pay to the median pay of their employees. The Act also requires disclosure comparing company performance against compensation paid to executives and, if the CEO is also the chairman, disclosure of the reasons why.

In conclusion, corporate governance in the USA could be considered as something of a patchwork of federal, state, regulator, stock exchange, investor and institution-led rules, regulations, principles and guidance supplemented by individual investor action with some companies.

Test yourself 3.4

Most countries have a corporate governance code and many have several. Does the US have a corporate governance code?

Chapter summary

◆ 120 countries now have a corporate governance code – many have more than one.

◆ The European Corporate Governance Institute maintains a list of most of the world's codes.

◆ The G20/OECD Principles of Corporate Governance were written for national policy makers to help countries ensure good corporate governance.

◆ The EU has followed a similar approach to the UK on corporate governance requiring companies to disclose their governance practices and let investors enforce good practice.

◆ The Dutch require bank employees to swear an oath to encourage ethical behaviour.

◆ External auditors are charged with assessing non-compliance with the Mauritian Code.

◆ The King IV Report on Corporate Governance™ for South Africa 2016 uses the 'apply and explain' principle requiring companies to state how they apply the principles. It emphasises ethics and stakeholder interests far more than most other codes.

◆ Enron was a catalyst for corporate governance reform highlighting problems with regulation, accounting and auditing standards, board oversight of companies, treatment of whistleblowers, ethical failure and other issues. It led to the wide-ranging US Sarbanes-Oxley Act 2002 and reforms in the UK, EU and elsewhere.

◆ The US does not have a single code for listed companies with which they are all expected to use. Instead there is a range of federal, state, regulator, stock exchange, investor and institution-led rules, regulations, principles and guidance supplemented by individual investor action with some companies.

Chapter four

Current corporate governance issues and likely developments

CONTENTS

1. Introduction
2. Overview of issues in corporate governance
3. Ethics, values, culture and behaviour
4. Value creation and corporate or organisational purpose
5. Sustainability and corporate social responsibility

1. Introduction

This chapter considers some of the main current issues in governance and likely developments. It looks at how recent scandals have meant that regulators are taking a greater interest in culture and ethics and the role of business in society. It explains how there is increasing interest in how organisations create value and how organisations need to be socially and environmentally responsible.

2. Overview of issues in corporate governance

2.1 Greed and misconduct

Some of the governance issues concerning greed and misconduct have already been picked up in earlier chapters.

The privately owned unlisted company BHS collapsed in April 2016, with the loss of thousands of jobs and a £570 million hole in the pension fund potentially affecting 20,000 ex-employees. This highlighted that the UK Code does not apply to large unlisted companies. Such companies are important to the economy, provide thousands of jobs and can leave large liabilities if they go bust. The BHS collapse suggests the company was run by one person for his and his family's benefit, at the expense of others. This is not against the law but BHS crossed a line in what is considered socially acceptable. Although BHS's parent board had a board with a chair, neither company did what would be expected in applying checks and balances over a dominant individual. There is arguably a strong case for applying governance standards to large, economically important private companies. As noted in Chapter 2, the Government announced action on this in August 2017, leading to the Companies (Miscellaneous Reporting) Regulations 2018.

There has been a stream of bad news in the banking sector, highlighting unethical and illegal behaviour by banks. Governor of the Bank of England, Mark Carney, in his capacity as Chairman of the Financial Stability Board (FSB) wrote in an open letter in 2015 to G20 leaders: 'in recent years, the incidence of financial misconduct has risen to a level that has the potential to create systemic risks by undermining trust in both financial institutions and markets.' Estimates of penalties for banks involved in foreign exchange manipulation, Libor-rigging and mis-selling in 2016 are around £53 billion for the UK and £190 billion worldwide. Banks have also been found to be involved in money laundering in a number of countries. Newspaper reports in March 2017 suggested UK banks helped process at least £15 billion and possibly up to £65 billion from Russia. Deutsche Bank was fined over £500 million by UK and US authorities for failing to prevent $10 billion of Russian money laundering.

The Serious Fraud Office (SFO) conducted a criminal investigation into Barclays, relating to when it raised new share capital in Qatar in 2008 during the financial crisis. The investigation centred on a US$3 billion loan facility made available from Barclays to the State of Qatar, acting through the Ministry of Economy and Finance in November 2008. Barclays plc and four senior Barclays executives, including John Varley, its CEO at the time, were charged in June 2017 with conspiracy to commit fraud and the provision of unlawful financial assistance contrary to the Companies Act 2006. The Serious Fraud Office made a similar charge against Barclays Bank Plc, the main operating company, in February 2018.

Banks which in the financial crisis were said to be 'too big to fail' became referred to as 'too big to jail', amid suggestions that governments had leaned on regulators to be soft on wrongdoing in case their actions triggered another financial crisis.

Test yourself 4.1

What is the estimate of fines in 2016 for banks involved in foreign exchange manipulation, Libor-rigging and mis-selling?

1   Department for Business Energy and Industrial Strategy (2017) Corporate Governance Reform: The Government response to the green paper consultation, www.gov.uk/government/uploads/system/uploads/attachment_data/file/640631/corporate-governance-reform-government-response.pdf

2   Carney, M. (2015) Building a resilient and open global financial system to support sustainable cross-border investment, Financial Stability Board open letter to G20 Leaders, 30 August, www.fsb.org/wp-content/uploads/FSB-Chair%E2%80%99s-letter-to-G20-Leaders-in-advance-of-their-meeting-in-Hangzhou-on-4-5-September.pdf

2.2 Short-termism

A persistent problem in financial markets has been short-termism: an excessive focus on short-term results at the expense of long-term interests by shareholders. This has led to short-termism in decision making by company executives, who then make decisions which benefit the company's share price in the short term at the expense of creating sustainable value over the longer term. This is considered in more detail in Chapter 6. This exacerbates what some argue has been a persistent problem in the UK of under-investment in infrastructure, research and development (R&D) and other long-term investment. Changes in share ownership over time has meant that UK insurance and pension funds now hold far fewer shares in UK companies than in 1990. There also seems to be fewer shareholders in companies who have a real interest in the long-term performance of their investment and consequently in ensuring a company is well governed. At the same time, fewer companies seem to want to have a Premium listing on the London Stock Exchange (LSE). AIM, intended to help smaller and growing companies raise capital for expansion, has grown while the number of companies with a Premium listing has fallen. Some people argue that stiff regulations, including corporate governance requirements, deter boards from wanting a Premium listing – which used to be seen as the pinnacle of corporate evolution and something to which all boards aspire. Executives are also finding there can be more lucrative opportunities working for private companies than working in Premium-listed companies, where pay is never far from the spotlight.

Test yourself 4.2

Why is short-termism a problem?

2.3 Unsuitable employment practices

Media reports have also revealed concerning employment practices where workers had poor working conditions and were paid less than the legal minimum wage.

Stop and think 4.1

Sports Direct

Sports Direct International plc is the UK's largest sporting goods retailer with around 600 stores throughout the world and with a Premium listing. It has grown rapidly but has been criticised over its working practices. It employs around 27,000 staff but less than 10% have a permanent contract; most of the others have zero hours contracts. In 2016 its UK headquarters had 200 permanent employees and over 3,000 agency workers employed through two agencies. The House of Commons Business, Innovation and Skills Committee investigated in

zero hours contract
A contract between an employer and a worker where the employer is not obliged to provide any minimum working hours and the worker is not obliged to accept any work offered.

2015/16. Their report in 2016[3] found the company business model involved treating workers as 'commodities rather than as human beings'. It found that workers 'were not being paid the national minimum wage, and were being penalised for matters such as taking a short break to drink water and for taking time off work when ill. Some say they were promised permanent contracts in exchange for sexual favours. Serious health and safety breaches also seem to have occurred.' East Midlands Ambulance Service records showed 50 cases of life-threatening conditions at the HQ between 2013 and 2016, including one woman who gave birth in the toilet in the warehouse. The BIS report noted 'for Sports Direct to pay £50 million to agencies that do not seem to have a basic understanding of employment law and practices seems irresponsible, if not reckless.'

The Committee found that Mike Ashley, the Deputy Executive Chairman, founder and majority shareholder did not seem aware of this practice and seemed shocked when he heard testimonies from workers. The Committee considered it 'incredible that the owner, whose name is inextricably linked with the brand of Sports Direct, and who visits the warehouse at least once a week, would have no idea of the working conditions and practices there, when they have been highlighted in the media and in Parliament since 2015'.

'Sports Direct always seeks to improve and do things better, listens to criticism and acts where appropriate. With that in mind, the board has agreed that Mr Ashley shall personally oversee a review of all agency worker terms and conditions to ensure the company does not just meet its legal obligations, but also provides a good environment for the entire workforce. We expect him to start that work in the New Year.'

The Committee concluded: 'Although Sports Direct is a particularly bad example of a business that exploits its workers in order to maximise its profits, it is unlikely that it is the only organisation that operates in such a way.'

What do you consider should be the board's role in ensuring proper working practices? Is it OK to leave it to the executive? What are the relevant director's duties?

2.4 Directors' duties

As highlighted in Chapter 1, the UK Companies Act 2006 lists director's duties in sections 171 to 177. These codified what had previously been established through common and case law. Section 172 confers a duty for directors to promote the success of the company and in doing so to have regard to a number of factors, including the interests of the company's employees, relations

---

3   House of Commons Business, Innovation and Skills Committee (2016) Employment practices at Sports Direct, 21 July, https://publications.parliament.uk/pa/cm201617/cmselect/cmbis/219/21902.htm

with suppliers and the desirability of maintaining a reputation for high standards of business conduct.

Cases such as BHS and Sports Direct highlight where boards seemed not to have had sufficient regard for the companies' employees. Similarly, Tesco has been strongly criticised for its treatment of suppliers, suggesting that its board gave insufficient attention to the need to foster relationships with suppliers. In all three cases, arguably, insufficient regard was also given to the desirability of maintaining a reputation for high standards of business conduct. The House of Commons Business, Energy and Industrial Strategy Committee report in April 2017[4] says there is 'a growing body of evidence that directors have not paid sufficient attention to the interests of wider stakeholders, whether it be those working for them, the local community or suppliers'.

The UK government in August 2017[5] announced its intention to pass secondary legislation to 'require all companies of a significant size (private as well as public) to explain how their directors comply with the requirements of s. 172 (CA2006) to have regard to employee interests and to fostering relationships with suppliers, customers and others'. This will be brought into law from January 2019 for large private companies by the Companies (Miscellaneous Reporting) Regulations 2018.

As described in Chapter 2, the new Corporate Governance Code includes a provision (5) requiring boards to explain in the annual report how they have engaged with the workforce and other key stakeholders during the relevant financial year, and how the interests of stakeholders and the matters set out in s. 172 of the Companies Act 2006 have been considered in board discussions and decision making.

Test yourself 4.3

Why is there an ambiguity around s. 172 of CA2006?

2.5 Stakeholders

One practical action boards may take to ensure they are sensitive to stakeholders would be to convene stakeholder advisory panels with representatives from the various different stakeholders. Boards and executives could sound them out on strategic changes and major decisions over investment and divestment. Practical problems may arise in balancing the need for commercial confidentiality with informing stakeholders sufficiently well. For the UK, stakeholder governance is an idea whose time has come.

---

4   See Chapter 2, Footnote 15.

5   See Chapter 2, Footnote 16.

Stop and think 4.2

Uber is a US technology company with an app which provides a taxi service in 630 cities worldwide by connecting people who want to travel with 'self-employed' Uber drivers.

A female former engineer at Uber published a blog alleging harassment, discrimination, and retaliation during her employment and ineffectiveness of the company's then-existing policies and procedures. While some companies might choose to try and bury such bad news Uber the next day instructed a law firm to conduct a thorough review of the workplace environment, including diversity and inclusion. The review was led by a former US attorney general. Since the investigation started there have been newspaper reports suggesting the claims of harassment were not isolated, attempts by investors to change the company culture, deceiving city authorities and theft of intellectual property rights (IPR).

The investigation included 200 interviews with current and former employees and review of 3 million documents. To say that Uber took this seriously could be an understatement. The 13-page 'Holder report' has been made public. It does not describe what poor practices were found but makes 48 wide-ranging recommendations which include working practices, diversity and inclusion enhancements, training, culture change and a complete overhaul of corporate governance arrangements including changes to the senior leadership and internal controls.

Meanwhile in the UK there are allegations that Uber lobbied senior members of the Conservative government who intervened to allow Uber to operate in the UK with minimal regulation. Uber also classed its 40,000 UK drivers as self-employed but an employment tribunal in October 2016 ruled that they are employed, should be paid the national living wage and holiday pay. In September 2017 Uber's application for a new licence in London was rejected by Transport for London after deciding the company was not a 'fit and proper' private car hire operator. The decision was taken after concerns about Uber's reporting of criminal offences by its drivers, obtaining medical certificates and driver background checks.

Why do you think Uber was so quick to order the investigation? Was it right to do so?

2.6 Worker representation on boards and advisory panels

German supervisory boards have had employee representation for years. The above examples of inappropriate employment practices have brought renewed calls for employee representation on UK company boards.

The UK government[6] invited the FRC to consult on changes to the Code to strengthen the voice of employees at board level. The FRC has implemented this in the 2018 Code in Principle E and in Provisions 5 and 6.

E. The board should ensure that workforce policies and practices are consistent with the company's values and support its long-term sustainable success. The workforce should be able to raise any matters of concern.

Putting employees on boards would, without change in the law, give employees the same legal responsibilities as any other director which inter alia would mean the employee director's duty would be to the company, not other employees who may have voted to appoint him/her. This could create conflicts of interest for employee directors and put them in a difficult position. Employee directors could also potentially find themselves facing claims and even criminal charges for acts of the company.

2.7   Executive pay

High executive pay has been a controversial issue since the early 1990s. Attempts to address the issue have not halted a gradual widening of the pay gap between chief executives and employees. This author, in 2003, in a response on ACCA's behalf to the Department of Trade and Industry consultation 'Rewards for Failure' recommended that 'directors should be required to demonstrate to shareholders that their pay is reasonable in relation to their own performance, company performance and employee pay' and having 'a standard measure ... to track the relationship of board pay to average employee pay and return on capital employed'. The suggestion fell on deaf ears at the time, as before the financial crisis there was a greater belief than now in efficient markets. It was felt the market for executive pay, like other markets, should be left to market forces.

Times have changed. The US Dodd-Frank Act 2010 requires companies to disclose the ratio of total CEO pay to median employee earnings and a similar requirement in the UK has been introduced. The Companies (Miscellaneous Reporting) Regulations 2018 will require listed companies with more than 250 UK employees to publish the ratio of the CEO's remuneration to the median, 25th and 75th quartile pay remuneration of their UK employees in the directors' remuneration report from January 2019. The requirements are complex. The ratio must be published with related information in the form of a prescribed table. Going forward, this must cover a 10-year period so that trends are clear. In addition to the table companies must explain, among other matters:

◆   Any reduction or increase in the relevant financial year's pay, including whether a reduction or increase is explained by changes to the CEO's or employees' pay and benefits (for example, if shares awarded to the CEO have vested in that year and/or there has been an increase in pay and benefits to employees).

◆   Changes to the company's employment models (including an increase in the proportion of employees not based in the UK, or an increase in the

---

6   Ibid.

proportion of the company workforce not employed under direct contracts of service).

◆   The use of a different pay methodology option that year.

◆   Any trend specifically in the median pay ratio.

◆   Whether, and if so why, the company believes that its median pay ratio for that year is consistent with the company's wider pay, reward and progression policies affecting its UK employees.

The Companies (Miscellaneous Reporting) Regulations 2018 also require listed companies with more than 250 UK employees to publish information on the possible impact of share price growth on executive remuneration outcomes that are linked to performance periods or other executive incentive periods of more than one financial year.

One of the generally accepted governance principles is that executive interests and shareholder interests should be aligned. It was felt the way to do this was to link pay for performance but studies have shown that linking executive pay to performance does not work as intended and can have perverse effects. Long Term Incentive Plans (LTIPs) are a relatively recent innovation to link pay to long-term performance. They were introduced after the practice of awarding share options was found to have unintended consequences. LTIPS give executives company shares which they can sell in three to five years. The theory was fine, but in practice they did not work as intended because of the inappropriate selections of metrics to measure performance. Such plans have also made it easier for companies to obfuscate how much it pays because the actual value of the award may not be known for years.

The House of Commons Business, Energy and Industrial Strategy Committee[7] concluded that LTIPS be phased out as soon as possible. Instead the Committee preferred deferred stock options in which a proportion of remuneration is paid in shares after a set period of time – say five years.

The Code gives remuneration committees an expanded remit to consider company remuneration and wider workforce policies. Provision 33 provides:

33. The remuneration committee should have delegated responsibility for determining the policy for executive director remuneration and setting remuneration for the chair, executive directors and senior management. It should review workforce remuneration and related policies and the alignment of incentives and rewards with culture, taking these into account when setting the policy for executive director remuneration.

2.8 Board diversity

Board diversity is widely seen as important for two main reasons. Boards have traditionally comprised members who were male, white and in late middle age or older. The term 'male, pale and stale' was coined. The lack of women and people from other ethnic backgrounds was seen as wrong on equality grounds

---

7   Ibid.

and because boards were losing out on talented people. Where UK plc boards fared better was that 'male, pale and stale' did not necessarily mean British and many British boards were well represented by other nationalities. There is some evidence to suggest having more women on boards makes better boards but metrics intended to measure what makes one board better than another are at best problematic.

Most women and people from non-white backgrounds are not in favour of positive discrimination and believe getting to the board should be based on merit – but they do want a level playing field without barriers which prevent their appointment.

The other reason for wanting diversity is to ensure diversity of thought. Major failures in corporate strategy have often been associated with 'groupthink' – a phenomenon where everybody in a group thinks as one person with nobody challenging ideas and decisions.

The UK government has commissioned significant reports on gender and ethnic diversity in board membership.

◆ The Davies review into gender diversity. Lord Davies in October 2015[8] concluded five years of work on gender equality by proposing a series of recommendations including a bold new target of all FTSE 350 boards having 33% female representation by 2020 – around 350 more women in top positions.

◆ The Hampton-Alexander review. In February 2016, Sir Philip Hampton and Dame Helen Alexander were appointed to carry out a new board review to continue the work of Lord Davies. Their most recent report was published in November 2017.[9]

◆ The Parker review[10] into ethnic and cultural diversity. The Parker Review Committee, led by Sir John Parker, in October 2017 published its Final Report urging business leaders to improve the ethnic and cultural diversity of UK boards to better reflect their employee base and the communities they serve. The Review's recommendations fall under the following three areas:

  – Increase the ethnic diversity of UK boards by proposing each FTSE 100 board to have at least one director from an ethnic minority background by 2021 and for each FTSE 250 board to do the same by 2024.

  – Develop a pipeline of candidates and plan for succession through mentoring and sponsoring.

  – Enhance transparency and disclosure to record and track progress against the objectives.

---

8   Improving the Gender Balance on British Boards, Women on Boards Davies Review Five Year Summary, October 2015.

9   Hampton-Alexander Review FTSE Women Leaders. Improving gender balance is FTSE leadership. November 2017.

10   A Report into the Ethnic Diversity of UK Boards, Sir John Parker, The Parker Review Committee Final Report, October 2017.

The 2018 Code has strengthened the requirements on diversity by including references to diversity in principles J and L and provision 23 in Section 3.

J. Appointments to the board should be subject to a formal, rigorous and transparent procedure, and an effective succession plan should be in place for board and senior management. Both appointments and succession plans should be based on merit and objective criteria and, within this context, should promote diversity of gender, social and ethnic backgrounds, cognitive and personal strengths.

L. Annual evaluation of the board should consider its composition, diversity and how effectively members work together to achieve objectives. Individual evaluation should demonstrate whether each director continues to contribute effectively.'

23. The annual report should describe the work of the nomination committee including.... the policy on diversity and inclusion, its objectives and linkage to company strategy, how it has been implemented and progress on achieving the objectives; and the gender balance of those in the senior management and their direct reports.

As the 2018 FRC Guidance on Board Effectiveness[11] makes clear in paragraphs 16 and 89, diversity is not just about gender.

16. The boardroom should be a place for robust debate where challenge, support, diversity of thought and teamwork are essential features. Diversity of skills, background and personal strengths is an important driver of a board's effectiveness, creating different perspectives among directors, and breaking down a tendency towards 'group think'.

89. Developing a more diverse executive pipeline should increase levels of diversity amongst those in senior positions. Improving diversity at each level of the company is important if there is to be more diversity at senior levels. Greater transparency about the make-up of the workforce could support this. This might cover a range of different aspects of diversity, including age, disability, ethnicity, education and social background, as well as gender.

3. Ethics, values, culture and behaviour

3.1 The importance of ethics, values, culture and behaviour

There are essentially two types of corporate governance scandal: those that involve a flawed strategy and those which involve misconduct. Most involve the latter.

It should be clear from the previous chapters how important sound ethics and values are to business and to good governance. Ethics and values, particularly as articulated and displayed by those at the top of the organisation strongly influence corporate culture, which in turn influences corporate behaviour. It is

---

11   www.frc.org.uk/getattachment/61232f60-a338-471b-ba5a-bfed25219147/2018-Guidance-on-Board-Effectiveness-FINAL.PDF

perhaps surprising therefore that, but for the notable exception of the South African King codes, most governance codes have been all but silent on ethics, values and culture. The UK Code was a case in point until 2018.

This was an omission for many years. The extent of unethical behaviour exemplified by the financial crisis and further scandals, including those referred to above, has highlighted that the UK Code so far had not been effective in either ensuring ethical behaviour or preventing misconduct. It is of course possible though that the extent of misconduct would be worse without the Code.

In 2015 the FRC launched a culture project, involving the Institute of Business Ethics, Chartered Institute of Management Accountants, Chartered Institute of Personnel and Development and the Institute of Internal Auditors. It issued a report[12] in 2016 called 'Corporate culture and the role of boards'. The FRC defined corporate culture 'as a combination of the values, attitudes and behaviours manifested by a company in its operations and relations with its stakeholders'. Stakeholders include 'shareholders, employees, customers, suppliers and the wider community and environment which are affected by a company's conduct'. The FRC said that it is the board's role to ensure that the company's values, strategy and business model are aligned to the company's purpose. It also made the point that a healthy culture is an asset and a 'source of competitive advantage and vital to the creation and protection of long-term value'. The FRC listed the following observations for boards who, it says, should not wait for a crisis before focusing on culture:

◆ 'Demonstrate leadership – leaders, in particular the chief executive, must embody the desired culture, embedding this at all levels and in every aspect of the business. Boards have a responsibility to act where leaders do not deliver.

◆ Be open and accountable – openness and accountability matter at every level. Good governance means a focus on how this takes place throughout the company and those who act on its behalf. It should be demonstrated in the way the company conducts business and engages with and reports to stakeholders. This involves respecting a wide range of stakeholder interests.

◆ Embed and integrate – the values of the company need to inform the behaviours which are expected of all employees and suppliers. Human resources, internal audit, ethics, compliance and risk functions should be empowered and resourced to embed values and assess culture effectively. Their voice in the boardroom should be strengthened.

◆ Align values and incentives – the performance management and reward system should support and encourage behaviours consistent with the company's purpose, values, strategy and business model. The board is responsible for explaining this alignment clearly to shareholders, employees and other stakeholders.

◆ Assess, measure and engage – indicators and measures used should be

12   FRC (2016) Corporate Culture and the Role of Boards, July, The Financial Reporting Council, www.frc.org.uk

aligned to desired outcomes and material to the business. The board has a responsibility to understand behaviour throughout the company and to challenge where they find misalignment with values or need better information. Boards should devote sufficient resource to evaluating culture and consider how they report on it.

◆ Exercise stewardship – effective stewardship should include engagement about culture and encourage better reporting. Investors should challenge themselves about the behaviours they are encouraging in companies and to reflect on their own culture.'

As noted in Chapter 2, the 2018 Code issued in July gives more emphasis to values, integrity and culture. Provision 2 requires boards to monitor and assess culture and explain in the annual report what they have done and any action taken. The FRC's report on culture, 'Corporate Culture and the Role of Boards', does not explain how boards should do this and there is no generally accepted approach. It seems likely that boards and their advisors will be giving this matter considerable thought. The 2018 FRC Guidance on Board Effectiveness, however, gives useful pointers on what to consider.

3.2 Understanding ethics

Interest in ethics dates back at least 2,500 years to the Greeks Socrates, Aristotle and Plato. Yet, as we shall see, business's attitude to ethics is still developing. There are many ethical theories and here we consider three main ones: virtue, utilitarianism or consequentialism, and duty or deontology.

Virtue ethics
Virtue ethics stems from Socrates, Aristotle and Plato c.400BC. For them, what is ethical depends on whether someone has good character and something is done for the right reasons.

Utilitarianism or consequentialism
Utilitarianism or consequentialism is concerned with the consequence or social utility of actions. It can also be called teleological deriving from the Greek telos, meaning end or purpose. The most ethical action is one which compared with alternative actions maximises the overall societal good. The term utilitarianism is attributed to Jeremy Bentham, the eighteenth-century British philosopher and founder of University College London, whose bones are still on display in the College North Cloisters. According to Bentham, an action is ethically right if it produces the greatest balance of pleasure or happiness versus pain or unhappiness compared with other actions. There is an obvious link with human motivation as nearly everybody desires pleasure or happiness.

The criteria used in assessing happiness, pain and pleasure were intensity, duration, certainty, proximity, whether more or less of the same will follow and its whether its pleasure would be followed by pain. John Stuart Mill was a follower of Bentham and developed Bentham's ideas. Mill emphasised that happiness and pleasure was about quality as well as intensity and the goal of morality would be the greatest happiness for the greatest number. Applying utilitarianism in practice of course is not necessarily straightforward, requiring for example balancing the happiness or pleasure of one person or group with another.

Duty, deontology and Kantian ethics

Deontology comes from the Greek for duty. Kant was an eighteenth-century German philosopher slightly younger than Bentham. Kant's view was essentially that the correct reasoning is what is important in deciding right action. Acts are good not for their consequence but whether they are done according to one's moral duty. His views on moral duty are not easy to follow but are determined by what he called categorical imperative. Simply put, one should act according to whether the principle behind the act could be a universal law by which everyone would hope to live. One should also act so as to treat others as having intrinsic value and not as means to achieve one's ends. So, principles based on honesty and truth, kindness and consideration of others could be regarded as universal.

3.3   Ethical theories in practice

Most people in an organisational setting are unlikely to give much thought to whether an action is right or wrong according to an ethical theory. They are more likely, if they consider ethics at all, to act by reference to what they think needs to be done, what others might think, whether it is legal and complies with regulations and whether it is in accordance with organisational policies, including any code of ethics.

Most large companies and many other large organisations have a code of ethics and such codes broadly come in two types: codes based on rules or instructions and codes based on values and principles or a combination of the two. The UK Institute of Business Ethics is of the view that codes based on values and principles are preferable. Codes based on rules are likely to be narrow in focus and unlikely to apply sensibly to all the different situations where ethical guidance is needed. They may also be interpreted narrowly such that a person argues they comply with the letter of the rule even if they do not follow its spirit. Codes based on principles should be sufficiently flexible to apply to most, if not all, circumstances and empower people to think and use their common sense. It is also harder to argue that an action is acceptable if it clearly flouts the spirit of a principle.

Some reflection will, however, show that these theories are very relevant even today to business decisions. A company which conspicuously does good things such as supporting charities, reducing its carbon footprint, having good labour policies and producing an ethical product could be said to be following a utilitarian approach. But what if it is doing all this just to look good? Would it matter? From a virtue perspective such a company would be considered unethical because it was not acting for the right reasons. It could also be accused of hypocrisy. From a Kantian perspective it would also be unethical as the principle which the company was acting under was something like 'do what it takes to look good' which could not be a universal principle as not everyone would hope to live that way.

It has been argued that the ethical standards of business life are different from private life and a degree of dishonesty in business is normal. Albert Carr argued in 1968 that business is like a game with its own rules. He cited as examples products advertised in a way that made them sound a great deal better than they actually were, such as built-in obsolescence, lying about one's age on a job application and employing lobbyists to push legislation. Some would say that a business person is ethical provided they comply with the law and do not tell malicious lies; and that being totally honest all the time does not make good business. Carr referred to one businessman's reinterpretation of the Golden Rule – do unto others as you would want them do unto you – that business people try to do to others what they hope will not be done to them.

Such practices are less accepted now than they may have been 50 years ago. One old definition of ethics which may go back to the ancient Greeks is 'norms of behaviour accepted by the majority of society'. With such a definition the ethics of business should be the same as in private life. What is accepted by society changes over time and some things which were considered acceptable years ago seem abhorrent to us today and some things which are accepted in one society or culture are not accepted in others. For example, in the UK it is not generally acceptable for managers in a large company or the public sector to give work to friends and family but in some African countries, where there is a strong allegiance to one's tribe, such preferment is not only expected but it would be considered wrong not to give it.

Test yourself 4.4

What are the three main ethical theories?

4. Value creation and corporate or organisational purpose

4.1 The role of business in society and the purpose of the organisation

There is a range of opinions on the purpose of a commercial organisation. These range from the view that the profit is all that matters or share price is all that matters to the purpose being about creating societal good.

Milton Friedman, an economist, argued that the social responsibility of business is to increase its profits. He said corporate executives are employees of the owners of the business and so have direct responsibility to them. That responsibility is to conduct the business in accordance with their desires, which generally will be to make as much money as possible while conforming to their basic rules of society, both those embodied in law and those embodied in ethical custom. Friedman's view has drawn much criticism as people focused on the making money part of what he saw as executives' responsibilities and ignored his qualification that they should conform with the legal and customary rules of society. Friedman makes it clear, however, that he regards executives spending money on social responsibility issues as unethical as it was spending stockholders' money not in their interests Stockholders could in any case choose to spend their own money on such things.

Kenneth Mason, a former Quaker Oats president, is widely reported as saying that a 'profits-are-everything' philosophy is 'a dreary and demeaning view of the role of business and business leaders in our society... Making a profit is no more the purpose of a corporation than getting enough to eat is the purpose of life'.

Jack Welch, former Chief Executive of General Electric, was seen as one of the exemplars of maximising shareholder value. Between 1981 and 2001, while he was CEO, GE's value increased from $14 billion to $484 billion. Fortune magazine named him 'Manager of the Century' in 1999.

CEOs' variable pay became linked to share value and what were seen as drivers of share value such as earnings per share and return on equity. Research suggests CEOs would engineer performance and the company structure to trigger bonuses. This included companies buying back their own shares to increase the earnings per share, taking on debt which was cheaper to finance than shares but brought added risk and sometimes falsifying accounts. GE Capital took on more debt and would have gone bust in 2008 but for government help. Welch then called shareholder value maximisation the 'world's dumbest idea'.

Founders of organisations sometimes have a broader vision in mind than simply making profit. During the nineteenth century many companies were formed by people with strong religious convictions who saw their work and the enterprises they ran as part of their religious calling. They wanted their businesses to improve the social and working conditions of their employees and the local community encouraging education, pension provision and housing. They also believed in fair dealing generally, which made them trusted, which in turn helped the businesses grow. The Quakers were particularly active in business and the names of some of the companies they established are still around today although in different ownership. These include Barclays and Lloyds banks, Price Waterhouse (now PwC) and Cadbury the chocolate maker.

Johnson and Johnson, a healthcare company established in 1886, has had a credo since 1943 setting out its responsibilities. Robert Wood, its chairman from 1932 to 1963 and a member of the founding family, drafted the credo just before Johnson & Johnson became a publicly traded company. It puts responsibilities to shareholders last, after all other major stakeholders.

Stop and think 4.3

Johnson and Johnson Credo

'Our Credo

We believe our first responsibility is to the doctors, nurses and patients, to mothers and fathers and all others who use our products and services.

In meeting their needs everything we do must be of high quality. We must constantly strive to reduce our costs in order to maintain reasonable prices. Customers' orders must be serviced promptly and accurately. Our suppliers and distributors must have an opportunity to make a fair profit.

We are responsible to our employees, the men and women who work with us throughout the world. Everyone must be considered as an individual. We must respect their dignity and recognize their merit. They must have a sense of security in their jobs. Compensation must be fair and adequate, and working conditions clean, orderly and safe. We must be mindful of ways to help our employees fulfil their family responsibilities. Employees must feel free to make suggestions and complaints. There must be equal opportunity for employment, development and advancement for those qualified. We must provide competent management, and their actions must be just and ethical.

We are responsible to the communities in which we live and work and to the world community as well. We must be good citizens – support good works and charities and bear our fair share of taxes. We must encourage civic improvements and better health and education. We must maintain in good order the property we are privileged to use, protecting the environment and natural resources.

Our final responsibility is to our stockholders. Business must make a sound profit. We must experiment with new ideas. Research must be carried on, innovative programs developed and mistakes paid for. New equipment must be purchased, new facilities provided and new products launched. Reserves must be created to provide for adverse times. When we operate according to these principles, the stockholders should realize a fair return.'

Less well known in the Western world is Panasonic's creed, which predated Johnson's.

Stop and think 4.4

Panasonic

Panasonic was formed by Konosuke Matsushita in 1918, who in 1929 formulated the Management Objective and Company Creed to guide the company's growth: 'While giving careful consideration to harmony between profit and social justice, we aim to devote ourselves to the development of national industry, to foster progress and to promote the general welfare of society.'

In 1932 he announced a new company mission:

'The mission of a manufacturer is to overcome poverty by producing an abundant supply of goods. Even though water from a tap is a processed product with a price, no one objects if a passerby drinks from a roadside

tap. That is because the supply of water is plentiful and its price is low. The mission of a manufacturer is to create material abundance by providing goods as plentiful and inexpensive as tap water. This is how we can banish poverty, bring happiness to people's lives and make this world into a paradise.'

Then, in an expression of long-term corporate thinking which is probably unrivalled, he announced a 250-year plan for the company to fulfil its mission.

He added Seven Principles, which today are said to form the philosophical base of Panasonic. Below are the headings which provide a sense of what the founder wished:

1.   **Contribution to Society**

2.   **Fairness and Honesty**

3.   **Cooperation and Team Spirit**

4.   **Untiring Effort for Improvement**

5.   **Courtesy and Humility**

6.   **Adaptability**

7.   **Gratitude**

There seems to be a growing debate about the purpose of the corporation which may be getting traction with the EU. A High-Level Expert Group on Sustainable Finance published a report in 2018, 'Financing a sustainable European economy',[13] which made a number of policy recommendations focusing on long-term outlooks and creating a 'sustainable financial system that benefits society'.

This is echoed in the first principle of the 2018 Code says that part of the role of the board is to contribute to wider society: 'A successful company is led by an effective and entrepreneurial board, whose function is to promote the long-term sustainable success of the company, generate value for shareholders and contribute to wider society'.

Test yourself 4.5

Who argued that the social responsibility of business is to increase its profits?

---

13   EU High-Level Expert Group on Sustainable Finance (2018), https://ec.europa.eu/info/sites/info/files/180131-sustainable-finance-final-report_en.pdf

4.2 Concepts of value

For many decades, in a corporate context, value has generally been expressed in terms of financial measures such as profit, assets, liabilities and share price and using ratios derived from these measures such as price earnings ratio. People have of course always been aware that value is not simply about financial metrics and other metrics are also relevant such as on social and environmental factors. Accountants have been keen to recognise other value drivers and the concept of the Triple Bottom Line with reports on three areas – financial performance, social wealth creation and environmental responsibility – was proposed in the early 1980s although the thinking behind it goes back further.

While the concept is simple, measuring value creation using the triple bottom line concept is difficult. After several hundred years, the accounting system for reporting financial performance is still problematic – as discussed in Chapter 7. Measuring social and environmental value is harder. There is no universally agreed set of measures and the best that can be done is for people to agree various metrics which can be used as proxies for measures. Such metrics can be reported as they are or can be weighted according to how important people decide they are relative to other metrics. These metrics are likely to include non-financial metrics so if value is to be expressed in financial terms the metrics would have to be converted. Such an exercise would involve so much judgement, which may be both arbitrary and subjective, it may not be worthwhile.

4.3 Reporting on value creation

The traditional view that a set of annual financial statements in combination with changes in share price described whether and by how much a company was creating or destroying value is now outmoded. For the reasons already covered, such focus gives too narrow a view and can be misleading, even if we are concerned only with financial value. There have been various initiatives to report on social and environmental issues which will be covered in the next section but there seems now to be a broad consensus among companies, institutional shareholders, accountants and **non-governmental organisations** on a new approach called 'integrated reporting'. This approach suggests that value should be considered in relation to six capitals: financial, manufactured, intellectual, human, social and relationship, and natural, and companies should report how their activities have changed these capitals.

5. Sustainability and corporate social responsibility (CSR)

5.1 How sustainability and CSR links to corporate governance

Sustainability and CSR are essentially the same things. The term CSR was more common in the 2000s and the term sustainability is more commonly used today. Other terms with a similar meaning are 'corporate responsibility', 'corporate

non-governmental organisation
A non-profit voluntary citizens' group organised on a local, national or international level, usually active in furthering a social or environmental purpose.

corporate and social responsibility
There are various definitions which include the concept of a company as a corporate citizen fulfilling its obligations to society and the environment, the efforts of a company that go beyond what is required in law to preserve the environment and be a good employer, supplier and customer and a company being ethical particularly as far as employees, society and the environment is involved.

citizenship' or the shorter 'responsibility' and 'citizenship'. The equivalent terms for investors are 'ESG' (environmental, social and governance) and 'responsible investment'.

For many years corporate governance and sustainability have been seen by regulators and companies as two distinct, albeit related, subjects. With the notable exception of the South African King Codes, most governance codes, including the UK Codes, have contained nothing about sustainability. In the EU, regulation and recommendations on corporate governance and sustainability have also developed separately. Academics and NGOs, however, have long argued that the subjects should be seen as more closely related. After all, whether an organisation behaves in a way that is responsible towards the environment and society is clearly an issue for boards and shareholders which should make it a governance issue.

It is perhaps investors who have led a more joined-up approach. The Principles for Responsible Investment (PRI)[14] is an investor initiative launched in 2006 in partnership with the UNEP (United Nations Environmental Programme) Finance Initiative and the UN Global Compact. The six principles which investors must commit to in order to become signatories to are:

1. We will incorporate ESG issues into investment analysis and decision-making processes.
2. We will be active owners and incorporate ESG issues into our ownership policies and practices.
3. We will seek appropriate disclosure on ESG issues by the entities in which we invest.
4. We will promote acceptance and implementation of the Principles within the investment industry.
5. We will work together to enhance our effectiveness in implementing the Principles.
6. We will each report on our activities and progress towards implementing the Principles.

Recent scandals involving banks, BHS, Sports Direct and Tesco highlighted once again that companies sometimes behave in ways that are seen as unfair on customers, employees, pensioners and suppliers. This time policy makers and regulators listened and, as discussed above, the FRC has included stakeholder interests in the 2018 Code. The Companies (Miscellaneous Reporting) Regulations 2018 similarly requires medium-sized companies to make disclosures on how directors have complied with their duty to have regard to the matters in Companies Act s. 172. The High-Level Expert Group on Sustainable Finance also wants to put 'sustainability at the heart of the financial system' and that ESG factors are at the heart of financial decision making'. The Expert Group also recommended that the fiduciary duties throughout the decision-making process – including directors – should be clarified such that their obligation extends to ESG issues.

---

14   Principles for Responsible Investment: The Six Principles, www.unpri.org/about/the-six-principles

5.2   CSR in regulation

EU directives on corporate reporting have gradually required organisations to report on environmental and stakeholder issues. The most recent is Directive 2014/95/EU, which amends a 2013 Directive on disclosure of non-financial and diversity information. Directives are binding on EU member states in the sense that countries are required to enact in their own laws equivalent regulation.

The Directive requires 'large undertakings which are public interest entities' with an average number of more than 500 employees to report 'to the extent necessary for an understanding of the undertaking's development, performance, position and impact of its activity, relating to, as a minimum, environmental, social and employee matters, respect for human rights, anti-corruption and bribery matters, including:

(a) a brief description of the undertaking's business model;

(b) a description of the policies pursued in relation to those matters;

(c) the outcome of those policies;

(d) the principal risks related to those matters linked to the undertaking's operations including, where relevant and proportionate, its business relationships, products or services which are likely to cause adverse impacts in those areas, and how the undertaking manages those risks;

(e) non-financial key performance indicators relevant to the particular business.'

In addition, the Directive requires a 'description of the diversity policy applied in relation to the administrative, management and supervisory bodies with regard to aspects such as, for instance, age, gender, or educational and professional backgrounds, the objectives of that diversity policy, how it has been implemented and the results in the reporting period'.

5.3   Reporting initiatives

There are a number of initiatives for corporate reporting on environmental and social matters. Some focus on single issues, such as:

◆   ISO 14000 which is a standard for environmental management;

◆   Good Corporation's standard on business ethics; and

◆   the Fair Wear Foundation's Code of Labour Practices which is based on the International Labour Organisation conventions.

There are also more holistic initiatives. These include:

◆   Islamic Reporting Initiative – a new initiative which aims to create a sustainability reporting standard based on Islamic principles;

◆   AccountAbility – a global consulting and standards organisation with the AA1000 series of principles based standards first published in 1999 based on the Triple Bottom Line concept for:

–   organisations reporting on sustainability,

–   people providing assurance on an organisation's sustainability practices, and stakeholders to engage with organisations; and

◆ The Global Reporting Initiative (GRI) which began in 1997, is another series of 36 standards for individual different components of sustainability reporting. It is probably the most comprehensive set of standards with the greatest international recognition.

5.4 Integrated reporting

As introduced above, integrated reporting (often written as <IR>) is a relatively new initiative (2013) of the International Integrated Reporting Council[15] (IIRC). Its stated mission 'is to establish integrated reporting and thinking within mainstream business practice as the norm in the public and private sectors' and its vision is to 'align capital allocation and corporate behaviour to wider goals of financial stability and sustainable development through the cycle of integrated reporting and thinking'. Its development has been strongly influenced by Judge Mervyn King who was behind the South African King governance codes. Indeed King III issued in 2009 in based on integrated reporting.

The IIRC has been widely supported by companies, investors, advisors, NGOs, accountants and professional bodies. An International Integrated Reporting Framework was developed and many large organisations are now producing integrated reports based on the framework. The essence of the framework is contained in Figure 4.1, which is a systems diagram showing inputs on the left, processes or activities in the middle and outputs on the right. Reporters should report how they have transformed the six capitals which are inputs to the system into the six capitals on the outcome side. So, for example, reporters might describe what natural resources they have used in the business and how their activities have changed – adding to or subtracting from – those resources. In theory the total value of the capitals on the outcome side less the total value of the capitals in the input side is the value created or destroyed over a reporting cycle (e.g. a year). Reports on capitals tend to be a mixture of narrative and figures such as key performance indicators and not all reporters report on each of the capitals. It seems unlikely that individual capitals will ever be expressed as a single figure and more unlikely still that total value added or reduced will be expressed as a single figure.

---

15   International Integrated Reporting Council (2013) The International, IR. Framework, http://integratedreporting.org/wp-content/uploads/2015/03/13-12-08-THE-INTERNATIONAL-IR-FRAMEWORK-2-1.pdf

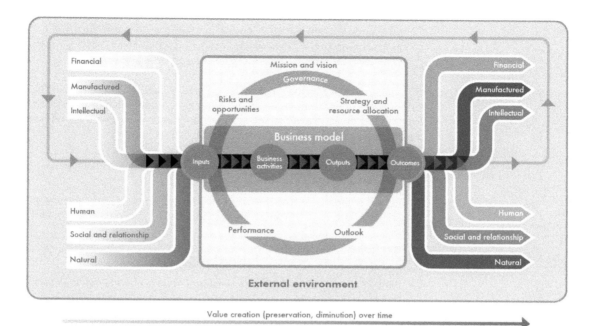

Figure 4.1 The <IR> value creation process

The widespread acceptance of Integrated Reporting could have eclipsed other initiatives such as the GRI. This does not seem to be happening though as reporters can use such frameworks as part of <IR>.

Reporters are still developing how best to communicate and considerable experimentation is still taking place. A danger of <IR> and indeed much reporting on sustainability or CSR is that reporters include what they want people to see and leave out or downplay what they do not want people to see. Balancing good with bad will always be a challenge. Former CEO of BP, John Browne, interviewed many senior executives of large companies for his book Connect. Browne argued that companies should connect better with society but found that CSR has failed in what he saw as its main purpose of building a stronger relationship between business and society. Browne gave the following reasons:

◆ CSR has proved irrelevant to a company's reputation in the face of scandals;

◆ executives view CSR as a largely irrelevant cost centre;

◆ CSR does not help build the business;

◆ CSR functions tend to be established for PR reasons in ghettos isolated from the business;

◆ CSR is fundamentally disconnected from the company's core commercial purpose; and

◆ companies with superb CSR records can also be hugely damaging to society. For example, Enron was widely lauded as a CSR champion winning six awards in 2000, yet CSR activities masked a rotten core. Also, banks in the run-up to the financial crisis claimed good CSR yet lost touch with what their businesses were doing for the economy and society.

<IR> in theory at least should not suffer the same flaws as Browne alleges for CSR. Integrated reporting, as the name suggests, is about integrating not just reporting but thinking and making reporters and readers alike understand how operations are connected and the role they all play in creating value.

Chapter summary

◆ Recent scandals, such as the failure of BHS and employment concerns at Sports Direct, have triggered renewed interest in governance reform in the UK.

◆ Key issues which need attention not hitherto part of most governance codes are: ethics, CSR, value creation and organisational purpose.

◆ Bank fines in 2016 for banks involved in foreign exchange manipulation, Libor-rigging and mis-selling are estimated at £53 billion in the UK and £190 billion worldwide.

◆ Short-termism by companies and investors continues to be a problem.

◆ Section 172 of CA2006 says directors must do what is most likely to promote the success of the company for the benefit of its members as a whole.

◆ Possible reforms include stakeholder and employee advisory panels.

◆ Executive pay continues to be a thorny issue. LTIPs, which were introduced recently as a better way to motivate executives, had unintended consequences.

◆ Diversity in the boardroom is recognised as an important issue.

◆ There is new interest by regulators, policy makers, companies and investors in corporate culture and behaviour.

◆ Three main ethical theories are utilitarianism or consequentialism, duty and virtue.

◆ Some companies claim to have a higher corporate purpose than just maximising profit. These include Johnson and Johnson and Panasonic.

◆ There is more to value than profit. There are several reporting initiatives which look at value creation in terms of social and environmental value as well as financial value.

◆ The most recent reporting initiative which is gaining widespread support is integrated reporting.

Part two

The board, shareholders and corporate reporting

Chapter five
The board

Chapter six
Shareholders

Chapter seven
Corporate reporting

Overview

This part looks at boards, shareholders and corporate reporting. Chapter 5 covers boards, their role and structure, how they are remunerated and the main board committees. It also looks at common problem areas for boards and directors in making good decisions. Chapter 6 explains the rights and responsibility of shareholders, the investor chain linking individual savers to legal share owners, engagement by shareholders with companies they invest in and some of the problem areas. Chapter 7 looks at corporate reporting – how companies report to shareholders. It looks at the purpose and contents of the annual report and some of the practical issues for reporting.

Learning outcomes

At the end of this part, students will be able to:

◆ understand directors' duties according to company law and governance codes;

◆ understand the concept of a balanced board;

◆ explain the different types of director;

◆ explain the role of non-executive directors;

◆   demonstrate ability to evaluate whether a director is independent;

◆   understand the role and functions of the main board committees;

◆   understand how boards are remunerated;

◆   appreciate some of the sensitivities surrounding board pay;

◆   explain shareholders' rights and responsibilities;

◆   understand how shareholders and companies engage;

◆   appreciate the main problem areas between shareholders and companies including the complexity of the investor chain;

◆   explain the purpose of and requirements for corporate reporting;

◆   explain what annual reports should include; and

◆   appreciate some of the main practical issues involved in producing a corporate report.

Chapter five
The board

CONTENTS

1. Introduction
2. The role of boards
3. The structure and composition of boards and the roles of different directors
4. Board committees
5. Directors' remuneration

1. Introduction

This chapter looks at boards, their role and duties, their structure and composition, board committees and how directors are remunerated. Section 1 sets out the responsibility of directors according to company law and governance codes. Section 2 covers the structure and composition of boards and the role of different types of director. Section 3 is about board committees such as the audit committee and section 4 is on director remuneration. Board decision making and board effectiveness are considered in Chapters 8 and 9.

2. The role of boards

2.1 Responsibility of directors according to company law

The duties of directors under company law have been summarised in Chapters 1 and 4. It is worth noting that the UK Companies Act 2006 (CA2006) does not refer to boards but instead talks about directors and meetings of directors. The model articles of association prescribed by the Secretary of State for both private and public companies set out the powers and responsibilities of directors and how they should make decisions. They state that decisions should be taken collectively and that any decision of the directors must be made either by a majority decision at a meeting or a unanimous decision confirmed in writing (not necessarily in a meeting). It follows that directors generally should not make decisions on their own unless they are acting within the delegated authority of the board.

It is good practice for all boards to document formally which decisions and matters are to be reserved to the board alone and what has been delegated by the board and to whom. This is covered more fully in Part 3.

2.2 Liability of directors

Generally, as agents of the company, directors are not liable for its actions and the company rather than its directors are responsible for its debts. There are many instances, however, where directors may have a personal liability. Directors could be liable in cases of breach of duty, trust, misstatement, misrepresentation, omission, libel or slander. Claims could be brought by shareholders, staff, creditors, regulatory and government bodies. Types of legislation which directors might breach include health and safety legislation, company law, financial regulation, employee, environmental and consumer protection, fraud and anti-bribery. A director may also be liable for wrongful trading if a company becomes insolvent and the company carries on trading after the director(s) knew or should have known that the company was or would become insolvent. In such a situation the directors could find that they have to contribute personally to the company's assets to pay creditors.

In the UK, in theory, all the directors on a board are equally responsible for what a company does so potentially an independent NED would have the same liability as, say, the chief executive. Fortunately, or unfortunately depending on your perspective, claims against directors have very rarely been settled in court so there is a lack of decided case law to clarify the situation.

Making it work 5.1

It seems likely that in practice, if a case was decided in court, a judge would take into account who knew or should have known what. Therefore in a case involving fraudulent accounting, for example, an audit committee chairman who was also a qualified accountant might be more culpable than an independent non-executive director (NED) from a non-business background. It is also likely that a court would take reward or remuneration into account so a lower level of responsibility might be expected of a voluntary non-executive director than a highly paid executive director (see Chapter 1).

Companies can take out directors' liability insurance which would cover many of the potential liabilities of directors but not for illegal acts.

2.3 The role of boards according to corporate governance codes

Whereas UK company law does not refer to boards, the UK Corporate Governance Code, other country governance codes, the G20/OECD governance principles and related guidance all address the role of boards in detail. There is a high degree of agreement generally about boards' roles although some codes emphasise particular issues. For example, the South African King Codes put more emphasis on the governing body's role in promoting ethics and corporate responsibility.

Principle 6 of the G20/OECD Principles of Corporate Governance sets out the responsibilities of boards which countries' corporate governance frameworks should encourage, irrespective of whether countries have unitary or two-tier board structures.

The 2018 UK Corporate Governance Code is effectively all about the role of the board and its committees. There are five sections of principles and provisions, covering:

1. leadership by the board including: setting the purpose, strategy and values of the company, ensuring necessary resources and controls, engagement with shareholders and other stakeholders, acting with integrity and processes for hearing concerns of employees;

2. division of board responsibilities including: the roles of the chairman and non-executive directors and independence;

3. board composition, succession and evaluation including: skills, training, commitment, appointments and re-election, board information and evaluation of the board, its committees and individual directors;

4. audit, risk and internal control including: the board's responsibility for fair, balanced and understandable reporting, the role of the audit committee, determining what level of risk the board is willing to take, establishing the risk and internal control framework and monitoring and reviewing all material controls; and

5. remuneration of the board and senior management (i.e. the first layer of management below board level including the company secretary).

The first section is perhaps the most important; the other principles and provisions essentially expand on it.

Stop and think 5.1

The first five 2018 Code principles are:

A. A successful company is led by an effective and entrepreneurial board, whose role is to promote the long-term sustainable success of the company, generating value for shareholders and contributing to wider society.

B. The board should establish the company's purpose, strategy and values, and satisfy itself that these and its culture are aligned. All directors must act with integrity and lead by example and promote the desired culture.

C. The board should ensure that the necessary resources are in place for the company to meet its objectives and measure performance against them. The board should also establish a framework of prudent and effective controls, which enable risk to be assessed and managed.

D. In order for the company to meet its responsibilities to shareholders and stakeholders, the board should ensure effective engagement with, and encourage participation from, these parties.

E. The board should ensure that workforce policies and practices are consistent with the company's values and support its long-term sustainable success. The workforce should be able to raise any matters of concern.

If boards did all this, would there be a need for other governance principles and provisions – or indeed governance codes?

2.4   The role of boards and governing bodies of organisations not required to comply with the UK Corporate Governance Code

Boards of other organisations may be subject to other codes or compliance requirements. For example, as discussed in Chapter 2, AIM companies and large listed companies will have to apply a governance code. Separate requirements exist for the National Health Service, charities and higher education. At a high level, the governance principles for any organisation will be similar. What will differ will be the mechanisms to ensure accountability of the governing body to an organisation's owners or principal stakeholders and the nature of risk facing an organisation. The G20/OECD principles and commentary on the responsibilities of boards and the principles of the UK Code, but not necessarily its provisions, should be applicable to any organisation with the qualified exception of the smallest organisations. The board of any organisation which applies the UK governance code principles with common sense is unlikely to go far wrong.

Test yourself 5.1

Does the UK Companies Act 2006 set out the role of the board?

3. The structure and composition of boards and the roles of different directors

3.1   Balance and size of board

Most governance codes encourage boards to have a balance of executive and non-executive directors (NEDS), including NEDs who are independent. Views on what constitutes a good balance have changed over time. As mentioned in Chapter 2, in the UK in 1992 a balanced board was one with two or three NEDs. As boards would typically have 8 to 12 members, NEDs were definitely a minority. Now in both developed and developing countries most codes, including the UK Code, expect independent NEDs to be in the majority. It is important to remember that, as far as UK company legislation is concerned, all directors have equal responsibility regardless of whether they are an executive director, a NED or the chairman.

A survey of over 4,000 directors from 60 countries of public and large private companies in 2016 conducted by researchers from Harvard Business School (Groysberg and Cheng[1]) for Spencer Stuart found that the average board size was 8.5 and the average percentage of NEDs was 67% (74% in public companies and 54% in private companies). The proportion ranged from 47% in Asia to 74% in North America, Australia and New Zealand. The percentage of NEDs in 2016 in the largest 150 UK listed companies was 61% (Spencer Stuart 2016[2]). The average board size for large listed companies in the UK and USA in 2016 was 10.2 and 10.8 respectively.

Balance these days is not simply about the proportion of NEDs. Diversity in the boardroom is now seen as important to ensuring good decision making and reducing the risk of groupthink. Having more women on boards is widely seen as a good thing. Several countries have introduced quotas to ensure more women are on boards of public companies and public sector organisations. Such countries include Norway, Finland, Spain and France with the highest quotas (40%), down to India which requires at least one female director on the board of listed companies.

Boards should be large enough to ensure they have the range of skills and experience needed to run the company and to ensure they have sufficient members to serve on the main board committees without over relying on individuals. The main committees are the nomination committee where a majority should be independent NEDs and the audit and remuneration committees which should be 100% independent NEDs. In practice, this would mean having at least eight independent NEDs if each one is only to serve on one committee.

Test yourself 5.2

Why have a balanced board?

3.2 Separation of the role of chairman and chief executive

A tenet of corporate governance is that the roles of chairman and chief executive should not be fulfilled by the same person. As noted in Chapter 1, the reasons are to improve the objectivity of the board and limit the risk of one

1   Groysberg, B. and Cheng, Y. (2016) 2016 Global Board of Directors Survey, Spencer Stuart and WomenCorporateDirectors Foundation, http://c.ymcdn.com/sites/www.womencorporatedirectors.com/resource/resmgr/Knowledge_Bank/WCDBoardSurvey2016_FINAL.pdf

2   Spencer Stuart (2016) UK Board Index, www.spencerstuart.com/~/media/pdf%20files/research%20and%20insight%20pdfs/ukbi_2016.pdf?la=en and Spencer Stuart 2016 Board Index A Perspective on U.S. Boards, www.spencerstuart.com/research-and-insight/spencer-stuart-board-index-2016

individual dominating the board. It should improve the board's ability to make decisions independently of management.

3.3   The chairman's role

The chairman is responsible for leading the board and ensuring the board is effective in all aspects of its role. This includes setting the board's agenda and ensuring members receive accurate, timely and clear information and that adequate time is available for all agenda items. The FRC Guidance on Board Effectiveness 2018 sets out the chairman's role in more detail.

A key agenda item will be for the board to decide which matters and decisions it wishes to reserve to itself and how it delegates other matters to board sub-committees, the chief executive and others.

The chairman should ensure directors continually update their skills, knowledge and familiarity with the company, and facilitate constructive discussion and challenge ensuring constructive relations between executive and non-executive directors. The chairman is also responsible for ensuring effective communication with shareholders and ensuring the board is aware of shareholder concerns. The 2018 Code includes a provision (9) that the chief executive should not become chairman and that on appointment the chairman, should meet the independence criteria in provision 10. Company secretaries will play a vital role in assisting the chairman (I).

Whereas in the UK it is not considered acceptable for the roles of chief executive and chairman to be held by the same person (UK 2018 Code Provision 9), it is still common in the US. This was the case for 52% of US Fortune 500 companies in 2016 (Spencer Stuart[3]).

3.4   The chief executive's role

The chief executive's role is not often set out in corporate governance codes or in legislation. Instead it is generally left to boards to determine the role and responsibility of the chief executive.

The FRC Guidance on Board Effectiveness covers the chief executive's role in paragraphs 70 to 73. It says that the chief executive is the most senior executive director with responsibility for proposing company strategy and for delivering the strategy as agreed by the board. The chief executive's relationship with the chair is a key relationship that can help the board be more effective. The differing responsibilities of the chair, senior independent director and the chief executive should be set out in writing and agreed by the board and be publicly available (Code Provision 14). Particular attention should be paid to areas of potential overlap.

The chief executive has primary responsibility for setting an example to the company's workforce, and communicating the expectations of the board to them in relation to the company's culture, and for ensuring that operational policies and practices drive appropriate behaviour. They are responsible for

---

3   Ibid.

supporting the chair to make certain that appropriate standards of governance permeate through all parts of the organisation. They will also ensure the board is made aware of views gathered via engagement between management and the workforce.

It is also the chief executive's responsibility to:

◆ ensure the board knows the views of the senior management on business issues in order to improve the standard of discussion in the boardroom and, prior to final decision on an issue, explain in a balanced way any divergence of view;

◆ ensure that management fulfils its obligation to provide board directors with:

 – accurate, timely and clear information in a form and of a quality and comprehensiveness that will enable it to discharge its duties,

 – the necessary resources for developing and updating their knowledge and capabilities, and

 – appropriate knowledge of the company, including access to company operations and members of the workforce.

It is good practice for the role of the chief executive to be set out formally and documented in writing.

The chief executive's role in terms of what they are expected to achieve and the means they can use to do so is discussed in the section on Policy Governance in Chapter 8.

3.5 The executive director's role

Neither legislation nor most codes set out the role of executive directors. Opinions differ on how many executive directors should be on a board. The UK tradition was for boards of commercial companies to be entirely or mainly executive. It is only since around 2001 that the balance has changed so that independent NEDs are in the majority. The trend has been for fewer executive board members on UK boards and for some companies the chief executive is the only executive director. This may not be ideal for decision making or for NEDs.

The FRC Guidance on Board Effectiveness states in paragraph 69 says that executive directors have the same duties as other members of a unitary board and that these duties extend to the whole of the business, and not just that part of it covered by their individual executive roles. The first part is potentially confusing, as in reality there are different expectations of what executive directors and non-executive directors will do – for example NEDs should, according to the Code, provide constructive challenge, strategic guidance and hold management (Principle H) to account and only independent NEDs should be on the audit committee (Provision 24). The real point the FRC is making is that on a unitary board all directors have an equal legal responsibility to the company and that executive directors should not, as it were, wear their executive hat in the boardroom. Executive directors should not see themselves only as members of the chief executive's team when engaged in board business.

Executive directors will have a greater knowledge of the company and its capabilities. They should welcome constructive challenge from non-executive directors as an essential aspect of good governance, and should encourage their non-executive colleagues to test their proposals in the light of the non-executives' wider experience outside the company. The chair and the chief executive should ensure that this process is properly followed.

Making it work 5.2

In South Africa King IV recommends that all boards should have at least one executive director in addition to the chief executive to ensure more than one point of interaction between the board and management.

The average number of executive directors of the largest 150 listed UK companies is 2.5.

It is more common in the USA for the chief executive to be the only executive director. In the USA, the average number of executive directors on boards of Fortune 500 companies is 1.5. Americans tend to take the view that having the chief executive as the only executive director is preferable because it provides clarity of delegation and the board knows the chief executive is responsible for everything that goes on. It has also been argued that other executive directors would not speak their minds as they would be subservient to and may be intimidated by the chief executive so there is no point having them on the board.

3.6 The non-executive director's role

As described in Chapter 2, Sir Derek Higgs led a review of the role and effectiveness of NEDs and reported his findings in 2003. His recommendations were reflected in the 2003 and subsequent codes and are still evident in the 2018 Code and FRC Guidance on Board Effectiveness. Among other things, the 2018 Code says that non-executive directors should provide constructive challenge, strategic guidance, offer specialist advice and hold management to account (Principle H).

Non-executive directors should appoint and where necessary remove executive directors, scrutinise and hold to account the performance of management and individual directors against agreed performance objectives (Provisions 13) and determine their remuneration. As part of their work on audit committees, independent NEDs should satisfy themselves on the integrity of financial information and that financial controls and systems of risk management are robust and defensible. As part of their work on remuneration committees, they are responsible for determining remuneration policy and appropriate levels of remuneration for executive directors and senior management.

NEDs fulfil their role through participation in board meetings and board committees. It is also important that NEDs understand the organisation and what is going on, so simply reading board papers and attending meetings is unlikely to be enough. They also need to see the organisation for themselves and talk to people other than senior executives.

In some countries it is common for directors to hold many other external directorships. The UK Code Principle H states that 'NEDs should have sufficient time to meet their board responsibilities'. External appointments should not be undertaken without prior approval of the board, with the reasons explained in the annual report. Full-time executive directors should not take on more than one non-executive directorship in a FTSE 100 company or equivalent (Provision 15).

By definition, NEDs do not have executive responsibilities but codes distinguish between NEDs as a whole and NEDs who are independent. Before the Cadbury Report in 1992 it was more common for boards to have members who did not have executive responsibilities but had a connection with the company, its shareholders or its directors. Companies where many of the shares were held by members of a family would often have family members on the board, some of whom might have executive responsibilities and some who would not. Significant investors may also have a representative on the board although such directors' duty should be to the company rather than particular shareholders. Such NEDs, while not independent, can play a valuable role but policy makers and codes now are more interested in NEDs who are independent as it is felt that they will better ensure effective challenge and oversight of executives. The Higgs Report proposed detailed criteria for determining whether a director is independent which is now part of the UK Code. Other codes have broadly similar requirements.

The 2018 UK Code says in Provision 10 that circumstances which are likely to impair, or could appear to impair, a non-executive director's independence include, but are not limited to, whether a director:

◆ is or has been an employee of the company or group within the last five years;

◆ has, or has had within the last three years, a material business relationship with the company either directly, or as a partner, shareholder, director or senior employee of a body that has such a relationship with the company;

◆ has received or receives additional remuneration from the company apart from a director's fee, participates in the company's share option or a performance-related pay scheme, or is a member of the company's pension scheme;

◆ has close family ties with any of the company's advisers, directors or senior employees;

◆ holds cross-directorships or has significant links with other directors through involvement in other companies or bodies;

◆ represents a significant shareholder; or

◆ has served on the board for more than nine years from the date of their first election.

Provision 10 however allows that a board may consider an individual non-executive to be independent notwithstanding the fact that any such circumstances apply. In such a case the board should provide a clear explanation of why an individual is nevertheless regarded as independent.

3.6   The senior non-executive director's role

The 2018 Code includes a provision (12) requiring boards to appoint one of the independent NEDs to be the senior independent director (SID) to provide a sounding board for the chair and serve as an intermediary for the other directors and shareholders. The SID should also lead a meeting of the NEDs at least once a year without the chair present to appraise the chair's performance.

The SID should hold meetings on other occasions as necessary and be prepared at times of stress for the company or board to intervene as necessary.

Test yourself 5.3

How should a board determine whether a NED is independent?

4. Board committees

The three main board committees prescribed in the UK Code (and many other codes) are the nomination committee, the audit committee and the remuneration committee. Companies may have other committees such as an ethics committee and a governance committee. Many financial services companies will also have a risk committee.

Apart from being called for by governance codes, boards have committees so as to reduce the workload on individual directors as the alternative would be for boards to consider all the matters which may more practically be covered by committees. It is important to note that the board remains responsible for the company, including decisions made or not made by committees. It is also important for the board to coordinate carefully which committee does what to avoid duplication and gaps. Clearly, it is essential to avoid omission of important items such as could be the case if one committee or the board thinks or assumes a matter will be dealt with by another committee. The work of the remuneration committee is considered in section 5 on directors' remuneration.

4.1   The nomination committee

The role of the nomination committee is set out in Provision 17 of the 2018 Code, with further guidance in the FRC Guidance on Board Effectiveness. Essentially the nomination committee should lead the process for board appointments and make recommendations for appointment to the board and to board committees. It should also evaluate the balance of skills, experience, independence and knowledge on the board and, in the light of this, describe the role and capabilities required for a particular appointment.

A majority of the nomination committee should be independent NEDs. It should be chaired by the chairman or an independent non-executive director, but the chairman should not chair the committee when it is dealing with the appointment of a new chairman. Annual reports should include a description of the work of the committee, which includes the board's policy of diversity and the name of any external search consultancy used or an explanation if neither an external search consultancy nor open advertising has been used.

ICSA and EY published research and thinking into the role of nomination committees in 2016 in 'The nomination committee – coming out of the shadows'.[4]

4.2 The audit committee

Section 4 of the 2018 Code sets out boards' duties on corporate reporting. Principle M states 'the board should establish formal and transparent policies and procedures to ensure the independence and effectiveness of internal and external audit functions and satisfy itself on the integrity of financial and narrative statements'. Principle N states 'the board should present a fair, balanced and understandable assessment of the company's position and prospects'.

Much of the board's work is delegated to the audit committee which comprises at least three independent non-executive directors (two for non-FTSE350 companies) but not the chair or any executive directors. At least one member should have recent and relevant financial experience. The committee as a whole should have competence in the sector in which the company operates. The FRC does not define financial experience but the FCA Handbook[5] for financial services firms narrows the requirement to 'at least one member of the relevant body must have competence in accounting or auditing, or both'.

The main roles and responsibilities of the audit committee are set out in Provision 25. The annual report should describe the work of the audit committee, including:

◆ significant issues (such as critical accounting judgements) considered and how they were addressed; and

◆ the assessment of the effectiveness and independence and objectivity of external audit.

Directors should explain in the annual report their responsibility for the annual report and accounts and state whether they consider them, taken as a whole, to be fair balanced and understandable and provides the information necessary for shareholders to assess the company's position, performance, business model and strategy.

4   ICSA and EY (2016) The nomination committee – coming out of the shadows, www.icsa.org.uk/assets/files/policy/research/ey-nomination-committee-digital.pdf

5   Financial Conduct Authority FCA Handbook, www.handbook.fca.org.uk/handbook/COBS/

5. Directors' remuneration

As introduced in Chapter 2, director remuneration has been a thorny subject since modern corporate governance began in the early 1990s. Concerns perpetuate about what are perceived as excessive levels of executive pay, high levels of pay when corporate performance is lacklustre and termination payments to leave a company which are perceived as a reward for failure. The concerns have generally been about the pay of the chief executive rather than other executive directors, NEDs or the chairman.

There is a vast disparity between the pay of the chief executive and the chairman and the pay of NEDs and the chairman. Chief executive average pay per day is nearly ten times the average NED pay per day.

NEDs are part time and work around 20 days a year, whereas a chief executive would probably work more than 200. NEDs and chairmen generally receive a fixed fee for their services. The remuneration of chief executives and other executive directors of large listed companies is more complex. Typically their pay will comprise fixed base salary, variable performance-related pay, pension and benefits. The following components are likely: base salary, annual bonus award which may be deferred, long-term incentive plans (discussed in Chapter 4) such as performance share plans, pension contribution, other benefits such as medical insurance and perquisites (or perks) such as a car.[6]

Making it work 5.3

According to the CIPD and the High Pay Centre[7] (2017) the make-up of a FTSE 100 chief executive package will typically be 20% base salary, 25% short-term incentives and bonuses, 48% long-term incentives (often paid in shares or options), 6% pensions and 2% other benefits. In the USA the package will typically be 30% base salary, 20% annual incentives, 40% long-term incentives and about 10% benefits.

The variable pay will be linked to various performance measures but there seems to be a consensus that the right formula for linking pay to performance is still to be found. Because the variable pay is variable within a specified range and based on performance metrics, there may be circumstances when the actual variable pay may be double the target pay or may be less. For example, if base pay is £1 million, target short-term incentives £1.25 million and target long-term incentives £2.4 million the actual incentive pay might be as high as £2.5 million and the long-term incentive payment £4.8 million.

6   See, for example, Deloitte (2010) CFO insights: Executive Compensation: Plan, Perform & Pay, www2.deloitte.com/us/en/pages/financial-services/articles/executive-compensation-plan-perform-pay.html.

7   CIPD and the High Pay Centre (2017) Executive pay Review of FTSE 100 executive pay packages, http://highpaycentre.org/files/2016_CEO_pay_in_the_FTSE100_report_%28WEB%29_%281%29.pdf

It used to be the case that formulas and the criteria for calculating variable pay were so complex it would be very difficult for shareholders and, indeed, remuneration committees, to form an accurate idea of what pay an executive might get.[8] Recent changes in the law now require listed companies to report more clearly both what individual directors receive and might receive in the next three years.

Advice from remuneration consultants is generally a major feature of deciding director pay. Consultants will advise executives on the structure of executive pay and advise the remuneration committee on the appropriateness of proposed pay. It would be poor practice for the same remuneration consultant to advise both parties in the same company and so-called 'independent remuneration consultants' will only advise remuneration committees. Following concerns about the independence and objectivity a 'Voluntary Code of Conduct in Relation to Executive Remuneration Consulting in the UK' was adopted by the Remuneration Consultants Group in 2009[9]; the latest version was issued in 2015.

Performance-related pay is now common practice for executives and managers, even in public sector organisations. It is widely believed that performance-related pay is a way of motivating people to perform better. Unfortunately evidence suggests this is rarely the case. Problems with performance-related pay include:

1. performance measures used to calculate variable pay are often not a good enough proxy for the performance which the organisation needs;

2. executive performance and the impact of executives on corporate performance are too complex to reduce to one or a few performance indicators;

3. executives cut costs excessively which gives a short-term boost to share price to hit a target and fail to invest for the future;

4. measures get gamed: for example, a person will focus attention on achieving a performance target while ignoring other key parts of their job or results are simply falsified;

5. higher paid chief executives may be prone to over-confidence; and

6. more pay may not equal better performance.

Making it work 5.4

Research by Cooper et al. in 201610 looked at CEO pay and company share price of US listed companies between 1994 and 2015. They

---

8   For further information, see for example Big Innovation Centre 2017 The purposeful company executive remuneration report, February, http://biginnovationcentre.com/media/uploads/pdf/TPC_ExecutiveRemunerationReport_26Feb.pdf

9   Remuneration Consultants Group (2015) Voluntary Code of Conduct in Relation to Executive Remuneration Consulting in the UK, www.remunerationconsultantsgroup.com/assets/Docs/RCG%20Code%20of%20Conduct%202015.pdf

10   Cooper, M., Gulen, H. and Rau, P. (2016) Performance for pay? The relationship between CEO incentive compensation and future stock price performance, http://online.wsj.com/public/resources/documents/CEOperformance122509.pdf

found that companies that pay their CEOs in the top 10 per cent of pay (adjusted for size of firm) have significantly negative abnormal returns in terms of future share price and profitability. The effect is stronger for CEOs who receive higher incentive pay relative to their peers; they undertake activities such as overinvestment and value-destroying mergers and acquisitions that lead to shareholder wealth losses. This suggests high pay and lower returns may be related to CEO over-confidence.

5.1 UK legislative and Code requirements

The UK Code requirements on remuneration should be considered in conjunction with relevant legislation. The main pieces of legislation are s. 439 of CA2006, The Large and Medium-sized Companies and Groups (Accounts and Reports) Amendment Regulations 2013[11] and the Enterprise and Regulatory Reform Act 2013.[12]

The legislation is complex and applies to companies with a main market listing on the London Stock Exchange. This includes companies with a primary market listing to which the UK Code applies, but is a larger group with around 1,000 more companies. In summary, companies must give detailed information in their annual reports about their policies for director remuneration, the projected and actual pay of individual directors and an analysis of their components. The remuneration report has three main parts:

1. Statement by the remuneration committee chairman summarising:
    ◆ the major decisions on directors' remuneration;
    ◆ any substantial changes relating to directors' remuneration made during the year; and
    ◆ the context in which those changes occurred and decisions have been taken.

2. An annual report on remuneration which is auditable, with comparative information for the previous year, which includes for each director:
    ◆ the total amount of salary and fees;
    ◆ all taxable benefits;
    ◆ money or other assets received or receivable for the relevant financial year as a result of the achievement of performance measures and targets for the year;
    ◆ money or other assets received or receivable for periods of more than one financial year as a result of the achievement of performance measures or targets relating to the relevant financial year (i.e. long-term incentives);

---

11   HM Government (2013) 'The Large and Medium-sized Companies and Groups (Accounts and Reports) Amendment Regulations 2013', www.legislation.gov.uk/ukdsi/2013/9780111100318/schedule

12   HM Government (2013) Enterprise and Regulatory Reform Act 2013, www.legislation.gov.uk/ukpga/2013/24/contents/enacted

◆ all pension-related benefits; and

◆ the total amount.

Considerably more information than this is required including graphical information containing performance graphs and tables.

3. Directors' remuneration policy, which sets out the proposed approach to remunerating directors over the next three years. This includes tables and graphs describing each of the components of the remuneration package, including:

◆ how that component supports the short- and long-term strategic objectives of the company or group; and

◆ how that component of the remuneration package operates:

  – the maximum that may be paid in respect of that component;

  – a description of the framework used to assess performance including:

    – a description of any performance measures which apply and the weighting of the measures;

    – the performance period; and the amount that may be paid in respect of the minimum level of performance that results in any payment under the policy, and any further levels of performance set in accordance with the policy (including the maximum that may be paid); and

◆ any provision for malus or clawback, explanation of how performance measures are set and details of directors' service contracts.

Listed companies are required to have a non-binding shareholder vote at a general meeting on the annual report and a binding shareholder vote on the remuneration policy at least every three years.

The UK government's response on remuneration has been to:

1. Ask the FRC to revise the UK Code, which it did in July 2018. As discussed in Chapter 4 the new Code significantly modifies the requirements on remuneration.

2. Introduce the Companies (Miscellaneous Reporting) Regulations 2018 to require quoted companies to report annually the ratio of CEO pay to the average pay of their UK workforce, along with a narrative explaining changes to that ratio from year to year and setting the ratio in the context of pay and conditions across the wider workforce; and provide a clearer explanation in remuneration policies of a range of potential outcomes from complex, share-based incentive schemes.

3. The Companies (Miscellaneous Reporting) Regulations 2018 also require quoted companies to provide a clearer explanation in remuneration policies of the range of potential outcomes, including the effect of growth in share price, from complex, share-based incentive schemes.

4. Invite the Investment Association to maintain, which it now does, a public register of listed companies encountering shareholder opposition to any

resolution of 20% or more, along with a record of what these companies say they are doing to address shareholder concerns.

The 2018 Code principles and provisions for remuneration are quite different from previous UK Codes and the schedule on the design of performance-related remuneration of executive directors has been removed. The 2018 Code emphasises the role of the board in exercising independent judgement. For example, Provision 37 says 'remuneration schemes and policies should provide boards with discretion to override formulaic outcomes.

Provision 41 says that annual reports should include a description of the work of the remuneration committee. The role of the remuneration committee is now included in the FRC Guidance on Board Effectiveness.

Share options, where for example an option to buy a share in an employer may be given in year 0 to buy a share in years 3 to 5 at the share price in year 0, were a major feature in executive remuneration packages in the 1980s through to the 2000s. They are no longer regarded as a good thing, as some executives would engineer the company to ensure a high share price when they could exercise the option and sell the shares. The share price later fell after profitability declined or bad news came out. Paying remuneration in the form of deferred shares is now preferred. The Listing Rules include provisions on approval and disclosure of share schemes (LR 9.4).

The 2018 Code includes a new requirement in provision 32 that that the chair of the remuneration committee should have been a member of that committee for at least a year before appointment as chair.

Code provision 36 says remuneration schemes should promote long-term shareholdings by executive directors that support alignment with long-term shareholder interests. Share awards granted for this purpose should be released for sale on a phased basis and be subject to a total vesting and holding period of five years or more.

Following the financial crisis some companies have introduced clawback arrangements where a bonus may be clawed back if, for example, the executive is dismissed or there is a restatement of the accounts. Provision 37 says that remuneration schemes should include provisions that would enable the company to recover and/or withhold sums or share awards, and specify the circumstances in which it would be appropriate to do so.

Making it work 5.5

Carillion plc's 2015 Annual Report stated in the Remuneration Report the existence of clawback and malus provisions:

◆ **A clawback provision is operated that gives the Remuneration Committee the right to recover all elements of bonus.**

◆ **A malus provision is operated that gives the Remuneration Committee the right to reduce any deferred bonus awards which** have not yet vested in relation to circumstances of corporate failure, which may have occurred at any time before malus is operated.

The 2016 Remuneration Report suggested that the conditions for applying the provisions had been restricted and would no longer include corporate failure.

'Malus' or 'clawback' may be applied if: (1) the results for the year in respect of which the award was made (or, in the case of a LEAP award, for a year in the performance period) have been misstated, resulting in a restatement of the Company's accounts (other than where the restatement is due to a change in accounting standards, policies or practices adopted by the Company); or (2) the participant is guilty of gross misconduct.

This attracted widespread condemnation in the media and suggestions that directors deliberately restricted the provisions knowing that corporate failure was a distinct possibility.

Chapter summary

- Boards are not mentioned in CA2006.
- Directors, although not generally liable for the actions of the company, may still be personally liable for various matters including breach of duty, trust, misstatement, misrepresentation, omission, libel or slander but such liability has rarely been tested in court.
- A successful company is led by an effective and entrepreneurial board, whose role is to promote the long-term sustainable success of the company, generating value for shareholders and contributing to wider society.
- Good practice board structure is to have an independent chairman, at least 50% independent NEDs including a senior independent NED and one or more executive directors including the chief executive.
- Learn the roles of the different types of director.
- Most boards will have three committees: audit, nomination and remuneration.
- There is now complex legislation regarding the disclosure of listed company directors' remuneration.
- Shareholders of listed companies have an advisory vote on the remuneration report which sets out individual directors' pay in the year and a binding vote at least every three years which will set out the company's board remuneration policy including how directors' pay will be determined and is likely to be paid in future years.

Chapter six
Shareholders

CONTENTS

1. Introduction
2. Engaging with shareholders
3. Shareholder rights
4. Shareholder responsibilities
5. The complex investor chain linking providers of capital with companies
6. Problem areas

1. Introduction

This chapter considers the corporate governance issues associated with shareholders and how they engage with boards and companies. It looks at their rights and non-legal responsibilities. It also discusses the structure of UK listed company share ownership and the complex chain linking individual shareholders and savers with companies. There are some serious problem areas with how shareholders can engage with companies and call them to account.

2. Engaging with shareholders

All private and public limited companies have a share capital. Most companies have just one class of share capital and the shares are normally called ordinary shares. A private company must have at least one issued share, which could be for any nominal value but will normally be £1. A public company has a minimum share capital of £50,000 (s. 763, CA2006). Companies can additionally have other classes of share capital which may have different rights to vote and receive a dividend. For example, a company may have ordinary voting shares and 'A' ordinary non-voting shares where the latter class has no voting rights but the same rights to a dividend. It may also have preference shares, which also have no voting rights but carry the right to a fixed dividend with payment taking priority over a dividend paid on ordinary shares.

The primary point of contact between a company and its shareholders is the general meeting. Until 1989 all companies, private and public, were required to hold an annual general meeting (AGM). Since 1989 private companies could opt out of holding AGMs by passing an elective resolution to that effect. Since the 2006 Companies Act (CA2006) only public companies are required to hold an AGM but private companies may choose to hold them. Any other meeting of shareholders is called an extraordinary general meeting. The notice required for general meetings is 14 days or 21 days for a public company. Such notice would include a written formal agenda and the time and place of the meeting.

Communication from a company to shareholders may be by electronic means or by posting communications on a website (for the entire notice period (s. 299 CA2006)). Shareholders may request communication from the company in written hard copy and if received in electronic form shareholders may respond electronically (s. 298, CA2006). The Listing Rules provide that consent is required from shareholders to be sent documents electronically or via the company website. If documents are posted on a website the shareholder needs to be suitably informed.

As a minimum, an AGM will include the following matters:

1. receiving and adopting the report and accounts, including the directors' and auditor's reports, of the company for the year, or other period, ended prior to the AGM date;

2. considering any recommendation of the directors that a dividend be declared for the year;

3. appointing or reappointing directors (Provision 18 of the 2018 Code requires all directors to be subject to annual re-election); boards should set out, in the papers accompanying a resolution to elect each director, specific reasons why their contribution is and continues to be important for the company's long-term success.

Other matters which might be included could be approval of a final dividend, amendments to the articles of association and alterations to share capital, such as new issues, buy backs or alteration of pre-emption rights. A listed public company would also put to separate votes its directors' remuneration report, the directors' remuneration policy and approval of any political donations and political expenditure. In addition, members may ask questions at an AGM which must be answered by the company unless it would:

◆ interfere unduly with the preparation for the meeting, or involve the disclosure of confidential information;

◆ if the answer has already been given on a website in the form of an answer to a question; or

◆ it is undesirable in the interests of the company or the good order of the meeting (s. 319A CA2006).

It is important to remember that ownership of a share in a company strictly speaking is not the same as ownership of a share (or portion) of a company. A shareholder who owns 50 £1 shares in a company with an issued share capital of £100 owns half the shares but not half the company and a person who owns all the shares does not own the company. Instead the shareholder has rights to vote and to receive dividends. A shareholder, even a 100% shareholder, may not help him or herself to the company's assets or tell the company what to do except in specific circumstances.

This is more than a semantic distinction. It is the board's job to run the company and shareholders generally can only exercise their rights by voting in shareholders' meetings (an annual general meeting or an extraordinary general meeting) or by taking legal action against the directors. In practice, however, shareholders also influence the directors on matters such as pay through discussion with them outside formal shareholders' general meetings as directors know that shareholders have the ultimate sanction to remove a director.

General meetings must be quorate. The model articles for private and public companies say that no business other than the appointment of the chairman of the meeting may be transacted without a quorum. The model articles do not state what a quorum is but s. 318 CA2006 says that if a company has more than one member the minimum present to constitute a quorum is two. Such people must be members (i.e. shareholders), a properly appointed proxy or a properly authorised person representing a corporate shareholder. The articles could prescribe a higher number for a quorum and almost certainly would if a public company. A meeting which is not quorate should be adjourned.

General meetings should have a chairman. If the directors have appointed a chairman, that person should chair the meeting if present and willing to do so. Otherwise the directors or the shareholders present may appoint a director or shareholder as 'the chairman of the meeting'. Shareholders and directors and others entitled to exercise the rights of shareholders are entitled to speak at general meetings. The chairman of the meeting may also permit others to attend and speak.

Test yourself 6.1

In what circumstances may a shareholder not be allowed to ask questions in a general meeting?

3. Shareholder rights

The rights of shareholders are set out in a company's articles of association and in company law – particularly CA2006. Shareholders have the following rights:

1. Shareholders have a reserve power to direct the directors to take or refrain from a particular action. This would be exercised by a special resolution of the company. To pass a special resolution requires, according to s. 283 CA2006, at least 75% of the votes cast to be cast in its favour.

2. Call a general meeting of the company.

3. Propose a resolution to be voted on at a general meeting.

4. Vote at a general meeting. Voting at general meetings of unlisted companies is normally by show of hands but any shareholder holding least 10% of the shares or two or more shareholders may demand a poll, in which case the number of voting shares held would be taken into account rather than a simple show of hands.

5. Appoint a director. This would be by an ordinary resolution which requires at least 50% of the votes cast to be in favour. However, shareholders cannot simply pass a resolution and appoint a director. A resolution to do so must first be put to a general meeting by the directors. A shareholder may request the directors call a shareholders' meeting and should the directors fail to do so within 21 days a shareholder, holding at least 5% of the shares, may call a general meeting him or herself.

6. Remove a director. Requires an ordinary resolution.

7. Appoint a proxy to vote on the shareholder's behalf.

Theoretically, shareholders can enforce the directors to discharge their duties under s. 172 of CA2006. However, no actions have been brought to court to do so.

The EU passed a directive on shareholders' rights in 2007, which was implemented in the UK in 2009 by amendment to CA2006. ICSA published guidance on the changes.[1]

Test yourself 6.2

Summarise the rights of shareholders.

4. Shareholder responsibilities

Owing a share does not confer any legal responsibility on the shareholder other than to be liable for full payment on any partly paid share. A widespread view among many shareholders is that if they do not like something about a company they simply sell the shares. Institutional shareholders and others who own shares financed by others act on behalf of their beneficiaries so have a fiduciary or ethical responsibility to the company and their beneficial owners, which at the very least means voting at general meetings. The efficacy of the UK corporate governance regime for listed companies depends on shareholders taking an interest in the corporate governance of the companies in which they hold shares and holding boards to account when appropriate.

According to the Cadbury Report (1992), 'shareholders' role in governance is to appoint the directors and the auditors and to satisfy themselves that an appropriate governance structure is in place'. The Cadbury Report also says

---

1   ICSA (2009) Changes resulting from the implementation of the Shareholder Rights Directive, www.icsa.org.uk/knowledge/resources/shareholder-rights-directive

stewardship
Acting as a good steward
looking after another
person's, group of people's
or an organisation's assets.

that directors act as **stewards** for shareholders who should 'call the directors to book if they appear to be failing in their stewardship'. While the AGM is the primary link between directors and shareholders the Report encouraged boards to find other ways to improve links with shareholders.

In 2010 the FRC adopted a Stewardship Code for institutional investors[2] based on Institutional Shareholders' Committee's Statement on the Responsibilities of Institutional Shareholders.[3] The most recent version was issued in 2012. The Stewardship Code is aimed at institutional investors and people who advise them such as proxy advisors and investment consultants who are invited to become signatories to it. The Stewardship Code contains principles and guidance. Signatories are expected to describe on their websites how they applied each of the principles and disclose information requested in the guidance; or if they have not applied any of the principles or not given the information required explain why not.

The seven principles say that to protect and enhance the value for the ultimate beneficiary, institutional investors should:

1. publicly disclose their policy on how they will discharge their stewardship responsibilities;
2. have a robust policy on managing conflicts of interest in relation to stewardship which should be publicly disclosed;
3. monitor their investee companies;
4. establish clear guidelines on when and how they will escalate their stewardship activities;
5. be willing to act collectively with other investors where appropriate;
6. have a clear policy on voting and disclosure of voting activity; and
7. report periodically on their stewardship and voting activities.

Previous FRC governance codes have all had a separate section on relations with shareholders. The 2018 Code does not and has covered relations with shareholders elsewhere within it. In particular, Principle D says:

'In order for the company to meet its responsibilities to shareholders and stakeholders, the board should ensure effective engagement with, and encourage participation from, these parties.'

The FRC is expected to review the Stewardship Code. The Stewardship Code is silent on matters of sustainability and corporate and social responsibility. As mentioned in Chapter 4, however, institutional investors have been active in this space and many are signatories to the six Principles for Responsible Investment[4]

---

2   FRC (2012) The UK Stewardship Code, The Financial Reporting Council UK, www.frc.org.uk/Our-Work/Publications/Corporate-Governance/UK-Stewardship-Code-September-2012.pdf

3   The 2007 version of the Institutional Shareholders' Committee (2007) The Responsibilities of Institutional Shareholders and Agents – Statement of Principles, www.ecgi.org/codes/documents/isc_statement_of_principles.pdf

4   ibid.

of the United Nations' Environmental Programme and the UN Global Compact.

The financial crisis revealed that shareholders in many cases supported managers' excessive short-term risk taking and in April 2017 the EU adopted a Directive[5] revising the 2007 EU Directive aimed at strengthening shareholders' engagement in listed companies by encouraging transparent and active engagement of shareholders. Among other things there were new requirements on directors' remuneration giving shareholders a 'say on pay' similar to the existing UK requirement.

The investor-led International Corporate Governance Network (ICGN) published Global Stewardship Principles[6] in 2016. These complement the FRC Stewardship Code but place considerably more emphasis on the need for investors to act in the interests of their beneficiaries and clients and on institutional investors' own governance practices. They also include a principle that investors should 'promote the long-term performance and sustainable success of companies and should integrate material environmental, social and governance factors in stewardship activities'.

These principles could be said to represent best practice for institutional investors' engagement with companies and are likely to be influential when the FRC reviews the Stewardship Code.

Test yourself 6.3

Summarise the responsibility of shareholders.

5. The complex investor chain linking providers of capital with companies

As previously discussed, the system of governance of UK listed companies depends on interested shareholders to enforce good governance. This is a foundation of governance. It is therefore important to understand the complex nature of shareholding, its complications, and how it has changed since the approach was first articulated by Cadbury in 1992. Shareholders are not a homogenous group: they have many forms and different, sometimes conflicting, interests.

In the 1960s individuals owned more than half the shares listed on the stock exchange with insurance companies and pension funds holding 10% and 6% respectively. By the 1990s the pattern had reversed, with individuals holding around 16% and insurance companies and pension funds holding around 45%. Ownership from outside the UK rose from around 7% in the 1960s to over 30%

---

5 Directive (EU) 2017/828 of the European Parliament and of the Council of 17 May 2017 amending Directive 2007/36/EC as regards the encouragement of long-term shareholder engagement

6 ICGN (2016) Global Stewardship Principles, http://icgn.flpbks.com/icgn-global-stewardship-principles/#p=5

and UK investors were also holding a higher proportion of their investments in shares of non-UK companies.

Since then the proportion of shares held by individuals has fallen further; so have the proportions held by insurance companies and pension funds as the proportion held outside the UK has risen to over 50%. The reasons for the changes are complex but tax advantages have, for several decades, encouraged savings through pension schemes and until the 1980s also encouraged savings in endowment life insurance funds. People were also encouraged to save through endowment funds to repay their mortgage. This century, pension funds have tended to hold a smaller proportion of their investments in shares as a result of changes in pensions regulation, actuarial assumptions and in financial reporting standards for the accounts of company pension schemes.

institutional shareholders (or investors)
A collective term for pension funds, insurance companies, unit trusts and other owners or managers of shares.

Institutional investors is an umbrella term for the following types of investor:

◆ occupational pension funds;

◆ insurance companies;

◆ pooled investment vehicles such as unit trusts, open-ended investment companies (OEICs);

◆ investment trusts; and

◆ other financial institutions such as charities, endowments and educational institutions.

UK-based institutional shareholders also invest considerable sums in other types of investment in the UK and around the world. Further information can be found in publications by the Investment Management Association.[7]

Hedge funds and investment banks may also be regarded as institutional investors. Their investment objectives and strategies may be very different from the other institutional investors which invest for the long term with a view to long-term growth in share price and/or dividends, generally on behalf of retail beneficiaries such as individual savers. Hedge funds may be more interested in short-term trading than investing for the longer term. Banks may also engage in short-term hedge fund style trading on their own account but also manage money on behalf of clients for long-term growth and in that sense are long-term institutional investors.

There is another distinction in institutional share ownership. Institutional investors fall broadly into two types: asset holders and asset managers.

Stop and think 6.1

Asset managers make the decisions to buy and sell shares on behalf of the asset holders. Asset holders are beneficial owners and include pension fund trustees and pension and insurance companies but do

7   See, for example, Investment Management Association 2016 Asset Management in the UK 2015-2016 – Full report, www. theinvestmentassociation.org/assets/files/research/2016/20160929-amsfullreport.pdf

so as agents for savers who should enjoy the economic benefit. A further complication is that some pension and insurance companies manage some of the funds themselves and place other funds with asset managers. The investment management sector is large, managing £5.7 trillion as at end of 2015, of which equities make up around £2.25 trillion with £570 billion invested in UK equities.

How important is it for companies to know who their shareholders are?

The UK system of corporate governance depends on engaged shareholders. The ability of UK pension funds and insurance companies to influence the governance of companies and hold them to account was much greater when they owned around half of UK listed company shares than now when their holding is down to around 10%. Many of the shares owned outside the UK are however managed by UK asset managers who can, and often do, use their votes to apply pressure on companies to ensure good governance.

Many asset owners take a less active interest in the corporate governance of companies leaving engagement with companies to the asset managers. This is the case unless an asset owner is also an asset manager. The majority of shares held by institutional shareholders in the UK and elsewhere are voted.

The FRC Stewardship Code distinguished the corporate governance involvement of asset owners and managers:

◆   Asset owners include pension funds, insurance companies, investment trusts and other collective investment vehicles. As the providers of capital, they set the tone for stewardship and may influence behavioural changes that lead to better stewardship by asset managers and companies. They may include engaging directly with companies or indirectly through the mandates given to asset managers. They should clearly communicate their policies on stewardship to their managers. Since asset owners are the primary audience of asset managers' public statements as well as client reports on stewardship, asset owners should seek to hold their managers to account for their stewardship activities. In so doing, they better fulfil their duty to their beneficiaries to exercise stewardship over their assets.

◆   Asset managers, with day-to-day responsibility for managing investments, are well positioned to influence companies' long-term performance through stewardship. An asset manager should disclose how it delivers stewardship responsibilities on behalf of the asset owners.

The ICGN published model contract terms[8] between asset owners and managers in 2012 which describe the respective governance roles of owners and managers in more detail.

---

8   ICGN (2012) Model contract terms between asset owners and their fund managers, www.icgn.org/sites/default/files/ICGN_ Model-Contract-Terms_2015.pdf

Figure 6.1 is a simplified representation of the complex investor chain.

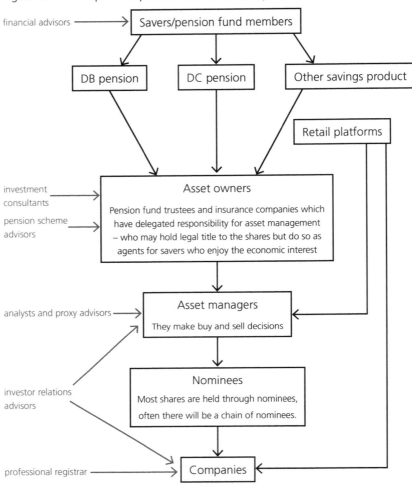

Figure 6.1: a simplified version of the chain linking savers and pension scheme members with companies.

Individuals may be advised by a financial advisor who may be independent or linked with a bank or institutional investor or make their own savings and investment decisions. Company defined benefit and trust-based defined contribution (DC) schemes will have trustees who will be advised by investment consultants, actuaries and pension scheme advisors. The trustees will select one or more asset managers who will make buy and sell decisions for shares. Contract-based DC schemes, which form the majority of DC schemes, will not have trustees but good practice is for them to have a governance committee, with employee and employer representatives, which would fulfil a similar function to trustees but without the legal responsibility.

Asset managers may choose to place money with other asset managers on advice from analysts. Proxy advisors will advise managers on how to vote at AGMs with their shares taking into account guidance on voting by asset owners. Investee companies may employ investor relations advisors to advise on how they should communicate with shareholders.

Individuals may invest directly in companies but are more likely to do so through products sold by a financial advisor or through a retail platform such as Hargreaves Lansdown, which will also take investments into unit-linked individual savings accounts and personal pensions.

Test yourself 6.4

Who are institutional investors?

6. Problem areas

Numerous problems have been found in the relationship between shareholders and companies. The most serious include:

◆ short-termism, where companies make decisions which benefit share price in the short term at the expense of creating sustainable value over the longer term;

◆ investor apathy, where investors do not engage with companies to ensure they are well governed, meaning that boards are not held to account and are effectively ownerless;

◆ inappropriate pressure from investors to pursue what may be an inappropriate strategy;

◆ conflicts of interest within the investment chain;

◆ an overly complex ownership chain and a lack of transparency within it; and

◆ a lack of accountability generally where savers cannot hold asset owners to account who don't hold asset managers to account who do not hold company boards to account.

Other issues include mergers and acquisitions where shareholder value is destroyed and/or jobs lost, concerns over share lending (also called stock or securities lending) and for small companies whether company law applies or a company is a quasi partnership.

The issues above are well known and have been the subject of numerous inquiries and reviews. Significant reviews were Paul Myners' Review of Institutional Investment in the United Kingdom in 2001[9] and John Kay's 2012

---

9   Myners, P. (2001) Institutional investment in the United Kingdom: A Review, http://uksif.org/wp-content/uploads/2012/12/ MYNERS-P.-2001.-Institutional-Investment-in-the-United-Kingdom-A-Review.pdf

Review of UK Equity Markets and Long-term Decision Making[10]. In spite of positive responses from government, many of the problems persist.

6.1 Short-termism

The problem is that some asset owners, but by no means all of them, judge a manager's record on the very short term. Lacking reliable indicators of future performance, owners will judge a manager on the change in value of the managed portfolio relative to relevant benchmark indicators such as global or national stock market indices. In practice, this means that a manager will be concerned that if they underperform a benchmark significantly for two quarters, without good reason, they might find asset owners place their money elsewhere. This encourages managers to be followers of investment fashion and like sheep may follow bubbles which then burst. Investors following a different strategy will underperform during a boom but outperform when a bubble bursts, but most asset managers may not be among those who avoid the burst.

Making it work 6.1

The share price of American conglomerate Berkshire Hathaway performed better over time than the S&P 500 index. In many ways the company acts like an investment fund: its policy has been to invest in sound businesses and hold the shares for the long term. Between 1965 and 2016 its compound annual growth has been 20.8% compared with 9.7% for the S&P. In some years the stock underperforms the market. In 1999, during the dotcom boom, the company stock price fell 19.9% while the S&P rose 21%. On such occasions people question the continuing value of the Berkshire Hathaway strategy of investing for the long term. During the dot com boom Berkshire Hathaway and investment funds which did not invest in dotcoms were criticised. Warren Buffet and Charles Munger, Berkshire Hathaway's chairman and vice chairman, were content to ignore the sentiment but fund managers would have felt pressure to invest in dotcoms and sell shares in traditional companies or risk being dropped by asset owners.

Managers therefore will try to ensure their portfolios do not underperform. Company executives understand this and are at pains to ensure the company share price does not disappoint as, if it does, the manager will dump the stock whose share price will fall causing others to join in in selling the stock. Short sellers may hasten the devaluation of the stock. This incentivises executives to focus on good short-term results rather than long-term results. The Kay Review implies that UK equity markets have not encouraged long-term value creation and may have discouraged high-performing businesses, asking why the UK does not have companies such as Amazon, Apple or Google. It has been suggested

10   Kay, J. (2012) Review of UK Equity Markets and Long-term Decision Making Final report, July 2012, www.ecgi.org/conferences/
eu_actionplan2013/documents/kay_review_final_report.pdf

that UK equity markets have discouraged risk taking and entrepreneurialism and that companies have been run more as bureaucracies than businesses.

The use of equity-based remuneration such as shares and options has also encouraged executives to focus on achieving a high stock price in the short term. This has sometimes been achieved by gaming performance measures and, on occasion, by fraud. Recent and ongoing changes in regulations for remuneration along with engaged shareholders may ameliorate this last problem.

Making it work 6.2

Somerset Webb, in a September 2017 issue of _Money Week_[11], bemoaned what she sees as 'incentive-driven short-termism that plagues the UK's corporate world'. It cites the Berkeley Group which builds houses. It had built around 6,000 houses in the previous three years during which time its chairman received £74 million and its chief executive £51 million. Around 90% of the remuneration was paid in shares under a long-term incentive plan. The remuneration works out at £48,000 per house which _Money Week_ suggests should not be allowed by shareholders.

6.2 Investor apathy

Investors have little financial incentive to take an interest in governance and engage with companies. Ensuring good governance should result in a lower likelihood of corporate failure and optimists claim it will result in better long-term financial performance. These factors should translate into a higher share price but this will benefit all shareholders giving a shareholder no relative advantage. This means that individually they have no incentive to engage and engagement is costly. Many funds under management are tracker funds which track stock market indices so arguably there is even less, if any, incentive to engage. Some managers of tracker funds do nevertheless engage actively with companies.

The interest in stewardship has now resulted in most institutional investors, asset owners and managers, becoming more proactive.

6.3 Inappropriate investor pressure

Some asset managers aim to distinguish themselves through active engagement but this has brought mixed benefits. While investors have been criticised for apathy some have been more active in influencing boards in ways which turned out to harm shareholder value. Before the financial crisis HSBC was criticised by shareholder activists for being too dull. Fortunately HSBC resisted pressure to be more adventurous. Other companies were less lucky. RBS acquired ABN Amro after the credit crunch started but shareholders overwhelmingly supported the purchase. Northern Rock was regarded by analysts as a role model

11   Somerset Webb, M. (2017) From the editor-in-chief, _Money Week_, 8 September.

which other banks should emulate. Marconi/GEC embarked on a misguided investment strategy, ditching its core business and pleasing shareholders, before it collapsed. BP was encouraged by analysts to cut costs which may have contributed to the fire at its Texas City refinery and the Deepwater Horizon oil spill.

6.4 Conflicts and misalignment of interest

Some of the conflicts have been discussed in the section on short-termism. There is a general lack of alignment in the interests of the various parties in the investor chain and their advisors. If we assume their primary incentive is to make money then the parties in between savers and companies have an interest in taking as much money as possible from savers, who lack any influence over any of the intermediaries and have to trust regulators to look after their interest. Such trust may not be justified, as events involving Equitable Life demonstrated. Equitable Life was a mutual institution owned by its members but the issue here was about how it was regulated, not how it was owned.

Making it work 6.3

The Equitable Life Assurance Society (Equitable Life) was established in 1762 and is the world's longest established life insurer. At its peak it managed £26 billion of funds on behalf of 1.5 million people. One of its products was a with profits pension contract offering a minimum guaranteed annuity rate. As interest rates fell in the 1990s the cost of the guarantee rose and it became clear that Equitable Life would not be able to meet those obligations. Equitable Life stopped taking new business in 2000 and policy holders found their policies were worth significantly less than they had thought. Protracted legal action took place on behalf of policy holders to recover money from the former directors, the auditors and the government as it was felt the regulator should have protected the policy holders.

The cases against the directors and the auditors collapsed but in 2008, the Parliamentary and Health Service Ombudsman[12] completed a four-year investigation which found 'comprehensive failure' by the regulators and called for a compensation scheme which the Government agreed in 2010.

Asset management companies and those who work for them are well remunerated. They are likely to be paid on the basis of a percentage of the funds under management, or a combination of this and a performance fee based on outperformance relative to benchmark indices. In theory their interests are aligned with savers who will also benefit from growth in the value of a portfolio but with annual charges of 1 or 2% there may not be much return left

12   Parliamentary and Health Service Ombudsman. Equitable Life: a decade of regulatory failure. Part one: main report. Fourth report Session 2007-2008. Ordered by The House of Commons to be printed on 16 July 2008. London: The Stationery Office.

for savers. Fund managers' main interest is to avoid underperforming compared with other funds and this may not drive the best allocation of shares for savers. As managers are well paid they may be more tolerant of what is widely seen as excessive remuneration paid to executives.

Asset owners such as trustees of pension funds may have little incentive to ensure investment growth. Being a trustee can be a regulatory nightmare and trustees' main incentive rather than making money is likely to be to ensure they do not fall foul of pensions regulation. All trustees have a duty to act in the best interests of the beneficiaries but their motivation may differ slightly according to who appointed them. Employee trustees will want to ensure a defined benefit pension scheme remains solvent so indirectly want a fund to perform well without excessive strain on an employer. Employer trustees may have a greater incentive to keep scheme costs as low as possible. Employee trustees of defined contribution schemes will want to ensure employees get a good choice of funds and information on which to make an informed choice. Employer trustees of DC schemes have may have less interest in choice, will want to keep their own costs low and may be less concerned with whether investments do well or not. All trustees will be guided by professional advisors and trustees often tend to act as a rubber stamp on what the advisor advises.

6.5 Complexity and lack of transparency

Section 6.4 outlines the complexity of the chain linking investors and companies. The system is criticised because there are too many parties involved, nearly all of whom extract some value from the system arguably at the expense of shareholders. The way in which they are remunerated may also not be ideal from the point of view of the providers of capital. The complexity makes it difficult for companies to know who their shareholders are. The fact that most shares are held through a chain of nominees also makes it harder, if not impossible, for smaller shareholders to exercise their right to vote.

6.6 Lack of accountability

Across the investment chain there is a lack of accountability and ability to hold other parties to account. Savers have no means of holding asset managers or any of the other intermediaries and their advisors to account. Asset owners have not been good at holding asset managers to account. Their main means of doing so are either to sack a fund manager who underperforms a benchmark or to reduce the funds allocated to that manager. As noted above, asset managers and owners lack a financial interest in engaging with companies although many have now felt the peer and moral pressure to engage with companies in accordance with the Stewardship Code.

Mergers and acquisitions have been problematic. Many result in destruction of shareholder value and investors would have been wiser to have voted against such deals. Evidence would suggest that investors put an immediate profit from sale of a share in a takeover target to an acquirer above all other considerations, including the impact of staff and other stakeholders.

Making it work 6.4

Cadbury was a UK company selling drinks and confectionery established in 1824. Its chairman in 1992 was Sir Adrian Cadbury who was the great great grandson of the founder. The company had a long track record of corporate and social responsibility, unique values and enjoyed a good reputation among customers.

The company was acquired by the US food company Kraft in 2010. Kraft's offer for Cadbury's shares caused controversy when many argued that Cadbury should continue as an independent company. Kraft made various assurances about retaining staff in the UK which may have made it easier for the UK government to remain uninvolved. In the end sufficient Cadbury shareholders voted to accept the offer and Kraft became the owner of Cadbury, including all its physical assets and brands.

The takeover valued Cadbury's shares at 850p which was 50% higher than the share price before Kraft's initial bid. A Reuters report[13] stated this was 'the lowest multiple of any major M&A deal in the global food space in well over a decade'. The Cadbury chairman was quoted as telling the BBC 'this is a bitter-sweet moment. As a chairman of a public company you are paid and required to focus on shareholder value and the process which we have undertaken has delivered shareholder value.'

There was widespread criticism that the UK system made it too easy for a company to be taken over and that the decision was exercised solely by shareholders without any reference to any other stakeholder such as staff or their interests. There was further criticism and censure by the UK Takeover Panel after Kraft went back on some of its commitments.

Share or stock lending, where an asset manager 'lends' or rents the voting rights to a share to more active investors such as hedge funds, is controversial. Technically the shares are not lent and title actually passes but the lender can later recall the share. The active investor may then use those votes to apply pressure on a company to take some action or short the stock in anticipation of being about to buy the share at a lower price. Fund managers derive income from the rent and many argue it adds liquidity to the market. Asset owners may also benefit from the income. Critics argue that the liquidity could vanish more quickly if market conditions deteriorate so share lending destabilises rather than stabilises markets. They would also claim that lending shares to a short seller will reduce the value of the share which is against the interest of investors investing for the long term. This is an example of the 'Tragedy of the Commons' where managers who allow short selling destroy value for everyone but as everyone suffers there is no relative underperformance to concern the manager. The ICGN

13   Jones, D. and Dorfman, B. (2010) Kraft snares Cadbury for $19.6 billion, Reuters, www.reuters.com/article/us-cadbury/kraft-snares-cadbury-for-19-6-billion-idUSTRE60H1N020100119

had published guidance[14] on stock lending which in essence says institutional investors should disclose their policy on share lending, lent shares should be recalled in time for the investor to vote at a general meeting, borrowers should not vote and the results of lending should be transparent to beneficial owners.

Finally, it is worth noting that in certain circumstances company law and shareholder rights may not apply. Companies where the shareholders have at some point had a relationship which is like a partnership may, if there is a shareholder dispute, find a court would decide a quasi partnership existed. This could mean, for example, that a majority shareholder could not force changes on the board. As a remedy a court is likely to rule that a majority shareholder offer to buy the minority's shares at a fair market value. This is more likely to apply to smaller companies with a small number of shareholders and very unlikely for a large listed company.

Chapter summary

◆ All private and public limited companies have a share capital.

◆ The primary point of contact between a company and its shareholders is the general meeting but shareholders may engage with directors and executives at other times.

◆ There are two types of general meeting: an annual general meeting and an extraordinary general meeting.

◆ AGM will include the following matters: receive and adopt the report and accounts, consider any recommendation to declare a dividend, appoint or reappoint directors, appoint or reappoint the auditors and authorise the directors to determine their remuneration.

◆ Shareholders own shares in a company which is not exactly the same as owning a share or portion of the company. Instead they have various legal rights such as to vote at general meetings and receive a dividend if declared.

◆ Shareholders do not have any obligations under the companies acts other than to pay in full for their shares. Most governance codes, however and would say shareholders have an obligation to appoint the directors and the auditors and satisfy themselves that the company is well governed and exercise their voting rights.

◆ The UK Stewardship Code sets out the stewardship responsibilities for institutional shareholders.

◆ The nature of shareholding in UK companies has changed significantly since 1992. Now most UK shares are held by shareholders outside the UK and the proportion of shares held by individuals, pension funds and insurance companies has fallen from over 60% to under 20%.

◆ There are many types of shareholder and not all of them have the same objectives in holding shares.

---

14   ICGN (2016) ICGN Guidance on Securities Lending, London, http://icgn.flpbks.com/icgn_securities-lending_2015/#p=2

◆   Most UK shares are held in multiple-ownership pooled nominee accounts which do not identify the beneficial owner.

◆   The nature of UK share ownership is problematic in many ways such as:

–   short-termism, where companies make decisions which benefit share price in the short term at the expense of creating sustainable value over the longer term;

–   investor apathy, where investors do not engage with companies to ensure they are well governed meaning that boards are not held to account and are effectively ownerless;

–   inappropriate pressure from investors to pursue what may be an inappropriate strategy;

–   conflicts of interest within the investment chain;

–   an overly complex ownership chain and a lack of transparency within it; and

–   a lack of accountability generally where savers cannot hold asset owners to account who don't hold asset managers to account who do not hold company boards to account.

Chapter seven
Corporate reporting

CONTENTS

1. Introduction
2. Overview of corporate reporting
3. The contents of the annual report
4. Practical issues

1. Introduction

A lot has been said already about corporate reporting, including reporting on directors' remuneration, corporate and social responsibility and integrated reporting. This chapter gives an overview of the other aspects of corporate reporting such as financial reporting and the strategic report. It looks at the legal and other regulatory requirements such as international financial reporting standards, the different components of annual reports and some practical issues for preparing an annual report, including the role of a company secretary.

2. Overview of corporate reporting

2.1 The origins of accounting and corporate reporting

Accounting and corporate reporting have their roots in stewardship. For thousands of years stewards who looked after assets belonging to others would have to give account to their owners for how they have stewarded or managed their assets. They would also need some means of keeping records. They would also need some means of keeping records. The need for accounting records evolved as activities became more complex and as economies developed from simple barter to a monetary system, to international trade, multinational conglomerates employing hundreds of thousands of staff and the giving and receiving of credit and, always present, taxation.

Accounting records consisted of little more than lists or a narrative of transactions until the double entry bookkeeping system emerged in the fifteenth century. The system is still used today in computerised form by most, if not all, organisations.

All companies must prepare annual accounts or financial statements – the terms are synonymous. If a company is part of a group of companies, a set of consolidated accounts showing the results of the whole group must also be prepared. Public sector and not-for-profit bodies must also prepare accounts annually.

2.2   The purpose of accounting and corporate reporting

Reports of financial transactions were and are needed to:

1.   keep track of what is owed by and to a business, by and to whom, and be able to demonstrate to them how much is due;

2.   enable the business to be properly managed and controlled;

3.   give an account to a business's owners of how it has been managed and what it has achieved;

4.   give information to investors to help them make investment decisions; and

5.   provide useful information for other users of accounts.

This list covers in general terms the main reasons for internal and external reporting. Internal reporting of financial transactions is sometimes also referred to as management accounting. It refers to what is reported within an organisation up to and including to the board. External reporting is what the organisation reports externally to shareholders, owners or stakeholders. What is reported externally should obviously be consistent with the internal reporting.

UK company law since the Companies Act 1900 requires companies to prepare accounts of financial statements for shareholders and for them to be audited. It is an obligation which goes with the privilege of incorporation and the fact that a company when incorporated is a separate legal person from its shareholders. Hence financial reporting is a core element of corporate governance. The requirement for directors to report reflects a stewardship purpose in that the directors of a company explain how they have stewarded the company. The requirement for an audit reflects an agency purpose as it could be expected that the directors might work in their own, rather than in the shareholders', interest.

Companies accounts originally were prepared according to what the company wanted to say, how they wanted to say it, what accounting judgements they wanted to make and what accounting policies they wanted to follow. There was little consistency in accounts preparation from year to year or from company to company. Although auditors would have ensured a modicum of consistency, comparisons of company performance from one year to another and between companies were difficult, if not a waste of time. The UK has been at the forefront of accounting development and attempts to introduce consistency and common policies began during World War II. Progress was slow: the first Statement of Standard Accounting Practice (SSAP) was issued in 1971 and a further 33 SSAPs were issued by 1990, when the FRC took over responsibility from the six UK accounting bodies for accounting practice. Leading accounting standard setters around the world acknowledged the need for accounts to be comparable from country to country and the first International Accounting Standards were issued in 1973.

The EU was keen to harmonise accounting standards across member states and from this IFRS developed. The new international accounting standards issued after 2001 are called International Financial Reporting Standards (IFRS). Many countries adopted IFRS with some, including the UK, requiring IFRS to be used for companies over a certain size and the consolidated accounts of groups of companies and continuing to allow use of local national accounting standards for individual companies. 118 countries now permit or require use of IFRS[1]. The big exception is the US, which instead uses US GAAP (Generally Accepted Accounting Principles). Some progress is being made on harmonising or converging IFRS and US GAAP.

The preparation of accounts is not an exact science. Financial accounts of companies are not all fact but contain judgements about, for example, whether the company will remain a going concern for the foreseeable future, how to value assets and liabilities and when to recognise income and expenditure. A clear understanding of the context and purpose of financial reporting, and the users' needs is important to reaching the best judgement.

The accounting profession has devoted considerable time over the last 40 years to how best to prepare so-called '**general purpose financial reports**' and financial reporting has gone through something of a revolution where the old, more UK and European, approach, based on the use of the four fundamental concepts of going concern, accruals, consistency and **prudence**, has been superseded by a US market value approach based on current costs and values which effectively ignored the prudence concept. The prudence concept, as the term implies, is about making prudent judgements about assets, liabilities, income and expenditure. For example, under the prudence concept, income is not recognised until it has been earned and will be paid for, profits are only recognised when they have been realised and provision is made for all anticipated future expenses and losses. The exercise of prudence should therefore ensure that assets and income are not overstated and liabilities and expenses are not understated.

general purpose financial report
A financial report intended to meet the information needs common to users who are unable to command the preparation of reports tailored so as to satisfy, specifically, all of their information needs.

prudence
The prudence concept, as the term implies is about making prudent judgements about assets, liabilities, income and expenditure. So, for example, under the prudence concept, income is not recognised until it has been earned and will be paid for, profits are only recognised when they have been realised and provision is made for all anticipated future expenses and losses.

Test yourself 7.1

For what type of company was the audit requirement first introduced in company law?

Making it work 7.1

Bank borrowings may be traded on public markets. The market value of such bank debt can change according to the market perception of the bank's creditworthiness, i.e. whether the bank will repay the debt in full. During the financial crisis accounts prepared under IFRSs showed that banks reported a profit when the market value of their debt went down because the market judged there was a risk they would be unable to repay their borrowing. This is counterintuitive but the accounting logic

1   PwC (2016) IFRS adoption by country, www.pwc.com

was that the bank, theoretically, could repurchase its own debt on the market for less money than it would otherwise have to pay. The fact that the bank would not have the funds to do so was ignored.

The situation is not that different from one child Anne (bank A) lending a pound to her friend Bob (bank B). Their school classmates (the market) think that Bob might not be able to repay the whole pound and will only repay 75p. If Bob was producing accounts he would report a profit of 25p because the rest of the class (the market) thinks he can only repay 75p.

According to a KPMG (2008) report 'Focus on transparency'[2] 12 European banks recognised such gains in 2007, which for three of the banks represented over 12% of pre-tax profit. The largest such gain reported was c£1.5 billion.

The financial crisis highlighted shortcomings in the market value approach and there have been renewed calls to give more prominence to stewardship and to reintroduce the prudence concept. These calls were recognised in the revised Conceptual Framework for Financial Reporting published by the International Accounting Standards Board (IASB) in March 2018[3].

2.3   The legal and other requirements for corporate reporting

The UK Companies Act 2006 (CA2006) Part 15 in sections 380 to 474 contains the detailed requirements for companies and groups of companies on keeping and reporting accounts. Sections 386 to 389 require companies to keep proper internal accounting records. Other sections set out the requirements for external annual reporting. Part 16 sets out the requirements for audit in sections 475 to 539. The Act has been revised a number of times to reflect changes considered necessary to respond to corporate events, such as the financial crisis, and to implement EC directives. Most of the recent changes have been to revise or introduce new non-financial reporting requirements.

With certain exemptions, such as a dormant non-trading subsidiary, all companies must prepare accounts in accordance with either International Accounting Standards (the Act does not refer to IFRS but no doubt the intention was to do so) or s. 396 or s. 404 (for groups of companies) which provides that individual accounts must comprise:

1.   a balance sheet as at the last day of the financial year that gives a true and fair view of the state of affairs of the company as at the end of the financial year; and

2.   a profit and loss account which gives a true and fair view of the profit or loss of the company for the financial year.

2   KPMG (2008) Focus on Transparency Trends in the Presentation of Financial Statements and Disclosure of Information by European Banks.

3   International Accounting Standards Board (2018) Conceptual Framework for Financial Reporting.

As discussed below, CA2006 regulations further prescribe what must be disclosed. Consolidated group accounts should show the aggregated balance sheet and profit and loss account of the parent company and, with certain exemptions, all its subsidiaries. Besides the detailed requirements for accounts in CA2006 and the Regulations there are other detailed and prescriptive requirements which include other regulations such as the UK Listing Authority Disclosure and Transparency Rules issued by the FCA, which implement the EC Transparency Obligations Directive and the Listing Rules.

Although accounts have to be laid before an AGM for the shareholders to approve, neither the Act nor case law say for whom accounts are to be prepared. UK accounting standards however acknowledge that investors (note: not shareholders) are to be treated as the defining class of user and UK, IAS, IFRS and US GAAP accounts are prepared primarily for investors. IFRS refers to users of accounts recognising that this includes creditors. Audit reports, however, are to the company's members (i.e. shareholders) as a body. UK case law has confirmed this, which means that although other persons such as creditors and providers of loan finance might rely on an audit report the auditor has no liability to them.

As noted above, UK company law has, since 1900, required all companies to have an audit. An exemption for small companies to have an audit has been part of UK company law since 1994. The thresholds for determining 'small' have gradually been raised and are currently any two of the three: (i) balance sheet assets <£5.1m; (ii) turnover <£10.2m; and (iii) <50 employees.

Corporate accounts continue to be misstated. This is despite several hundred years of development in accounting, financial reporting and auditing, which has led to sophisticated and complex company law, disclosure and listing regulations and thousands of pages of accounting and financial reporting and audit standards. Misstatement is sometimes deliberate by company management and sometimes companies make mistakes. An external audit of the financial statements is no guarantee that misstatements will not happen but it should make them less likely.

The responsibility of boards and audit committees in relation to approving annual reports is set out in Chapter 5.

Stop and think 7.1

Tesco

For many years Tesco enjoyed a dominant position in the UK grocery sector but its profitability came under threat from the low-cost rivals. It lost £10 billion in its stock market value in 2014 after it announced its first drop in annual profit in 20 years. Tesco's half-year accounts for 2014 overstated profits by £326 million by incorrectly booking payments from suppliers. It has been suggested that the company used aggressive accounting to hide, rather than fix, problems with its business model. The overstatement was a result of Tesco's treatment of financial contributions from Tesco's suppliers determined by sales volume. These

contributions were conditional on hitting sales targets that it was not going to reach but Tesco nevertheless booked them. It was a case of premature or, possibly, just fictitious recognition in the profit and loss account of income which had not yet been earned and might never be earned.

The Serious Fraud Office agreed a deferred prosecution agreement in April 2017, which meant Tesco paid a £129 million fine but escaped criminal prosecution. The FRC was to investigate the role of Tesco's auditor PwC but in June 2017 dropped its investigation after deciding there was 'not a realistic prospect that a tribunal would make an adverse finding against PwC'.

In September 2017 it was reported that three former Tesco UK executive directors had been charged with one count of fraud by abuse of position and one count of false accounting. It was alleged that they 'bullied and coerced' and 'encouraged the manipulation of profits and pressured others under their control to misconduct themselves in such a way that the stock market was ultimately misled'.

Using inappropriate accounting to misstate results is a very old practice going back to the South Sea Company and before. Enron and WorldCom were more recent examples. Why do you think companies still do this when so often the facts come out, meaning shame for the perpetrators? And why do you think auditors either fail to notice or go along with what their client wants?

3. The contents of the annual report

ICSA issued the guidance note 'Contents list for the annual report of a UK company'[4] in 2015, which explains what goes into an annual report. When CA2006 talks about accounts it means the financial accounts, which are also known as financial statements. The Companies Act Part 15 Accounts and reports specifies a company's annual report will comprise:

◆ Balance sheet as at the last day of the financial year which must give a true and fair view of the state of affairs of the company as at the end of the financial year.

◆ A profit and loss account which must give a true and fair view of the profit or loss of the company for the financial year.

◆ Strategic report (s. 414A to D not required for smaller companies).

◆ Directors' report (s. 415 to 419A not required for smaller companies).

◆ Directors' remuneration report including report on remuneration policy (s. 420 to 422A required only for quoted companies).

---

4   ICSA (2015) Guidance note Contents list for the annual report of a UK company, www.icsa.org.uk/assets/files/free-guidance-notes/contents-list-for-the-annual-report-of-a-uk-company.pdf

◆ Governance statement (s. 419A required for companies with a primary London Stock Market listing).

Part 16 requires:

◆ An auditor's report on the financial statements, the strategic report, directors' report and parts of the remuneration report and governance statement (s. 495 to 497A).

Most quoted companies' annual reports will normally also include financial highlights, a chairman's statement, letter or report and a chief executive's statement. None of these are legal requirements.

CA2006 sets out the high level requirements for annual reports. The Large and Medium-sized Companies and Groups (Accounts and Reports) Regulations 2008[5] add the detail. They set out the permitted formats for the various components of the financial statements and requirements for accounting policies.

Annual reports of public companies now commonly run to several hundred pages and successive additions to reporting standards have meant annual reports got longer. Financial reporting standards for financial institutions require more information to be disclosed than most other types of company. HSBC's 2008 Annual Report possibly held the record in length, which was 472 pages. There was a widespread view that annual reports were too long to understand. Its 2011 report was much shorter at 207 pages, but its 2016 report was longer at 286 pages. UK companies with a US listing also need to comply with the US Form 20-F requirements. BP's combined 2016 annual and form 20-F report is nearly 300 pages long. The financial statements will typically occupy around half an annual report and come at the end of the report. The annual financial statements of US companies are filed on Form 10-K and large US companies will also prepare a glossy annual report.

3.1 The financial statements or accounts

Under IAS 1[6] Presentation of Financial Statements a complete set of financial statements comprises:

◆ statement of financial position as at the end of the period (i.e. a balance sheet);

◆ statement of profit or loss and other comprehensive income for the period;

◆ statement of changes in equity for the period;

◆ statement of cash flows for the period;

◆ notes, comprising significant accounting policies and other explanatory information; and

◆ comparative information in respect of the preceding period.

---

5 HM Government (2008) The Large and Medium-sized Companies and Groups (Accounts and Reports) Regulations 2008, www.legislation.gov.uk/uksi/2008/410/schedule/1/mad

6 International Accounting Standards Board (2007) (first issued in 1975) IAS 1 Presentation of Financial Statements, IFRS Foundation.

The IAS requirement is similar to the Large and Medium-sized Companies and Groups (Accounts and Reports) Regulations 2008. The balance sheet shows the assets and liabilities of a company which are valued on the basis that the company is and will be for a period (at least a year) a going concern, that is that the company will remain in business. If there are doubts about going concern the values would be on a break-up basis so that assets would be valued at the price at which they could be sold in the short term. Accounts are generally prepared on the basis of what assets and expenses actually cost (the historic cost basis) with adjustment for assets which are not expected to realise that cost if/when sold but with further adjustment for certain assets and liabilities to reflect a fair value (essentially a market value, or an estimate of market value).

3.2 Strategic report

The requirement for a strategic report was introduced in CA2006 (Strategic Report and Directors' Report) Regulations 2013[7] as an amendment to the Companies Act. Previously directors' reports included a 'business review' with largely similar content. The FRC published guidance on the strategic report in 2014.[8]

The Regulations state the 'purpose of the strategic report is to inform members of the company and help them assess how the directors have performed their duty under section 172 (duty to promote the success of the company)'.

The Regulations, in summary, require:

◆ A fair review of the company's business, and a description of the principal risks and uncertainties facing the company.

◆ A balanced and comprehensive analysis of: (a) the development and performance of the company's business during the financial year, and (b) the position of the company's business at the end of that year, consistent with the size and complexity of the business.

◆ To the extent necessary for an understanding of the development, performance or position of the company's business: (a) analysis using financial key performance indicators, and (b) where appropriate, analysis using other key performance indicators, including information relating to environmental matters and employee matters.

◆ Quoted companies to the extent necessary for an understanding of the development, performance or position of the company's business: (a) the main trends and factors likely to affect the future development, performance and position of the company's business, and (b) information about
   (i) environmental matters (including the impact of the company's business on the environment),

---

7   HM Government (2013) Companies Act 2006 (Strategic Report and Directors' Report) Regulations 2013, www.legislation.gov.uk/uksi/2013/1970/contents/made

8   FRC (2014) Guidance on the Strategic Report, www.frc.org.uk/accountants/accounting-and-reporting-policy/clear-and-concise-and-wider-corporate-reporting/narrative-reporting/guidance-on-the-strategic-report

(ii) the company's employees and

(iii) social, community and human rights issues, including information about any policies of the company in relation to those matters and the effectiveness of those policies.

◆ Quoted companies:

(a) a description of the company's strategy,

(b) a description of the company's business model, and

(c) a breakdown showing at the end of the financial year

(i) the number of persons of each sex who were directors of the company,

(ii) the number of persons of each sex who were senior managers of the company and

(iii) the number of persons of each sex who were employees of the company.

◆ Where appropriate references to, and additional explanations of, amounts included in the company's annual accounts.

◆ The Companies (Miscellaneous Reporting) Regulations 2018 amends s. 414 and from January 2019 requires large companies to describe how the directors have regarded the matters set out in s. 172 when performing their duties.

Companies are not required to disclose information about impending developments or matters in the course of negotiation if the disclosure would, in the opinion of the directors, be seriously prejudicial to the interests of the company.

3.3 Directors' report

Since the introduction of the requirement to prepare a strategic report, the directors' report is much shorter and not all listed companies provide a separate directors' report. The large and varied number of legal requirements for what to include are spread across the 'Companies Act and the Large and Medium-sized Companies and Groups (Accounts and Reports) Regulations 2008' rather than conveniently located in one place. The ICSA Guidance note 'Contents list for the annual report of a UK company' fortunately lists them. Some of the main things to include are:

◆ names of the directors during the financial year;

◆ the dividend (if any) recommended by the directors;

◆ details of changes concerning share capital and voting rights;

◆ details of political donations;

◆ details of any post year-end important events;

◆ a description of various matters relating to employee engagement and how account has been taken of their interests (for companies with over 250 employees); and

◆ a summary of how the directors have had regard to the need to foster the company's business relationships with suppliers, customers and others including the effect on principal decisions taken by the company (for large companies).

3.4   Directors' remuneration report

The requirements for the directors' remuneration report including remuneration are given in Chapter 5.

3.5   Governance statement

Details of what needs to be disclosed are set out in the UK Code of Corporate Governance, the FCA Disclosure and Transparency Rules, the FCA Listing Rules and the Companies (Miscellaneous Reporting) Regulations 2018 and are discussed throughout this book. Readers may find it useful to refer to Appendix B of the FRC Guidance on Board Effectiveness, which lists the disclosure requirements for each of the three sources.

3.6   The audit report

As noted above, auditors should report on the financial statements, the strategic report, directors' report and parts of the remuneration report and governance statement (s. 495 to 497A). Audit is highly regulated as it is a legal requirement for all companies which are not 'small' to have an audit. Auditors are governed by their professional bodies and in the UK by the FRC. Auditors must comply with the FRC's Ethical Standard[9] and with approximately 40 UK versions, which are issued by the FRC, of International Standards on Auditing (ISA) issued by the International Auditing and Assurance Standards Board (IAASB). The auditing standards are detailed: the IAASB handbook which includes the ISAs is almost 1,000 pages long.

The current requirements for audit reports are set out in 'ISA (UK) 700 – Revised June 2016'[10]. The contents of a public company audit report would include:

◆   The date of the audit report.

◆   The addressee (normally the shareholders as a whole).

◆   The respective responsibilities of the directors and the auditor.

true and fair
This is a simple term which broadly means a set of financial statements are reasonably accurate, balanced and not misleading. There is no statutory definition however and pages of legal opinion have been given on what is an extremely complex subject.

◆   An opinion on the financial statements and whether the opinion is modified as to whether they give a **true and fair** view of the companies affairs at the balance sheet date and the profit for the year and whether they have been prepared in accordance with the Companies Act and applicable accounting and financial reporting standards.

◆   The auditor's assessment of the risks of material misstatement (such as concerning going concern, revenue recognition, value of goodwill, pensions liability and asset valuations) including a discussion of those risks and how the auditor responded to them. This can occupy several pages of the report.

---

9   FRC (2016) Revised Ethical Standard, The Financial Reporting Council, www.frc.org.uk/getattachment/0bd6ee4e-075c-4b55-a4ad-b8e5037b56c6/Revised-Ethical-Standard-UK-June-2016.pdf

10   FRC (2016) ISA (UK) 700 – Revised June 2016, The Financial Reporting Council, http://frc.org.uk/getattachment/a08b0906-f40c-4735-bbc7-45908bee2b32/ISA-(UK)-700-Revised-June-2016_final.pdf

◆ The auditor's application of **materiality** and an overview of the scope of our audit.

◆ The auditor's opinion on other matters required by the Companies Act:

- Whether the part of the Directors' Remuneration Report to be audited has been properly prepared in accordance with CA2006.

- Whether the information given in the Strategic Report and the Directors' Report, for the financial year is consistent with the financial statements.

- Based solely on the work required to be undertaken in the course of the audit and from reading the Strategic Report and the Directors' Report whether the auditor has identified material misstatements in those reports.

- Whether the auditor has anything to report on the disclosures of principal risks, the directors' statement of longer-term viability, the management of risks and the directors' assessment and expectations of the company/group's continuing in operation; or the disclosures in the financial statements concerning the use of the going concern basis of accounting.

- Any material inconsistency with either the auditor's knowledge of the company or the financial statements.

- Whether the annual report and financial statements taken as a whole is fair, balanced and understandable, and provides the information necessary for shareholders to assess the group's position and performance, business model and strategy.

- Whether the Audit Committee Report appropriately addresses matters communicated by the auditor to the audit committee.

- Whether adequate accounting records have not been kept.

- Whether the Directors' Remuneration Report to be audited is not in agreement with the accounting records and returns; or certain disclosures of directors' remuneration specified by law are not made.

materiality
In an audit context materiality refers to misstatements, including omissions, that are considered to be material if they, individually or in the aggregate, could reasonably be expected to influence the economic decisions of users taken on the basis of the financial statements (ISA 320).

3.7 Reporting on corporate and social responsibility

Reporting on corporate and social responsibility and sustainability and integrated reporting is covered in Chapter 4.

Making it work 7.2

The annual report and financial statements of Carillion published in March gave the impression of a profitable healthy company with a strong order book. The external auditor issued an unqualified audit report. A few issues were highlighted but the report implied the board was on top of things and the company had all the resources needed for continued growth. Some investors were concerned at what appeared to be an inability by the company to reduce debt and fragile profitability with low margins. The detailed disclosures in the notes to the accounts

told of critical accounting judgements on issues such as valuation of long-term work in progress but gave no indication that these judgements were suspect.

In July, a few weeks after publication of the annual report, £845 million in provisions against these contracts was made and a further £200 million in provisions made in September.

The directors later confirmed to the Parliamentary Inquiry that that these provisions related to events after the annual report was published, a view which was supported by the external auditor. There was widespread scepticism about this and board minutes from May 2017 board meetings made public after the evidence given by directors and auditors to Parliament, suggested that concerns with the 2016 accounts and audit were known to the board in May.

Test yourself 7.2

What is required by CA2006 Part 15 Accounts for the contents of a company's annual report?

4. Practical issues

4.1 Corporate reporting is a team effort

The preparation of an annual report is a major undertaking for any company. Even for smaller companies, which will be exempt from many of the requirements for listed companies, the preparation of financial statements which comply with legal and reporting standards requires planning and occupies considerable staff time and professional costs. The accounts preparation process for a medium-sized company requiring an audit is likely to involve planning before the year end, procedures at the year end including counting any stocks and confirming balances at banks, procedures after the year end to ensure that transactions taking place in the accounting records are reflected in the correct year and preparation of the financial statements from the accounting and other records. Finally an AGM should be called and take place to approve, inter alia, the financial statements.

A public listed company will require all of the above, plus will need to:

1. carry out more detailed initial planning and design the annual report (liaising with external agencies as required);
2. select a designer and printer;
3. carry out the same steps above for all group companies;
4. agree inter-company trading balances for companies within the group;

5.   compile required information on shareholdings from company share register;

6.   compile the information necessary, with supporting documentation for the auditors, for and prepare the chairman's statement, chief executive's statement, strategic report, directors report, directors' remuneration report including remuneration policy and governance report;

7.   as above for corporate and social responsibility reporting;

8.   finalise design of report;

9.   prepare a draft of the annual report;

10. audit committee to consider the annual report and recommend its approval to the board;

11. board meeting to approve the financial statements and the annual report;

12. proofread annual report; and

13. print annual report and post on website.

It will be a team effort involving most of the accounting staff, company secretarial staff, investor relations staff, share registration staff, the chairman, chief executive, chief financial officer and CSR staff. The chief financial officer will be responsible for the financial statements but the company secretary, or one of his/her staff, is likely to be the main person coordinating all the activities.

4.2 Challenges when producing the annual report

The above exercise is unlikely to be trouble free. Likely problems with the preparation of the financial statements include:

◆   difficulties agreeing balances between group companies and making the adjustments to consolidate the results of all the companies in the group;

◆   provisions for impairment of values; critical accounting judgements such as with fair value accounting and hard to value assets and liabilities;

◆   ensuring transactions are recorded in the correct financial year, providing evidence to the auditors; and

◆   finessing the wording in the annual report, ensuring the auditor is happy with everything and agreeing any adjustments with the auditor.

The work is often done to a tight timescale, resulting in considerable pressure on all involved. It will be important to monitor progress against the timetable carefully.

Making it work 7.3

Non-accountants, many accountants and some auditors do not think about the inherent lack of accuracy of the financial figures in a set of accounts. Financial statements express figures with more precision than they can be known accurately yet they do not highlight this. Figures are typically given with four significant figures precision but the margin for

uncertainty for some figures may be two significant figures, that is + or - 10%. Apart from items such as cash at the bank and dividends paid, most figures in a set of accounts are not known exactly and are subject to estimates or judgements of one kind or another. When all the margins for error in an income statement or balance sheet are added together the total error or uncertainty might be large. Thus the net assets reported by a company may be £1,234,000 but there may be sufficient uncertainty with some of the components which mean the error may be £123,000 so this figure can only be reported accurately to £1.2 million.

Another weakness in accounting is that it does not distinguish between essential costs and costs which may not be essential. Shareholders and analysts generally encourage companies to cut costs but it is possible to cut too far. Profit can be boosted by cutting costs but some costs, such as concerning safety or maintenance or to ensure the business model is robust, are essential to maintain the long-term value of the business. If these are cut it may boost profit in the short term which could please shareholders and raise the share price but reduce the business value, future profitability and share price in the longer term. It is possible for executives motivated to achieve performance targets on which their remuneration depends to cut essential costs to boost short-term profitability and achieve the performance targets.

Chapter summary

◆ The first accounting records date back 7,000 years.

◆ Accounting is important for economic growth.

◆ Double entry bookkeeping is the foundation of accounting systems.

◆ Company law requires companies to maintain accounting records and prepare an annual report each year for shareholders.

◆ Giving such an account is a key aspect of stewardship.

◆ There is continuing debate in the accounting profession about the purpose of an annual report and the role in it of stewardship and prudence.

◆ Company law also requires companies' accounts to be audited because mistakes happen and because directors' interests may not be the same as shareholders'.

◆ UK accounts may be prepared under UK GAAP or IFRS. There is a move to IFRS which all public companies will use. The requirements are detailed and complex.

◆ Audits will comply with (UK) international auditing standards on auditing. The standards are nearly 1,000 pages long.

◆ The whole process for preparing the accounts and the annual report and having it audited is lengthy and requires coordination and planning.

Part three

Chapter eight
Good meeting
practice

Chapter nine
Board effectiveness

Board procedure and governance administration

Overview

This part looks at board procedure and governance in practice. Chapter 8 looks at good meeting practice for boards, including purpose, chairing, time allocation and challenge. It also looks at the documentation that boards can use to improve meeting practice such as a board charter and the procedures for running a meeting. Chapter 9 looks at board effectiveness and the role of the company secretary in helping to ensure meetings are effective. It also considers how boards should evaluate their effectiveness and some of the things that can challenge effectiveness in making good board decisions.

Learning outcomes

At the end of this part, students will be able to:

◆ understand the essentials of good meeting practice;

◆ explain what is needed for effective chairing;

◆ demonstrate how to mitigate the risks posed by groupthink and other cognitive biases;

◆ appreciate the importance of boards setting the right values and ethical tone for the organisation;

◆ explain the systems of documentation which good boards use to help to ensure good meeting practice;

◆ appreciate and explain good procedures for running meetings;

◆ demonstrate how the company secretary contributes to effective meeting practice;

◆ explain the role of the company secretary in meetings;

◆ appreciate the benefits of board evaluation and what it involves; and

◆ appreciate the main challenges to ensuring good meeting practice and how to address them.

Chapter eight
Good meeting practice

CONTENTS

1. Introduction
2. Overview of good board meeting practice
3. Key documents that should be available to boards
4. Running the meeting

1. Introduction

This chapter looks at good meeting practice for boards, including being clear about a meeting's purpose, chairing a meeting, allocating time for the meeting and encouraging constructive challenge from board members. It also looks at the documentation such as board policies and a scheme of delegation which boards can use to improve meeting practice and run an effective meeting.

The role of the company secretary/governance professional is discussed in detail in the next chapter but for this chapter it should be noted that they will play a vital role in good meeting practice assisting and facilitating the board before, during and after meetings.

2. Overview of good board meeting practice

As explained in Chapter 5, company law refers to directors rather than boards but the model Articles of Association state that decisions should be taken collectively, which in practice means they should be made by the board. The model articles also say that any decision of the directors must be made either by a majority decision at a meeting or be a unanimous decision confirmed in writing but not necessarily in a meeting. Directors have a duty under Companies Act 2006 (CA2006) s. 172 to promote the success of the company for the benefit of its members (shareholders), having regard to various matters including stakeholder interests (see Chapter 1). Directors' decision making therefore will generally be in a board meeting and to a lesser extent in board committee meetings. It is obviously important the board makes good, well-informed and considered decisions for the company.

2.1   Good chairing

A prerequisite to having an effective meeting is good chairing. The basic role of a chairman is outlined in Chapter 5; here we look at what is needed for being an effective chair. The chairman needs to do more than chair a meeting well; it also involves preparation and planning of a meeting, ensuring the directors are properly prepared and following up after a meeting and between meetings. The company secretary can assist in this. It means ensuring that the directors are giving their best in a common cooperative cause during and outside of meetings.

Making it work 8.1

Adrian Cadbury likened the role of a chair to a conductor of an orchestra, except that chairs do not have a score to work from so chairs also have to be their own composer. Unlike a conductor a chair cannot be sure in advance what tunes their soloists (the directors) will play, whether one or more of them will want to take over as conductor or whether they will perform well or limply.

2.2   Having a clear aim

The aim of a board meeting is for the board to make the soundest decisions on the matters with which it should deal. The board is at the apex of an organisation and the top decision-making body so the potential scope for what a board meeting might consider is almost unlimited in a large complex organisation. It could easily overwhelm a board. Its members have limited time so it is important that boards avoid getting bogged down in detail which could or should be left to management.

The chairman should ensure the board is clear both about the overall purpose of the meeting and the organisational objectives about which decisions are made. Not everything a board may consider will require a decision. Some items discussed will have the objective of informing members so they are in a better position to make decisions sometime in the future. Another reason for bringing a matter to a meeting is that executives may want the board's opinion on something. It is important to remember why such items are being discussed and avoid aimless debate. Good chairing involves ensuring discussion keeps to the point, contributes to making a good decision in line with the aim of the meeting and understanding what the meeting is to achieve.

2.3   Effective time management

The chairman should allow sufficient time to debate an issue before making a decision. Some chairmen try to ensure a meeting covers all it needs to by planning the time allowed for each agenda item. This can be a good idea but runs the danger that insufficient time will be given to debate an issue properly and a poor decision is made. It can also mean more time than necessary spent on other items. The chairman and boards must be prepared to take the time needed. The chairman could use such a timetable as a guide but avoid making strict adherence to it an aim of the meeting. The company secretary might want to take note of how long each item takes as a guide to how long a similar item might need in future.

2.4   The need for constructive challenge

As noted in Chapter 2, a common feature of corporate governance scandals has been lack of challenge by NEDs. Chapter 5 highlights that a key task of NEDs is to provide constructive challenge and that one of the chairman's roles is to facilitate it. Without constructive challenge a course of action, advocated by a dominant chief executive or faction of the board, that requires board approval will effectively be rubber stamped. That may suit some directors but is far from ideal for the company. Good discussion and constructive challenge should ensure board members build on one another's analysis and ideas and make wiser decisions. Thorough debate may be required to ensure the important issues and options are considered.

Corporate governance codes have tried since the Cadbury Code to ensure that NEDs really do give constructive challenge. Provisions on the matter get longer and much guidance has been written. The problem persists although it is impossible to know if the problem would have been worse without the provisions and guidance. The reason for lack of challenge is to do with culture and behavioural dynamics rather than any lack of detail or imperfection in governance codes.

Becoming a director for the first time for most people is an honour and the realisation of an ambition. A new director will want to make a good impression in their first board meeting. They will want to avoid saying anything that may appear ignorant and will want to avoid upsetting anyone. They are likely to observe closely what other directors say and how they behave and take their lead from them. Unfortunately this passive habit adopted early in a board career can become entrenched. They may remain passive, asking the occasional question or making uncontentious remarks to show that they have read the board papers and show an interest. They still feel the need to avoid saying anything which may reveal any ignorance and, feeling part of a prestigious group and having strong respect for other board members, will want to avoid rocking the boat.

The financial crisis revealed that many directors of financial institutions did not really understand their bank's business. In particular, they did not understand the nature of risk taken by creating and trading in sub-prime asset backed securities or their derivatives such as collateralised debt obligations. The crisis also highlighted that some directors lacked sufficient relevant experience. The chief executive of failed bank HBOS was a retailer not a banker, nor was its chairman a banker. The chief executive of failed bank RBS was an accountant working in the profession until 1995 who became chief executive just six years later. The chairman of Northern Rock was a journalist.

Stop and think 8.1

The Co-operative Bank, part of the Co-op Group, attempted in 2012 to acquire 630 Lloyds Bank branches. Co-op Bank was chaired by a local politician and Methodist minister Reverend Paul Flowers; its board had few directors with banking experience and, as reported in the Guardian[1], included a plasterer, a nurse and horticulturalist. The intended acquisition stalled after a £1.5 billion capital shortfall was uncovered in 2013 by the Prudential Regulation Authority (part of the Bank of England). The Co-op Bank had to be bailed out, which its bondholders did, and the Co-op Group lost control of the group to hedge funds. The Financial Services Authority had approved Flowers becoming a NED and approved his appointment as chairman a year later.

The Treasury Select Committee, considering the circumstances behind the Co-op Bank's capital shortfall, heard that Flowers had no previous banking experience and had been appointed because he did better on psychometric tests than other candidates. The Committee chairman Andrew Tyrie said it was apparent that the Co-op Group rather than the bank had been driving the takeover of the Lloyds branches.

How would you determine whether a person has the necessary skills, knowledge and experience to be on a board or chair it? Should psychometric tests be part of the evaluation process?

Board members cannot reasonably be expected to know everything. It is tempting for boards of complex organisations to rely on the advice of specialists, particularly if the organisations are highly regulated. The danger is relying too much on others and avoiding thinking critically about the advice. Specialists are prone to missing the bigger picture and directors, particularly NEDs with their outside perspective, can help bring the bigger picture into view. An action that might make sense to a specialist may not in the wider scheme of things. NEDs should be prepared to ask what they might fear to be 'dumb questions'. They may ask questions which everyone else would like answered and reveal flaws in thinking and assumptions and gaps in knowledge.

Making it work 8.2

The full facts may never come out about why engineers at VW fitted software into cars which cheated emissions tests. It is possible though to imagine engineers thinking they had found a clever way to make their engines compliant. What's harder to understand is why no one stopped it from happening. A modern car is a mobile computer with perhaps 100 million lines of software code. Very few people will know how that software works. It may have been difficult for individuals who did know

1   (The) Guardian (2013) The Co-op and the mutuals have failed us almost as badly as the banks, Leader on 23 November 2013, www.theguardian.com/business/2013/nov/23/co-operative-mutual-failed-badly-as-banks

some of the detail to air their concerns and easier to say nothing. Others may have chosen not to look for problems and turn a blind eye.

A company culture which prizes engineering expertise may have been slow to question what was going on. The culture and values of a large corporation may become different from that of the society in which its people work. People who work long hours for a corporation may end up thinking alike and losing touch with the values and accepted norms of society. What might have made sense to an engineer in such an environment would have been considered corrupt by someone outside it.

Groupthink, as mentioned in Chapter 2, and other cognitive biases should be a major concern for boards. Groupthink occurs when individuals in a group think alike. Alternatively, real or perceived group pressures prevent individuals from questioning either a dominant individual or faction in the group or a paradigm of thinking held by the group. It leads the group to make poorer decisions because it fails to evaluate different options or appreciate risks. Groupthink can also lead groups to lose their capacity for moral judgement and they may behave in an inhumane way. Groups are likely to take more risk than do individuals. A group whose members share a similar background or is insulated from outside opinions is particularly vulnerable to groupthink. Groupthink is likely to be a symptom of lack of diversity of thinking on the board. The growing recognition of the importance of gender and ethnicity diversity on boards was discussed in Chapter 4. There are other cognitive biases which affect everyone but we are usually unaware of them when we make decisions. Biases to which executives and boards are prone include optimism bias and confirmation bias. Optimism bias tends to make us unaware of the risks and make an exaggerated assessment of the likelihood of success of an action. Optimists believe their plans will succeed. Confirmation bias is where people make a decision based on evidence which confirms their view and ignore or undervalue evidence which conflicts with their view.

A good chair will be aware of these thinking risks. They will encourage people to express their views and consider different options. They will ensure board members are aware of the risk these biases can pose and guard against them. This may require adjourning a meeting as happened at General Motors.

Making it work 8.3

Alfred Sloan was CEO, then chairman, of General Motors between 1923 and 1956. He was known as 'Silent Sloan' as he ran the business from behind the scenes. At one senior executive meeting he is reported[2] to have said: 'Gentlemen, I take it we are all in complete agreement on the decision here.' Everyone nodded their heads. He then said: 'I propose we postpone further discussion of this matter until the next meeting to give ourselves time to develop disagreement, and perhaps gain some

---

2   (the) Economist (2009) Alfred Sloan, January, www.economist.com/node/13047099

understanding of what the decision is all about.' Sloan could see that the lack of any challenge meant people did not understand or were unwilling to question.

2.5 Different board styles

The aim of any chairman, and its members, should be to have a professional board style where decisions are informed and considered and the members respect each other but are willing to give constructive challenge. Not all boards will have this style. Less appropriate styles include:

◆ where the board agrees to what the chief executive and/or chairman wants without proper discussion or challenge;

◆ where the members are all from a similar background and board meetings are more like a social gathering;

◆ where the board seldom meets and when it does just goes through the motions;

◆ where members are selected because of their fame or prestige rather than what they can contribute to the organisation;

◆ where the members are mostly alumni of the same school, college or university;

◆ where the members are friends of the chief executive or chairman;

◆ where all the members are like partners, all enthusiastically closely involved in managing the organisation; and

◆ where all the members are from the same family and may lack business expertise.

Stop and think 8.2

Do you know why these other styles of board could make poorer decisions than a professional board?

3. Key documents that should be available to boards

3.1 Powers reserved to the board

Boards will find they are more effective if they introduce structure, procedure and policies. As a minimum the board of even a small company should have a Schedule of Powers Reserved to the Board and a Scheme of Delegation from the board to the executive directors. The Schedule of Powers Reserved to the Board (also known as a Schedule of Reserved Powers) will list the matters that should be considered by the board and cannot be delegated. One of these matters will be agreeing the Scheme of Delegation, which specifies how other matters can be delegated to individual executives or managers.

Even a board with no NEDs should have such documents as they can prevent conflict later on. They clarify in advance what will require consideration and decision by the whole board and what decisions can be taken by individual directors. The FRC Guidance on Board Effectiveness says ensuring there is a formal schedule of matters reserved for board decision will assist the board's planning and provide clarity to all over where responsibility for decision-making lies.

The model Articles of Association[3] have a general enabling provision that the directors are responsible for managing a company's business and may exercise all the powers of the company (Article 3). Article 5 provides that directors may delegate any of their powers to a person or committee as they think fit. This gives boards a high degree of flexibility over what to delegate and what to retain.

It is therefore up to boards to decide which powers and matters they want to reserve to themselves and what is delegated. This flexibility is tempered by some company law and other requirements, which make the board responsible for various matters such as:

◆ approving financial statements;
◆ calling a general meeting of the shareholders;
◆ making political donations;
◆ appointing auditors;
◆ paying interim dividend and recommending a final dividend to shareholders;
◆ changes to the company's capital;
◆ authorising conflicts of interest; and
◆ board appointments.

The 2018 Code also sets out specific matters which should be dealt with by the board. The following comes from the principles in section 1 on board leadership and company purpose and section 2 on division of responsibilities:

◆ Establishing the company's purpose, values and strategy, and satisfy itself that these and its culture are aligned.
◆ Ensuring that the necessary resources are in place for the company to meet its objectives and measure performance against them.
◆ Establishing a framework of prudent and effective controls, which enable risk to be assessed and managed.
◆ Ensuring effective engagement with, and encourage participation from shareholders and stakeholders.
◆ Ensuring that workforce policies and practices are consistent with the company's values and support its long-term sustainable success.

---

3   HM Government (2014) Model articles of association for limited companies, www.gov.uk/guidance/model-articles-of-association-for-limited-companies and HM Government (2014) Model articles for public companies, www.gov.uk/guidance/model-articles-of-association-for-limited-companies

◆ Ensuring that it has the policies, processes, information, time and resources it needs in order to function effectively and efficiently.

Other good practice matters for boards are:

◆ approving a scheme of delegation to board committees, individual directors and executives;

◆ approving changes in strategy;

◆ approving significant acquisitions and divestments;

◆ approving budgets and forecasts;

◆ approving significant expenditure, contracts or commitments to spend above a prescribed threshold;

◆ approving significant treasury and financing matters;

◆ approving whistleblowing or speak up policies;

◆ considering reports from committees;

◆ appointment and removal of company secretary; and

◆ making changes to the board.

ICSA issued a guidance note on this subject, 'Matters reserved for the board' (2013).[4]

3.2 Scheme of delegation

The South African King IV Report recommends that governing bodies should approve a delegation framework which includes authority for executive appointments. It is up to the board how it chooses to delegate anything it does not reserve to itself. Boards may simply delegate everything to the chief executive and leave the CEO to get on with things. They may choose to set out formally what at high level it delegates to other committees, the chief executive, other executive directors, the company secretary and possibly other senior executives or managers. Responsibility for financial control may, for example, be delegated to a chief financial officer or finance director. It should be remembered that although the board may delegate matters to individuals the board remains responsible in law for what the organisation does.

Public sector organisations, such as the NHS, have standing orders (SOs) and standing financial instructions (SFIs) which imply a scheme of delegation. Since 1997 the NHS model SOs and SFIs[5] issued to all NHS organisations have included a model reservation of powers to boards and a model schemes of delegation to officers. The latter listed the significant matters delegated such as management of budgets, operation of bank accounts, ordering and payment procedures, capital expenditure, tendering and contracting, relations with the press, whistleblowing and engaging and employing staff. For each matter it also

---

4   ICSA (2013) Guidance note Matters reserved for the board, www.icsa.org.uk/download-resources/download0?fileId=1120

5   Moxey, P. (1997) NHS Trust Example Standing Orders and Example Reservation of powers to the Board and Delegation of Powers Health Authority and Trust Model Standing Financial Instructions. and Example Fraud Policy and Response Plan NHS Executive.

listed the person (job title) or committee to whom authority had been delegated and, where relevant, financial authority limits and reference documents. Many NHS bodies now publish their matters reserved for the board, the SOs, SFIs and scheme of delegation online.

3.3 Board policies

Schedules of matters reserved for the board and schemes of delegation are matters of board policy.

The board may want to have, or approve, other policies covering such matters as:

◆ code of ethics;
◆ conflicts of interest;
◆ corporate and social responsibility;
◆ directors' remuneration;
◆ diversity and equal opportunity;
◆ dividend payments;
◆ employment of staff and contractors;
◆ environmental protection;
◆ financial and treasury management;
◆ health and safety;
◆ litigation;
◆ non-audit services provided by the auditor;
◆ press and media relations;
◆ speak up or whistleblowing procedures; and
◆ succession planning.

If a board chooses to have policies on these matters it should avoid too much detail or being too prescriptive. It would be better to keep most policies high level giving a framework and principles, and for more detail, if needed, to be provided by management. Some policies, however, will need full detail as they are required by company law or the UK Code of Governance. These include, for public companies, policies on directors' remuneration and provision of non-audit services by the external auditor.

3.4 A board charter

The IFC encourages boards to have a board charter. This locates board procedures and policies in one place. A charter can cover:

◆ board composition, structure and independence criteria;
◆ board appointments, terms and resignation;
◆ responsibilities of the chairman, NEDs, company secretary and committees;
◆ duties and powers of the board including supervision of management, decision making, schedule of matters reserved to the board and matters

delegated;

◆   board evaluation;

◆   external reporting;

◆   audit matters;

◆   directors' remuneration;

◆   relations with shareholders;

◆   board meeting procedures;

◆   conflicts of interest;

◆   director induction and training;

◆   trading in company shares; and

◆   confidentiality.

Test yourself 8.1

What are the two most important board policy documents?

3.5   Policy governance

Policy governance[6] is an approach to, and theory of, governance developed by John and Miriam Carver. The model is used mainly in not-for-profit organisations but has also been used in the NHS. Aspects of policy governance have been used by BP.

With policy governance, boards govern through four sets of policies on: (i) governance process; (ii) delegation to management; (iii) the ends the CEO is expected to achieve; and (iv) the limitations placed by the board on the CEO:

1.   Governance process. This covers how the board manages itself. It would include:

   –   the fundamental accountability of the board to the organisation's 'owners' (meaning e.g. the government, trustees and shareholders);

   –   its social responsibility to other stakeholders;

   –   the board's governing style and structure (e.g. separate chairman and CEO, proactive or reactive and decisions to be taken collectively rather than individually);

   –   how the board adds value, board–shareholder engagement, agendas, committees and evaluation.

2.   Board delegation to management. The Carver approach delegates all operational matters to the CEO as, arguably, it makes accountability cleaner than delegating some matters to the chief executive and other matters to other executives. Policies would include:

   –   only formal resolutions of the board are binding on the CEO;

---

6   Carver, J. and Oliver, M. (2002) Corporate boards that create value, Jossey Bass, San Francisco.

- all authority and accountability for operational achievement and conduct is delegated to the CEO;
- the board instructs the CEO through written policies; and
- the CEO's performance is rigorously and systematically monitored against the board's ends policies and limitations policies.

The last policy is fundamental to the effectiveness of the model and forms the bulk of the board's work once the policies have become established.

3. Ends policies. These set out the ends which the CEO is expected to achieve. These may be expressed as priorities, aims and objectives, which would include financial matters and other matters considered by the board to be in the owner's direct or indirect interests. This allows for ends to include social and environmental matters.

4. Limitations policies. These set out the constraints placed on the CEO. The CEO is authorised to do anything except what is precluded in the limitations policies. This would include precluding doing or allowing anything which is unlawful, violates generally accepted business practices, breaches regulatory standards, places the organisation in jeopardy and activity which is unsafe.

Policy governance may seem similar to a board charter and the policies could be implemented as a board charter. The difference is that it is a systematic approach which makes a clear distinction between what the board does (which is governance) and what the CEO does (which is management). The system makes it harder for a board to omit doing things which are its responsibility and harder to interfere in management.

If the system has a weakness it is that the system relies on the CEO providing detailed reports to the board setting out (a) how the ends policies are being achieved while (b) staying within the boundary set by the limitations policies. These reports need to be sufficient, accurate and balanced. It would be possible for a CEO to mislead the board accidentally or intentionally and the board remain ignorant. Internal audit can provide an objective check on the CEO's monitoring reports as might the external auditor on financial aspects of the monitoring reports.

3.6 Directors' and officers' insurance

Although not a board policy in the same sense as the policies above, a directors' and officers' insurance policy is nevertheless an important board document. The model Articles of Association for both private and public companies provide that the company may indemnify directors out of the company's assets against liability incurred through negligence, default, breach of trust or any other liability incurred as an officer of the company. It does not authorise indemnity for anything which would be illegal.

4. Running the meeting

4.1 Calling meetings

The model Articles of Association prescribe that any director may call a board meeting by giving notice of the meeting or authorising the company secretary to do so. The notice must give the proposed time, date and location. The articles also provide for meetings where not all the participants will be in the same place, in which case the notice should state how they will communicate. Notice must be given to each director but need not be in writing. No minimum notice period is prescribed but seven days is generally regarded as sufficient.

4.2 Agenda and agenda planning

Company law does not require an agenda but they are standard practice and would normally be issued with the notice calling the meeting. The notice may alternatively invite directors to submit items to be included on the agenda which would then be issued afterwards. The agenda will of course vary according to the nature of the meetings but should normally explain the matters to be discussed and whether the matters are for information only, consideration or a decision. Standard matters to include are:

◆ date, time and location of the meeting;

◆ any apologies for absence;

◆ approval of the minutes of the previous meeting;

◆ matters arising from the previous minutes unless specifically included on the agenda;

◆ brief details of each item to be discussed in the meeting and whether it is for information, consideration or decision (supporting information such as management reports or accounts will normally be provided with the agenda);

◆ other business (it is customary for the chairman of the meeting to invite those present to add additional items for discussion at the beginning of or end of the meeting); and

◆ date of the next meeting.

Most chairmen discourage directors from including substantive or contentious items under any other business. It could take other directors by surprise and other directors would not have time to prepare.

The agenda should not be so full that the board cannot get through it in a reasonable time. Meetings lasting over three hours are unlikely to be as productive as shorter ones. Company secretaries should work with their chairmen to plan the time but bear in mind that items can overrun. It makes sense therefore to put the high priority most important items at the top of an agenda. Matters which are for information and do not require consideration or decision and can be dealt with quickly could be placed before or after items requiring decision. Information items are on the agenda as the board needs to be informed so it can carry out its monitoring role. Any director should be free to ask for a discussion on such items. Such matters could include sales reports and management accounts. Some matters may not require a decision but require consideration: executives may want to bring them to the board's attention to seek the board's view on a subject. For example, there may be pressure from stakeholder groups or non-governmental organisations about an aspect of the company's activities; the board could be asked to advise on what priority to give the matter.

Not all decisions need take much time and may be more like a formality, such as if a document requires sealing. A preliminary discussion near the start of the meeting about what the board feels is important may be appropriate.

Test yourself 8.2

What is an appropriate notice period for calling a board meeting?

4.3 Quorum

A quorum is the minimum number of people needed for a meeting to take place. For board meetings the model articles prescribe that if the company has more than one director the minimum quorum for a meeting is two but the directors can agree a higher number. If the total number of directors falls below what is required for a quorum the only decisions the remaining directors can take is to appoint other directors or call a general meeting to enable shareholders to appoint more directors. If the company has sufficient directors for a quorum but there is not a quorum at a meeting the only decision that can be taken is to call another meeting.

The chairman or company secretary should check a quorum is present before proceeding with a meeting and adjourn it if the number subsequently falls below a quorum.

4.4 Board and sub-committee papers – how much information is appropriate?

In order for boards and their committees to make good decisions they need to be properly informed. A director should not regard the board and committee papers as their only source of information. They should talk to other directors, executives, management and staff and have seen sufficient of the organisation's operations to have a first-hand understanding of the business model. Board and committee papers are nevertheless an essential source of information for information and decision making.

It is not easy to get their content right. They may be too short, leaving out essential detail or too long so that the detail obscures what really matters. The people responsible for preparing information for the board may have little idea what the board really needs, wants or already knows. Board members may not know what information is available and may also be unsure what information they need. What boards will need is information which is relevant to the matter being considered and any decision needing to be taken. It should be objective, factual, fair, balanced, understandable by all directors, just sufficient and timely. Information which is irrelevant, subjective, biased or out of date is obviously not wanted. The company secretary will have an important role in collating the board information and advising on what content is appropriate.

Not all directors will have the same level of prior knowledge. NEDs are likely to have less than executives. In deciding what is sufficient information the principle to apply is that NEDs should not be disadvantaged. Additional background information may be needed, such as about how a situation, which needs a decision, developed or occurred. Board information should be understandable to a non-expert.

Providing information that is objective, balanced, free from bias and understandable can be a challenge, particularly if the matter to be decided on is a course of action favoured by management, such as a new strategy, project or acquisition. Bias can be deliberate. Executives and their subordinates will naturally want to get board approval and be tempted to avoid including anything in the board information which does not support their case. Executives and their staff will also want the board to think well of them and leave them to do their jobs. They will therefore be tempted to sanitise board reports and remove or downplay things which would invite difficult questions.

Bias can also be unintentional. Executives and their staff are likely to have an optimistic disposition and see the positive side of what they want to do and possibly not recognise the downside. They will naturally look for information which supports their case and are less likely to look for anything which does not (optimism bias). They may also innocently reject contrary information as it does not feel or look right to them (confirmation bias). NEDs should be aware of this and ask searching questions.

4.5 Governing not micromanaging

It is easy for boards to be distracted by detail or indulge themselves in matters which interest them. They may be tempted to offer helpful advice to management on how they do their jobs. This is not really the board's job, can be wasteful of their time and blur the boundary between governing and managing. It is up to the chairman to draw the line.

Making it work 8.4

Adrian Cadbury[7] gives advertising as an example. Everyone has a view on it, particularly if advertising is aimed at the public. It is proper for the board to consider advertising policy but not advertising execution unless it does not comply with policy. The system of policy governance described above creates a clear demarcation between what the board should do and what the board should leave to management.

7   Ibid.

4.6 Decision making

It is not necessary for all directors to be in agreement although that may be desirable. The chairman should judge whether an issue is contentious. The chairman should decide when to end a discussion and sum up the arguments for and against. Voting may not be a good way to resolve a matter on which the board is divided. If there is insufficient agreement to reach a decision it may be better to adjourn the decision to another occasion.

4.7 Minute taking

Company secretaries are likely to be actively involved in many of the matters covered above as they assist their chairmen. Much of what they do is unnoticed and behind the scenes. Minute taking is more conspicuous. Minutes are the written record of the business transacted at a meeting and of the decisions reached. Minutes are important. CA2006 s. 248 prescribes:

◆ every company must record minutes of all proceedings at meetings of its directors;

◆ records must be kept for at least ten years;

◆ failure to comply means an offence is committed by every officer of the company who is in default; and

◆ a person guilty of an offence is liable to a fine.

Minutes are evidence, if authenticated by the chairman, of the proceedings at the meeting and until the contrary is proved, that the meeting was duly held and convened, the proceedings took place and appointments at the meeting are valid (CA2006 s. 249).

What to include in addition to decisions is a matter of judgement for the chairman and company secretary. The fact that minutes may be used as evidence in a legal or regulatory action encourages minutes to be brief. Brevity and succinctness are virtues but there may be times when more information is needed, such as why a decision was made or not; in such cases a background brief filed with the minutes may be appropriate. A dissenting director may also want the minutes to record his/her disagreement with a decision.

Stop and think 8.3

Cadbury was once a Quaker company and Quaker practice in minute taking is to agree a minute with those present at the meeting for each agenda item as the meeting progresses. This is time consuming but has the advantage that everyone present has agreed what was decided and agreed that they have agreed.

This minute taking practice is unusual but do you think it has merit?

If the minutes are not agreed in the meeting the company secretary should prepare the minutes soon after the meeting and agree them with the chairman.

It would be preferable to circulate them as draft minutes to the rest of the board once the chairman is happy with them rather than waiting until shortly before the next meeting. The draft minutes must be discussed and confirmed at the next board meeting.

ICSA has published a guidance note on minute taking[8].

Chapter summary

- Good chairing is essential for an effective meeting and so is constructive challenge.
- Good meetings will start with a clear aim of what is to be achieved.
- The time of a meeting should be managed appropriately.
- Boards, like other groups, can be victims of groupthink leading to unchallenged flawed decisions.
- They are also susceptible to other cognitive biases such as optimism bias and confirmation bias.
- NEDs should be prepared to ask questions that may make them seem ignorant.
- Boards should be careful about relying on advice of specialists as they are fallible.
- Boards should have a schedule of matters and powers reserved to the board and a scheme of delegation from the board to its committees and executives.
- Consider if policy governance would be appropriate for your board.
- Make sure board meetings are quorate.
- Getting right the amount and quality of information to support a board meeting is a challenge.
- Board minutes are an important record which company law requires to be kept for ten years.

8   ICSA (2017) Guidance note Minute taking, www.icsa.org.uk/knowledge/resources/minutetaking/minute-taking-sign-up

Chapter nine
Boardroom effectiveness

CONTENTS

1. Introduction
2. The company secretary
3. Board effectiveness evaluation
4. Problem areas for directors and boards in effective decision making

1. Introduction

This chapter builds on the previous chapter on good meeting practice, setting out what else makes boards effective. Section 1 is about how the company secretary supports the board, including their role and responsibilities. The next section looks at board evaluation, what it involves and ways of doing it. The last section considers some of the problem areas for directors and boards in effective decision making not already covered in this or the previous chapter.

2. The company secretary

2.1 The legal and code requirement

All public companies are required to have a company secretary (CA2006 s. 271). The model articles for public companies contain a number of references to the company secretary in relation to meetings and documents. Together with the directors a company secretary is an 'authorised signatory' under s. 44 for executive documents.

Private companies were required to have a company secretary until the Companies Act 2006 but they may still choose to have one (CA2006 s. 270). If a private company does not have a secretary, anything required to be given or sent to its secretary may be given or sent to the company itself. Anything else required to be done by the secretary may be done by a director or person authorised by the directors.

Principle I of the 2018 Code says 'the board, supported by the company secretary, should ensure that it has the policies, processes, information, time and resources it needs in order to function effectively and efficiently. Provision 16 provides 'all directors should have access to the advice of the company secretary, who is responsible for advising the board on all governance matters. Both the appointment and removal of the company secretary should be a matter for the whole board'.

So the company secretary's role is one of supporting the board, and particularly the chair, in the performance of their duties. Exactly how much each company secretary does will differ from board to board.

2.2 The role and responsibilities of the company secretary

As the ICSA Guidance note, 'The corporate governance role of the company secretary' (2013),[1] says, the company secretary is at the heart of the delivery of good quality corporate governance. Much of the governance work described in this study text will be done by the company secretary.

The FRC confirms this in its Guidance on Board Effectiveness. In a section entitled 'Board support and the role of the company secretary', it says that 'the company secretary is responsible for ensuring that board procedures are complied with, advising the board on all governance matters, supporting the chair and helping the board and its committees to function efficiently'.

Other responsibilities set out in the guidance include ensuring good communication and facilitating induction, training and general professional development. Another responsibility is to ensure that directors have access to independent professional advice at the company's expense. The company secretary should report to the chair on all board governance matters. This does not preclude the company secretary also reporting to the chief executive in relation to their other executive management responsibilities. The remuneration of the company secretary should be determined by the remuneration committee.

Another aspect of the company secretary's role is assisting in the establishment of policies and processes that the board needs in order to function. The company's governance processes, for example board and committee evaluation, should be regularly assessed by the company secretary and the chair, along with any potential improvements that arise from the assessment.

The King IV Report™ says that governing bodies should have 'access to professional and independent guidance on corporate governance and its legal duties', and 'support to coordinate the functioning of the governing body and its committees'. It says 'the governing body should approve the arrangements for the provision' of such guidance and ensure that the company secretary 'is empowered and carries the necessary authority'. It recommends that even companies and other organisations not required to have a company secretary should consider appointing one. King IV™ says the company secretary 'should have unfettered access to, but for reasons of independence … not be a member of, the governing body'. Finally, King IV™ says that the company secretary

---

1   ICSA (2013) The corporate governance role of the company secretary, www.icsa.org.uk/download-resources/download0?fileId=7960

'should report to the [board] via the chair on all statutory duties and functions performed in connection with the governing body'. The company secretary may report to executive management on other matters.

It follows that company secretaries should develop and maintain a professional, objective and effective relationship with the chairman and other board members. They should be seen as trusted advisers who enjoy board members' confidence and be a confidential sounding board on matters that concern them. They can be an unobtrusive but, if necessary, firm voice in board discussion. They are not, however, board members and should not vote in a board meeting. They should be abreast of new governance legislation, regulation and codes and any other governance developments relevant to the company and brief the board appropriately.

Agendas will normally be prepared by the company secretary in consultation with the chairman. As part of the agenda setting they should agree what the meeting needs to achieve, including any decisions that are required.

The company secretary will attend board meetings and be the chairman's right hand. The effectiveness of the chairman and of the board meeting will, to a considerable extent, depend on the company secretary. They are responsible for board and committee administration and the issue of board papers including calling meetings, agendas, resolutions, supporting board papers and board minutes after a meeting. They can also advise on procedure during the meeting and on regulatory matters. The company secretary, or one of his/her team in a large organisation, will have the same role in committee meetings.

The company secretary will draft the minutes of the board or committee meeting. As discussed in Chapter 8, this is likely to be as soon after the meeting as possible, if not actually done during the meeting. The minutes of one meeting will normally be approved at the next meeting if not before. Once approved, they should be signed by the chairman and filed in the Minute Book.

Test yourself 9.1

Which legislation removed the requirement for private companies to have a company secretary?

The company secretary is likely to be responsible for many of a company's compliance requirements. This will include maintaining the various statutory registers and Companies House filing requirements and compliance with legislation.

The statutory registers which should be maintained at the registered office include:

◆ register of members and share ledger;
◆ register of directors and secretaries;
◆ register of directors' residential addresses;
◆ register of charges;

◆ register of people with significant control (PSC register); and

◆ minutes of board and company meetings including shareholder resolutions.

These registers may be inspected by the public. Information to be filed at Companies House includes:

◆ the company's financial statements once approved;

◆ an annual confirmation statement (this replaced the Annual Return in 2016);

◆ company resolutions (passed by the members);

◆ changes in directors or the secretary;

◆ changes in share capital or the rights of shares;

◆ changes to the articles of association or a new memorandum and articles;

◆ change of company name or registered address; and

◆ changes in mortgages or charges.

This information can be filed by post, courier or online. There are time limits for filing and penalties for late filing. Apart from the financial statements, resolutions and the memorandum and articles, changes should be notified on prescribed forms.

The company secretary will also be responsible for much of the work associated with shareholder general meetings, also called company or members' meetings. There are two types: the annual general meeting (AGM), at which matters to do with the accounts, audit, directors' remuneration, appointment of directors and dividends will be transacted. Any other matter for the members such as alterations to share capital can also be transacted at an AGM. Any other shareholder meeting is an extraordinary general meeting (EGM). An EGM would be called if business needs to be transacted at a different time from the AGM. Notice to convene a general meeting will be by the board (but see also Chapter 6) but will usually come from the company secretary by order of the board.

It follows that company secretaries must be well organised and have access to up-to-date compliance requirements. A timetable or series of timetables covering the main events such as production of an annual report, company general meetings and board meetings should be helpful, as would checklists for the various standard procedures.

In addition to all the responsibilities above the company secretary may also be the executive with overall responsibility for all other administrative matters.

Test yourself 9.2

Which documents must be filed at Companies House?

3. Board effectiveness evaluation

All boards should benefit from board effectiveness evaluation. The benefit of having one is likely to be proportional to the effort made in carrying it out. Benefits for boards, committees and individual directors can include:

◆ recognising mistakes and learning from them;

◆ surfacing uncomfortable issues which no one wants to raise (identifying the elephant in the boardroom) and dealing with them;

◆ identifying what works and what can be improved;

◆ considering boardroom dynamics: are they healthy or do they need help?;

◆ reviewing the evidence of the outputs of the board and committees such as: whether good decisions been made, whether the strategy was a good one and whether the values and standards the board wanted are embedded in the organisation;

◆ identifying and addressing any gaps in knowledge or experience on the board; and

◆ the satisfaction of knowing the board, its committees and members are doing a good job.

Stop and think 9.1

The 2016 Carillion Annual Report described in three pages the annual review of board effectiveness which it said 'is an important process for helping to identify key areas for future improvement or focus'. The 2016 review was led by the chair and facilitated by Linstock Limited, an independent corporate advisory firm. At the December 2016 board meeting, the directors reviewed the results of the evaluation, which confirmed that the board, each of its committees and the directors continue to be highly effective.

Can the board of a company which a year later ran out of money justifiably have considered itself highly effective?

The requirement for boards of companies with a primary listing to evaluate their effectiveness was one of the recommendations by Sir Derek Higgs in his Review of the Role and Effectiveness of Non-executive Directors for the Department of Trade and Industry in 2003[2]. He recommended that the performance of the board as a whole, of its committees, and of its members, be evaluated at least once a year. It was a controversial suggestion but was included in the Combined Code later in 2003. It has now gained general acceptance and some now say it is the most useful part of the UK Code.

Many national codes of corporate governance and the New York Stock Exchange require board effectiveness evaluations.

---

2   Derek Higgs (2003) Review of the Role and Effectiveness of Non-executive Directors, The Department of Trade and Industry.

The 2018 Code principle L says 'annual evaluation of the board should consider its composition, diversity and how effectively members work together to achieve objectives. Individual evaluation should demonstrate whether each director continues to contribute effectively'. Provision 21 says this evaluation should be rigorous and include the board, its committees, the chair and the individual directors. In FTSE350 companies, evaluation should be facilitated externally at least every three years, in which case the external evaluator should be named in the annual report.

The Higgs Report includes guidance on how evaluations should be carried out, part of which has been carried over into the FRC's 2018 Guidance on Board Effectiveness. The latter guidance suggests 16 areas which might be considered as part of an evaluation:

1. the mix of skills, experience and knowledge on the board, in the context of developing and delivering the strategy, the challenges and opportunities, and the principal risks facing the company;

2. clarity of, and leadership given to, the purpose, direction and values of the company;

3. succession and development plans;

4. how the board works together as a unit, and the tone set by the chair and the chief executive;

5. key board relationships, particularly chair/chief executive, chair/senior independent director, chair/company secretary and executive/non-executive directors;

6. effectiveness of individual directors;

7. clarity of the senior independent director's role;

8. effectiveness of board committees, and how they are connected with the main board;

9. quality of the general information provided on the company and its performance;

10. quality and timing of papers and presentations to the board;

11. quality of discussions around individual proposals and time allowed;

12. process the chair uses to ensure sufficient debate for major decisions or contentious issues;

13. effectiveness of the company secretary/secretariat;

14. clarity of the decision-making processes and authorities, possibly drawing on key decisions made over the year;

15. processes for identifying and reviewing risks; and

16. how the board communicates with, and listens and responds to, shareholders and other key stakeholders.

These areas are mainly input issues for the board. The areas underlined represent process issues. None of the areas represent outputs, i.e. what the board actually achieves in terms of results.

Test yourself 9.3

Who introduced the requirement for UK listed companies to have a board effectiveness evaluation?

Board evaluation is the responsibility of the board but it is the chairman's responsibility to lead it and ensure the board has sufficient time and resources for it. The company secretary is likely to be the key facilitator making sure it runs smoothly.

Making it work 9.1

After HBOS failed in 2008 the deputy chairman and senior independent NED told the Parliamentary Commission on Banking Standards[3] investigating the failure that 'I have no doubt that the HBOS board was by far and away the best board I ever sat on. My recollection of the culture and characteristics of the board was one of openness, transparency, high intellect, integrity, good working relationships between the chair and chief executive, and a suitable diversity of backgrounds, mix of experience and expertise to maximise effectiveness [...] If with the benefit of hindsight I was asked if I wanted to sit on this board again I would be saying yes.'

The HBOS chair told the Commission that he did not accept that the board he chaired failed in its challenge to the executive. He said that much thought was given to ensuring that 'there was a lot of challenge and different ways of challenging ... There was an atmosphere where people were able to be very direct and blunt. There were one or two occasions when great offence was caused, but we had a very open society. There was constant challenge, not just of corporate, but of the other divisions'. He concluded: 'I think the governance was rather good.'

Other directors reported positively about their experience on the board. The Commission concluded: 'the corporate governance of HBOS at board level serves as a model for the future, but not in the way in which Lord Stevenson and other former board members appear to see it. It represents a model of self-delusion, of the triumph of process over purpose.'

The more detailed report[4] by the FCA and PRA after the Parliamentary Commission report commented on the bank's disclosures on board effectiveness reviews in the 2005, 2006 and 2007 Annual Reports and Accounts. They all stated that 'performance and effectiveness of the Board and each of its Committees is evaluated annually'.

The FCA/PRA report implies that such evaluations were weak. It reports

---

3   An accident waiting to happen': The failure of HBOS, https://publications.parliament.uk/pa/jt201213/jtselect/jtpcbs/144/144.pdf

4   Financial Conduct Authority (FCA) and the Prudential Regulation Authority (PRA) (2015) The failure of HBOS plc (HBOS).

that the bank chair said that he met with individual directors about once every two or three years to obtain and give feedback, and then he produced a report which would be discussed as a board. The Review was 'unable to form a view on this ... as no records of any such reviews have been found'. Nor had the Review seen evidence to confirm that the 'reviews were carried out, or what the outcomes if any, were'.

The report concludes there was insufficient evidence to suggest that the evaluations were in line with the guidance at the time or a formal and rigorous evaluation advocated in principle B.6 of the Combined Code and 'in none of these years did the evaluation identify material failings or weaknesses'.

Clearly, one lesson from HBOS is that board effectiveness evaluation should be properly documented.

Disclosures by UK listed companies about their board evaluations seldom reveal useful detail or insights. For many companies which actually give information about the process used, the main evaluation tool is a questionnaire, the results of which are collated and discussed in a board meeting. Some companies use a questionnaire followed by interviews between each of the directors and an external facilitator or one or more of the chairman, the senior independent NED or the company secretary. Some disclosures say that evaluation includes review of documents. A few companies disclose brief information about the findings of the evaluation and the action taken but most are silent or simply conclude the findings were satisfactory.

Stop and think 9.2

A 2016 study[5] of board evaluation of 187 North American public and private companies by the Rock Center for Corporate Governance at Stanford University and The Miles Group found:

◆   55% of the companies that conducted board evaluations evaluated individual directors (leaving 45% which did not evaluate individual directors).

◆   36% believed that their company does a very good job of accurately assessing the performance of individual directors.

◆   52% believed their board is very effective in dealing with directors who are underperforming or exhibit poor behaviour, while a quarter (26%) do not.

---

5   Rock Center for Corporate Governance at Stanford University and The Miles Group, 2016 Board Of Directors Evaluation And Effectiveness, Stanford USA, www.gsb.stanford.edu/sites/gsb/files/publication-pdf/cgri-survey-board-directors-evaluation-effectiveness-2016.pdf

Group dynamics and culture

◆   **46% believed that a subset of directors has an outsized influence on board decisions.**

◆   **74% said directors allow personal or past experience to dominate their perspective.**

◆   **53% did not express their honest opinions in the presence of management.**

◆   **47% said directors are too quick to come to consensus.**

◆   **44% said directors do not understand the boundary between oversight and actively trying to manage the company.**

◆   **39% said fellow board members derail the conversation by introducing issues that are off-topic.**

This survey suggests a number of problem issues for boards in how they handle group dynamics. Do you recognise any of them in your own experience? On the positive side, 46% strongly believed that their board tolerates dissent.

A need to document effectiveness evaluations could encourage a formulaic box-ticking approach to provide evidence of their having taken place. This is a danger, especially if the primary reason for having an evaluation is to comply with the UK Corporate Governance Code. It would be better if the whole board sees board evaluation as an opportunity to improve the way they work and make decisions. This is of course easier for boards which already work well together and if the organisation they direct and control is also doing well. The board of an ailing organisation has a harder job and is more likely to have signs of dysfunction. Facing up to the challenge through a rigorous evaluation may be hard.

If we think of the board as a system with inputs, processes and outputs, the 16 areas listed above which the FRC suggests might be considered in an evaluation mostly consider what could be termed input issues. They are the ingredients of what is needed for an effective board. The areas which have been underlined in the list above are process issues although number five, 'key board relationships, particularly chairman/CEO, chairman/senior independent director, chairman/ company secretary and executive/non-executive', is both an input and a process issue.

The list above does not include output issues which consider whether the board actually does its job well. The example of HBOS above revealed a board which thought it was doing a good job. If it had considered its effectiveness in the light of what was really going on within HBOS it might have reached a different view. It is therefore important that boards consider their effectiveness in relation to the effect it has on the organisation and whether or not the decisions it made had been sound ones. An organisation which fails is unlikely to have had an effective board.

3.1   Asking good questions

Additional considerations for boards therefore include the following.

◆   How well does the board lead the organisation?

◆   Were all the decisions made by the board good ones?

◆   How well does the board set strategy?

◆   Is that strategy the best one available?

◆   Is that strategy being achieved?

◆   How well does the board ensure the necessary financial, human and other resources are present to achieve objectives in line with the strategy?

◆   How well does the board monitor organisational performance?

◆   How clear is the board that the organisation always operates within its risk appetite and tolerance?

◆   How confident is the board that it understands all the significant risks facing the organisation?

◆   How satisfied is the board that all these risks are managed, mitigated or transferred so that any residual risk is within the board's set risk tolerance?

◆   How well does the board set the values and standards, including ethical values, for the whole organisation?

◆   How sure can the board be that the values and standards it sets are indeed embedded throughout the organisation?

The above considerations also apply to committees but it is the board which ultimately is responsible for its effectiveness.

The FRC has highlighted culture, including board culture, as an important issue for companies. The Stanford University survey referred to above suggests a number of cultural issues which boards should be wary of, such as 74% or respondents saying directors allow personal or past experience to dominate their perspective and 39% saying fellow board members derail the conversation by introducing issues that are off-topic.

Not surprisingly, perhaps, annual report disclosures about the board evaluations which have taken place do not reveal whether such cultural issues were present in their boards nor do they reveal whether the evaluation was designed to include such cultural issues.

3.2   Methods of evaluation

Board evaluations will usually consist of a combination of questionnaires, interviews, group discussions, reporting of findings and discussion of findings, development of an action plan and implementation.

The questionnaires may use only closed questions (where the respondent would choose an answer from two or more options given), a mixture of closed and open (where the respondent could write a narrative response) questions or only open questions and each director will be asked to respond. The questionnaires may be designed within the organisation, be one of the standard formats widely available or developed by an external facilitator. Open questions allow a rich source of information but closed multiple choice questions have the advantage of being quick, allowing comparison with other responses and easy to interpret. They may also be easy to misinterpret if the questions are not well designed or do not fit the particular circumstances of the board or organisation at the time. Questionnaires can be detailed: one Middle East bank uses a questionnaire with nearly 200 questions but length does not necessarily indicate quality. A shorter, more targeted questionnaire could be better.

Interviews with individual directors would be with the chairman, senior independent NED, external facilitator or company secretary. The interviews can build on the responses from the questionnaires. Both questionnaires and interviews will consider the board and committees. They may also consider the performance of individual directors. Individual directors will be asked to evaluate their own performance and they may also be asked to evaluate other directors. Criteria considered for individual directors will include input issues such as independence and number of meetings attended or been absent. More useful, but harder to consider, are matters such as the quality of constructive challenge and their contribution to the work of the board and its committees. Executive directors will also have a review of their performance as executives.

Interviews or discussions may also be held with investors and other stakeholders. The depth and scope of the evaluation will vary. A thorough review will take much time and effort. Evaluations carried out soon after they were required by the Combined Code were relatively perfunctory and focused on compliance with the Code. They would have been designed partly to enable the board to say they had performed an evaluation and that the results were satisfactory rather than uncover problems to be addressed. As experience of evaluations has improved, and boards have gained confidence in them and appreciate their benefits, boards are undertaking more rigorous evaluations. It can be difficult, however, for boards to be self-critical when directors want to retain their positions. As explained above, the evaluation should include board culture and output issues which link the performance of the board and individual directors to organisational performance.

4. Problem areas for directors and boards in effective decision making

This chapter and the previous chapter have already outlined a number of problem areas for boards which harm their effectiveness and good decision making, such as:

◆   adequacy of information available to make decisions;
◆   lack of clarity about the aim of a meeting and lack of focus;
◆   maintaining strategic overview and avoiding micromanagement;
◆   lack of constructive challenge; and
◆   cognitive biases.

Other problem areas are:

◆ personality and group dynamics issues;
◆ a dominant CEO or chairman;
◆ not knowing what is going on;
◆ maintaining independence and objectivity;
◆ illegal or unethical conduct; and
◆ conflicts of interest.

4.1 Personality and group dynamics issues

The Stanford University survey above highlights some of the problems caused by personality and group dynamics issues. Some people are just awkward. The vast majority are not and want to do a good job. Problems can arise if people feel they are not being listened to. Good chairing will help ensure that each director is able to speak and be listened to. Other problems can arise from genuinely held difference of opinion. Good chairing can help find any common ground from which to build some agreement. Problems in meetings can be reduced by good preparation smoothing the way before a meeting. A thorough and professional board effectiveness evaluation properly handled should help to identify and address more deep-seated issues.

The company secretary can assist, working with the chairman, in making sure people are as fully informed as practicable and alert for signs of trouble ahead.

Test yourself 9.4

List two of the examples of dysfunctional group dynamics and culture in the study of board evaluation of 187 North American public and private companies by Rock Center for Corporate Governance at Stanford University and The Miles Group.

4.2 Dominant CEO or chairman

Years of code development have sought to eliminate the problem of one person, usually the CEO or chairman, dominating board proceedings. It is human nature though that one person is likely to have more influence and other people defer to that person, choose not to confront him/her or choose to leave. A good effectiveness evaluation should identify the problem and the dominant person might moderate his/her behaviour. Having raised the issue it should then be easier for other directors to assert themselves.

4.3 Knowing what is going on

Knowing, or rather not knowing, what is going on in the organisation is a problem facing all managers and board members everywhere except in the smallest organisations. Good induction procedures for new board members and updating for current directors can help ensure the board is as well informed as reasonably possible. It simply is not possible, however, to know everything which happens yet directors, in legal terms theoretically at least, remain responsible for what goes on. The financial crisis highlighted examples not just of banks being too big to fail but seemingly too big to manage.

The solution is to accept that it is not possible to know everything but take care to ensure that the organisation:

◆ only employs good people with integrity;

◆ has a framework of prudent and effective controls;

◆ has good values and standards which are embedded throughout the organisation;

◆ sets clear aims or objectives for the organisation, team's and individuals which are all aligned;

◆ understands the significant risks and is resilient enough to deal with them;

◆ has sufficient resources to achieve what is expected;

◆ has clear delegation of responsibility and accountability;

◆ has effective monitoring; and

◆ has staff who feel free to speak up where they have concerns.

4.4 Maintaining independence and objectivity

Governance codes attach great weight to the appearance of independence for NEDs. Too much independence could mean detachment and disinterest. Too great an involvement in something means objectivity could be lost. What really matters is that all directors think independently and objectively and are engaged in a common purpose. A clear policy of what powers the board reserves to itself and what it delegates can help boards maintain independent and objective thinking, and stay concerned enough to be engaged but not so close as to lose objectivity.

4.5 Illegal or unethical conduct

Illegal or unethical conduct is a common problem affecting most large organisations. A web search looking for examples of illegal or unethical conduct in Fortune 500 companies will show most have had issues and some multiple issues. Illegal conduct at board level is rarer but does happen.

Boards will want to ensure as far as possible that this does not happen in their organisations. Surveys suggest that the most effective ways to ensure ethical behaviour are to have a good tone at and from the top of the organisation and to have a work culture where people feel free to raise any concerns they have without fear of any retribution. Creating such a culture may be difficult. Most boards and top management will say that values are important, that the code of ethics or conduct must be followed and violations will be severely dealt with. Such things may fall on deaf ears if the managers are set over-demanding performance targets and then managers, whose career and livelihood may depend on keeping their job, push staff to deliver. Whistleblowing procedures, discussed in Chapter 12, can help deter unethical or illegal behaviour provided staff have confidence there will be no retribution against them for raising a concern.

Making it work 9.2

This example is based on an article[6] in Vanity Fair by Bethany McLean in 2017.

Wells Fargo was founded in the USA in 1852 as a stagecoach express. By 2016 it had become one of the six major US banks after a series of acquisitions and mergers. It was focused on growth and customers. The bank had an initiative to sell each customer eight additional products. Each morning there was a conference call where staff had to tell management how they were going to make the sales goal for the day. Those who could not make the goal had to explain why and how they were going to fix it. 'It was really tense,' according to one employee. Achieving sales goals was difficult, especially with competition from other banks.

Unusual things happened. Customers took out large loans and then immediately repaid part of them so that the bankers could get credit for the bigger loan. New customer bank accounts were created without the customers' knowledge. Some customers were charged fees on these accounts. Managers ignored concerns raised by employees about such practices. Staff who failed to make their targets were dismissed.

An internal report in 2004 highlighted concerns of staff who felt they could not make sales goals without gaming the system. The incentive to cheat was based on the fear of losing their jobs. The report recommended reducing or eliminating sales goals as several peer banks had done, and warned that the issue could lead to loss of business and diminished reputation in the community.

Between 2011 and 2015 Wells Fargo employees opened over 2 million deposit accounts and credit card accounts that may not have been authorised. In September 2016, Wells Fargo agreed to pay a $185 million penalty to various enforcement agencies to settle charges of fraudulent conduct. As part of the agreement Wells Fargo admitted no wrongdoing.

4.6 Conflicts of interest

One of the directors' duties in company law (CA2006 s. 175) is to avoid conflicts of interest. A director of a company must avoid a situation in which they have, or can have, a direct or indirect interest that conflicts, or possibly may conflict, with the interests of the company. This applies in particular to the exploitation of property, information or opportunity. It is immaterial whether the company

---

6   McLean, B. (2017) How Wells Fargo's Cutthroat Corporate Culture Allegedly Drove Bankers To Fraud, Vanity Fair Summer 2017, www.vanityfair.com/news/2017/05/wells-fargo-corporate-culture-fraud

could take advantage of the property, information or opportunity. If the articles allow it, the board may decide to authorise the decision provided the director concerned is not counted as part of the quorum.

The model Articles of Association for both private and public companies also provide that if a director is concerned in an actual or proposed transaction or arrangement with the company they should not take part in the decision-making process. The director may, however, take part in the decision if:

◆ the company allows it by an ordinary resolution of its members;

◆ the director's interest cannot reasonably be regarded as likely to give rise to conflict of interest; or

◆ the conflict arises from a permitted cause:
(i) a guarantee,
(ii) a subscription, and
(iii) arrangements which benefit employees and do not provide special benefits to directors.

Chapter summary

◆ Public companies are required to have a company secretary, private companies may choose to have one.

◆ The company secretary is at the heart of the delivery of good quality corporate governance.

◆ The company secretary will be the first source of independent professional advice for the board; all directors should have access to their advice and services.

◆ The company secretary is likely to be responsible for many of a company's compliance requirements including maintenance of statutory registers and filing with Companies House.

◆ The company secretary will also be responsible for much of the work associated with shareholder general meetings.

◆ Many national codes of corporate governance and the New York Stock Exchange require annual board effectiveness evaluations.

◆ The UK requirement for board evaluation is in the UK Corporate Governance Code principle L.

◆ Board evaluation is the responsibility of the board but it is the chairman's responsibility to lead it and ensure the board has sufficient time and resources for it.

◆ Companies are required to explain in the annual report how the board effectiveness review was conducted.

◆ HBOS in 2008 highlighted an example of a board which claimed board effectiveness reviews had been carried out each year but there was no evidence of this and HBOS board was clearly ineffective.

◆ Effectiveness reviews should include consideration of cultural dynamics of the board and its effectiveness in terms of outputs.

◆ Effectiveness reviews consist of a combination of questionnaire, interview, group discussion, reporting of findings and discussion of findings, development of an action plan and implementation.

◆ Further problems which can harm board effectiveness, in addition to those already covered include: personality and group dynamics issues, dominant CEO or chairman, not knowing what is going on, maintaining independence and objectivity, illegal or unethical conduct, and conflicts of interest.

◆ Wells Fargo provides an example of fraudulent behaviour caused by staff being expected to achieve over ambitious performance targets.

Part four

Risk governance

Chapter ten
Board oversight of risk

Chapter eleven
Sources of risk

Chapter twelve
Practical issues in the management of risk

Overview

This part looks at risk governance, explaining the role of the board in relation to ensuring the resilience of the organisation and its strategy in the face of risk. Chapter 10 introduces the subject, what risk is, key risk terms and the board's role in risk governance. Chapter 11 looks at sources of risk, including consideration of what can be learned from the financial crisis. Finally, Chapter 12 looks at the practical issues and challenges of managing risk.

Learning Outcomes

At the end of this part, students will be able to:

- understand what risk is;
- explain key risk terms such as internal control and risk appetite;
- explain the board's and audit committee's role in relation to risk;
- appreciate the requirements of the UK Corporate Governance Code on risk, risk management and internal control;
- appreciate what is required in other sectors and countries from boards in relation to risk;
- understand key sources of risk in organisations;
- explain some of the standard approaches to managing risk;

◆ demonstrate ways in which organisations protect themselves from wrong doing; and

◆ appreciate the need for boards to get assurance on risk management.

Chapter ten
Board oversight of risk

CONTENTS

1. Introduction
2. What is risk?
3. Important risk terms
4. What is the board's role in relation to risk?

1. Introduction

This chapter outlines the role of boards in the oversight of risk meaning, risk taking and risk management. It also introduces the key components of risk management and a sound understanding of risk in an organisational setting. No organisation operates in an environment that is risk free over the long term. Even where an organisation has a monopoly, and may not be subject to commercial or market risks, it faces other risks; for example, it may lose its monopoly, demand for what it does disappears or it falls victim to a natural disaster. Public sector and not-for-profit organisations also face risk: their funding may disappear or the need for their services changes. These risks are all external to an organisation. All organisations are also potentially prone to internal risks, such as an operational mistake or failure, non-compliance with laws or regulations and ethical failure.

The following sections set out:

◆ what is meant by risk;

◆ some key terms with technical meanings, knowledge of which is essential to understanding the board's role in relation to risk, including risk appetite and internal control; and

◆ the role of boards in relation to risk and internal control according to influential authorities such as the Financial Reporting Council (FRC).

This chapter outlines what boards of UK organisations should do. The focus of the chapter is on the requirements for listed companies but these requirements are relevant for any type of organisation with a board. Chapter 12 addresses the important practical issues affecting boards and challenges to having effective risk management, such as to do with corporate culture and decision making.

ISO (International Standards Organisation) 31000 Risk Management Principles and guidelines
ISO is an independent, non-governmental international organisation based in Switzerland whose members are the 162 national standards bodies. ISO has published over 21,000 standards including 31,000 on risk management.

BS (British Standards) 31100 Risk Management
The British Standards Institute was established in 1901 and has 76 offices worldwide and over 36,000 current British standards including BS31100 on risk management.

2. What is risk?

In a corporate or organisational setting, the word risk can have a variety of meanings. Often it will have the same meaning a layperson would give it; especially when discussed by most directors and executives . The risk management profession and standards setters, however, have given 'risk' a more specialist meaning. The **International Standards Organisation (ISO) Standard 31000**[1] and the **British Standards Institution Risk Management Standard BS31100**[2] define risk as the 'effect of uncertainty on objectives' where an effect is a positive or negative deviation from the expected. Objectives are organisational objectives or goals at any level within an organisation from strategic to detailed process. They could relate to matters such as finance, operations, compliance, health and safety, and environment. Uncertainty according to ISO 31000 is the 'state, even partial, of deficiency of information related to, understanding or knowledge of an event, its consequence, or likelihood'.

The ISO definition is harder to make sense of than the layman's definition. The key differences are that the ISO definition:

◆ puts risk in the context of what an organisation is trying to do; and

◆ allows that risk can have a positive or beneficial effect on objectives so could be a good thing and not just a bad one. It also makes risk just a noun and not a verb.

A layman might view risk as either a cause or an effect, for example the risk of failure to follow a safety feature causing the risk of a fire. When considering how to manage risk it is a good idea to consider both but the ISO standard clearly defines risk as an effect only. For these and other reasons some risk specialists are not entirely happy with the ISO definition. This is discussed further in Chapter 12.

Risk is often regarded as a combination of potential events and their consequences. Risk managers will often assess and rank different risks in terms of the impact of an event (singular) and its likelihood of happening using a simple two-by-two matrix (Figure 10.1). Risks with a high predicted impact and high predicted likelihood will be considered more important than ones with low impact and likelihood. Many risk managers and internal auditors use a simple traffic light colour coding, using red for the biggest risks, green for minor risks and amber for something in between. Figure 10.1 uses light shading in place of green, medium shading in place of amber and dark shading in place of red. This simplistic approach can be problematic, as will be discussed in Chapter 12.

---

1   ISO (International Standards Organisation) 31000 Risk management – Principles and guidelines.

2   British Standards Institution, Risk Management Standard BS31100 Risk management – Code of practice and guidance for the implementation of BS ISO 31000.

Risk Assessment	Likelihood	
Impact	High impact, low likelihood	High impact, high likelihood
	Low impact, low likelihood	Low impact, high likelihood

Figure 10.1: Risk assessment

3. Important risk terms

As well as understanding what the word risk can mean in different contexts, there are other terms that you will need to know, set out below.

3.1 Going concern

The term 'going concern' is used in the general sense to mean an organisation is viable, is able to meet its financial obligations and will remain in business over the medium to long term. There is also a stricter accounting meaning. Companies should prepare accounts using the going concern basis of accounting which assumes, broadly, that the company will remain in business for at least a year. The requirements are complex and set out by the FRC (2016) in Guidance on the Going Concern Basis of Accounting and Reporting on Solvency and Liquidity Risks[3]. It is important for boards to know whether their organisation is a going concern and whether it can use the going concern basis of accounting.

3.2 Internal control

There is some disparity of view on what internal control is. Originally an auditing term, it came into wider use after a series of corporate failures in the late 1980s in the US which led to several control frameworks to help organisations assess whether control was effective. One very broad view of (internal) control set out by the Canadian Institute of Chartered Accountants in Guidance on Control (1995) (known as the CoCo Report[4]) is that control is 'all the resources, processes, culture, structure and tasks that taken together support people in achieving the organisation's objectives'. This could be more simply put as the means by which an organisation achieves its objectives. The US Committee of Sponsoring Organizations of the Treadway Commission[5] (known as COSO) defines it more narrowly: 'internal control is a process effected by an entity's board of directors, management, and other personnel, designed to provide reasonable assurance regarding the achievement of objectives relating to operations, reporting, and compliance.' Thus, in the CoCo sense of the term, internal control can include everything by which an organisation achieves

---

3   Financial Reporting Council (2016) Guidance on the Going Concern Basis of Accounting and Reporting on Solvency and Liquidity Risks, Financial Reporting Council (2016) Guidance on the Going Concern Basis of Accounting and Reporting on Solvency and Liquidity Risks Guidance for directors of companies that do not apply The UK Corporate Governance Code.

4   Canadian Institute of Chartered Accountants Criteria on Control Board (1995) Guidance on Control, Canada.

5   Committee of Sponsoring Organisations of the Treadway Commission (1992) Internal Control – Integrated Framework, USA.

objectives, where everything includes deliberate actions and passive aspects of an organisation such as good teamwork, people using their common sense, judgement and taking responsibility for their actions and having an ethical corporate culture. COSO sees it as a deliberate process to provide assurance about achievement of objectives.

Examples of internal controls affected by management include separation of duties such that one person does not see a process through from beginning to end. An example would be to have a separate buying department so that the person who wants a good or service does not have the opportunity to negotiate with a supplier a kick back for him/herself. Another example is to have one person signing off another person's work. Other controls include having procedures for a senior manager to review invoices, expense claims and requiring two signatures, or the electronic equivalent, before a payment can be made. Clearly such controls come at a price as they create added cost and can slow work down. Higher level examples of internal control include a budgetary control system and review of financial ledger adjustments.

Test yourself 10.1

How would you define internal control?

3.3   Risk management

risk management
Coordinated activities to direct and control an organisation with regard to risk' or simply managing risks.

One aim of **risk management** which, according to its broader definition, could also be said to be the same as the aim of internal control, is to ensure an organisation remains a going concern. ISO 31000 defines risk management as 'coordinated activities to direct and control an organization with regard to risk'. This is a logical definition yet, like the COSO definition of internal control, refers only to activities which have been deliberately devised by management. It ignores the fact that a lot happens in organisations which can contribute to ensuring risks are 'managed' in a broader sense and may not be actively coordinated such as the people factors discussed above in the comments about COSO.

At its simplest, risk management involves just three essential elements:

◆   risk identification;

◆   risk assessment and evaluation; and

◆   a decision to take, treat, avoid or transfer a risk (or a combination of these actions).

Risk identification means identifying by all means practicable what risks the organisation may face. There will be risks people are aware of and other risks about which they won't. Activities such as brainstorming and scenario planning may bring some of the unknown risks into awareness but others will remain unknown and may be unknowable.

Risk assessment and evaluation are about assessing and evaluating the risks which have been identified. It will often include making decisions on the expected likelihood of a risk happening and its impact if it does (see Figure 10.1). Evaluation should include considering the possibility that a risk assessed as having a high likelihood of happening but a low impact or consequence might, with lower likelihood, could also happen with a high impact or consequence. Risk assessment is also likely to include risk categorisation, where risks are categorised according to who is responsible for owning or managing them, or their type – such as reputational, strategic, financial, reporting, operational, external, internal, legal, compliance, credit, market, and so on. These separate types will be covered in more detail in the next chapter.

Risk evaluation includes deciding whether a risk is within or outside the defined risk appetite or tolerance and decisions as to what action to take. Evaluation should take into account that risk management is not like a game of cricket where a risk is a ball which a bowler bowls one at a time. It is more like a game where all the fielders are also bowling at the wicket from all around the field so that several balls may come from different directions to the wicket at once. Evaluation should therefore consider several risks happening at the same time and organisations should be resilient enough to survive them.

The choice of what to do with risk is between taking a risk, treating or mitigating it so it is within the risk appetite, avoiding it, for example by refraining from an activity, or transfer, for example transferring a risk to an insurance company. It should be borne in mind that risk treatment does not mean every risk has its own risk management action. Some risks are best controlled by a sound internal control system which ensures, among other things, having a sound risk culture where staff take responsibility for things which might go wrong and can use their common sense and where everyone has high moral or ethical values.

The above is risk management at its most simple. Doing this in a large organisation requires a lot more, as discussed below.

Test yourself 10.2

How would you evaluate different risks?

3.4   Risk appetite

Risk appetite is broadly the level of risk the board of an organisation is willing to take. The Financial Stability Board (2013)[6] (an international body whose members are mainly national central banks that monitor and make recommendations about the global financial system) defines risk appetite as 'the aggregate level and types of risk a financial institution is willing to assume within its risk capacity to achieve its strategic objectives and business plan'. Being clear about risk appetite is generally considered a foundation of good risk

---

6   Financial Stability Board (2013) Principles for An Effective Risk Appetite Framework, www.fsb.org/wp-content/uploads/r_131118.pdf

management and risks should be assessed in relation to risk appetite. ISO 31000 defines it as 'the amount and type of risk (2.1) that an organization is prepared to pursue, retain or take'.

risk tolerance
Organisation's or stakeholder's readiness to bear the risk after risk treatment in order to achieve its objectives.

Risk tolerance is regarded by the FSB as the effectively the same as risk appetite but is defined in BS31100 as 'organization's or stakeholder's readiness to bear the risk after risk treatment in order to achieve its objectives'. According to the Institute of Risk Management[7] (IRM) 'risk appetite is about the pursuit of risk whereas risk tolerance is about what you can allow the organisation to deal with'.

Decisions on whether to take, treat, avoid or pass on a risk should be taken with reference to risk appetite (or tolerance). In practice, as will be discussed in the next two chapters, this is easier said than done.

Although risk appetite or tolerance is widely regarded as a fundamental component of risk management, prior to the financial crisis it was rarely used in a systematic way outside of financial services. Within financial services it was expressed as one or more numerical measures.

Making it work 10.1

After Lehman collapsed in 2008 its website still claimed 'the effective management of risk is one of the core strengths that has made Lehman so successful. We rely on it to identify, measure and monitor the issues associated with doing business in the global capital markets'. The SEC and ratings agencies also thought Lehman's approach to risk was particularly good. When things started to go wrong for the bank in the early stages of the financial crisis Lehman increased the risks it would tolerate. The SEC supported this action but unfortunately with hindsight this turned out to be flawed.

The IRM advised that risk appetite is not a single, fixed concept, there will be a range of appetites for different risks which need to align and these appetites may well vary over time.

Risk appetite should be considered whenever a significant decision is made. It should be considered with reference:

◆   to the context in which the decision is being made; and

◆   in relation to the reward or benefit which may accrue if the outcome of a decision is positive and an assessment of both the likely risk: reward ratio and the expected likelihood of a positive or a negative outcome.

It follows that risk appetite is a concept that needs to be used with judgement. It will rarely be sensible for the board to be too prescriptive and it would be better to give general principles to be applied in different situations. There are some things however that the board can be categorical about. Any act which

7   Anderson, R. (2011) Risk Appetite and Tolerance, The Institute of Risk Management.

breaks the law, risks harm to a person or would be considered highly unethical by society is considered outside the risk tolerance.

4. What is the board's role in relation to risk?

UK company law does not say anything explicit on directors' responsibility for risk but s. 172 of the UK Companies Act 2006 (CA2006) strongly implies it in 'a director of a company must act in the way he considers, in good faith, would be most likely to promote the success of the company for the benefit of its members'. Most people agree that promoting a company's success means taking and managing risk and being resilient in an uncertain environment. It also means that the company remains in business – a going concern.

4.1 UK Governance Code requirements

The present UK requirements have developed since 1992 in response to various corporate scandals and are now embodied in the 2018 Code, further guidance from the FRC and in the Listing Rules. The Cadbury Committee in 1992 (GEE 1992) wanted directors to report on the effectiveness of the company's system of internal control and report that the business is a going concern. However the Committee recognised that criteria for assessing effectiveness needed to be developed. In the UK, this criteria was first set out in the **Turnbull Report**[8] (ICAEW 1999). Criteria was published before this in the USA in 1992 in the form of the COSO report and in Canada in 1994 in its Criteria on Control referred to above.

Turnbull Report 1999
Guidance issued by the Institute of Chartered Accountants in England and Wales on internal control and risk management.

The 2018 Code in principle C says the board should establish a framework of prudent and effective controls, which enable risk to be assessed and managed. Provision 1 includes the board 'should describe in the annual report how opportunities and risks to the future success of the business have been considered and addressed, the sustainability of the company's business model and how its governance contributes to the delivery of its strategy'.

Although not explicitly referring to risk or internal control, other parts of the 2018 Code are highly relevant. For example, a healthy culture is a vital component of good control. Principle B says the board should establish the company's purpose and values and Provision 2 says the board should monitor and assess culture to satisfy itself that behaviour throughout the business is aligned with the company's values.

Making it work 10.2

The failure of Marconi is one of the few examples of corporate governance failure where there was no suggestion of wrongdoing or excessive greed. Marconi was a simple example of failure caused by a

---

8   Institute of Chartered Accountants of England and Wales (1999) Internal Control: Guidance for Directors on the Combined Code. Commonly known as the Turnbull Report.

bad strategy at the wrong time.

As GEC, its previous name, it had been an industrial giant with a record in engineering respected around the world and with large cash reserves. In 2000 its stock market value was £35 billion. A year later it was in debt and shares were worth just £500 million. A debt for equity swap to its banks and bondholders left shareholders with only 0.5% of the business. Five years earlier its new chief executive sold the defence and other businesses and spent the proceeds and its cash reserves of £11 billion investing in telecommunications. That sector was going through a bubble phase along with the dotcom boom and the investments proved disastrous.

With the benefit of hindsight the new strategy was a mistake. We do not know exactly what was discussed at board meetings but it is worth reflecting on what the directors might have done which could have prevented failure.

In principle H non-executive directors should provide constructive challenge.

The main section on risk in the 2018 Code is Section 4, Audit, risk and internal control. In this section, principle O says 'the board should establish procedures to manage risk, oversee the internal control framework, and determine the nature and extent of the principal risks the company is willing to take in order to achieve its long-term strategic objectives'.

Provisions 28 to 31 provide:

28. The board should carry out a robust assessment of the company's emerging and principal risks (those risks that could result in events or circumstances that might threaten the company's business model, future performance, solvency or liquidity and reputation). The board should confirm in the annual report that it has completed this assessment, including a description of its principal risks, what procedures are in place to identify emerging risks, and an explanation of how these are being managed or mitigated.

29. The board should monitor the company's risk management and internal control systems and, at least annually, carry out a review of their effectiveness and report on that review in the annual report. The monitoring and review should cover all material controls, including financial, operational and compliance controls.

30. In annual and half-yearly financial statements, the board should state whether it considers it appropriate to adopt the going concern basis of accounting in preparing them, and identify any material uncertainties to the company's ability to continue to do so over a period of at least twelve months from the date of approval of the financial statements.

31. Taking account of the company's current position and principal risks, the board should explain in the annual report how it has assessed the prospects of the company, over what period it has done so and why it considers that period to be appropriate. The board should state whether

it has a reasonable expectation that the company will be able to continue in operation and meet its liabilities as they fall due over the period of their assessment, drawing attention to any qualifications or assumptions as necessary.

These last two provisions are about what are termed 'viability' statements. The FRC Guidance on Board Effectiveness provides further guidance for boards in making such statements.

Provision 25, inter alia, sets out the audit committee's responsibility to review 'the company's internal financial controls and internal control and risk management systems, unless expressly addressed by a separate board risk committee composed of independent non-executive directors, or by the board itself'.

The remuneration section of the Code also considers risk in Provision 40. It says that 'when determining executive director remuneration policy and practices, the remuneration committee should address (among other matters) 'risk – remuneration arrangements should ensure reputational and other risks from excessive rewards, and behavioural risks that can arise from target-based incentive plans, are identified and mitigated'.

Excessive remuneration and inappropriate forms of financial incentive have contributed to things going wrong for organisations. In the early 2000s it was found that executives manipulated financial performance to trigger performance-related pay. The financial crisis provided numerous examples of where individuals were financially incentivised to do things which were ultimately bad for their employer, customers and society (see the FCA guidance 'Risks to customers from financial incentives').[9]

4.2 FRC guidance on risk management and related matters for listed companies applying the Code

Guidance on applying the Code principles and provisions on risk management was issued by the FRC in 2014 in 'Guidance on Risk Management, Internal Control and Related Financial and Business Reporting'[10]. This superseded the guidance published by ICAEW in 1999, 'Internal Control: Guidance for Directors on the Combined Code and Going Concern and Liquidity Risk: Guidance for Directors of UK Companies', then the Turnbull Report. This latest guidance has the ambitious aim of:

◆ bringing together best practice for risk management;

◆ prompting boards to consider how to discharge their responsibilities in relation to the existing and emerging principal risks faced by the company; and

---

9   Financial Conduct Authority (2013) Risks to customers from financial incentives, https://www.fca.org.uk/firms/risks-customers-financial-incentives

10   FRC 2014 Guidance on Risk Management, Internal Control and Related Financial and Business Reporting, The Financial Reporting Council UK, www.frc.org.uk/getattachment/d672c107-b1fb-4051-84b0-f5b83a1b93f6/Guidance-on-Risk-Management-Internal-Control-and-Related-Reporting.pdf

◆   reflecting sound business practice, whereby risk management and internal control are embedded in the business process by which a company pursues its objectives; and highlighting related reporting responsibilities.

The need for new guidance stemmed from the financial crisis, after which two things became clear:

◆   risk management, particularly in banking, left something to be desired and the sense that something was missing from the guidance at the time; and

◆   financial institutions became illiquid almost without warning so the guidance ongoing concern needed review.

The rest of this section summarises the board's main risk-related responsibilities under the following six headings:

1.   Design and implementation of appropriate risk management and internal control systems.

2.   Ensuring appropriate culture and reward systems.

3.   Determining the principal risks faced and what risks the organisation is willing to take.

4.   Agreeing how the principal risks should be managed or mitigated.

5.   Monitoring and reviewing the risk management and internal control systems.

6.   Ensuring sound internal and external information and communication processes on risk management and internal control.

These requirements could seem daunting, particularly for smaller companies. Remember that success in business involves taking risk so it is not the board or management's job to avoid risk. Nor should risk management and internal control considerations get in the way of sensible business judgement. Rather it should help enable good judgement. The board's job is to ensure that the risks to which the organisation is exposed are known and understood. It is management's role to implement and take day-to-day responsibility for board policies on risk management and internal control, ensure internal responsibilities and accountabilities are clearly established, understood and embedded at all levels of the organisation and provide the board with timely information.

4.3   Design and implementation of appropriate risk management and internal control systems

The board should ensure that appropriate risk management and internal control systems have been designed, implemented and are in place that identify the risks (including their likelihood and impact) facing the company and enable the board to make a robust assessment of the principal risks. It should consider risk in conjunction with other matters normally considered by the board such as company strategy, business model and new projects such that, for example, the effect on risk of a new strategy or commitment is understood.

The board may delegate aspects of risk management to, or seek advice from, a committee or management but should satisfy itself the people concerned have the necessary skills, knowledge, experience, authority and support. Boards should consider specifically assessing this as part of their regular evaluations of their effectiveness.

4.4 Ensuring appropriate culture and reward systems

The board should ensure that appropriate culture and reward systems have been embedded throughout the organisation. It should ensure the remuneration committee takes appropriate account of risk when determining remuneration policies and awards, and whether the links between the remuneration committee and the risk and/or audit committee are operating effectively. As part of this the board should establish the tone from the top to establish the culture it wishes to embed and ascertain whether it has been embedded.

4.5 Determining the principal risks faced and what risks the organisation is willing to take

The board should determine the nature and extent of the principal risks faced and those risks which the organisation is prepared to take in achieving its strategic objectives. In other words, the board should determine its 'risk appetite' or 'risk tolerance' and whether the risks it faces are within this. The board should then satisfy itself that management have understood the risks, implemented and monitored appropriate policies and are taking risk that is within the accepted risk appetite. The 'principal' risks are those that, given the company's position, could threaten the business model (see Chapter 2), future performance, solvency, liquidity or reputation. The board should understand the extent to which these risks are managed or mitigated.

The board should consider:

◆ the likelihood of risks materialising, and the impact of related risks materialising as a result or at the same time (risks can come in bunches);

◆ the company's ability to reduce their likelihood or impact on the business of risks that do materialise (to get them with the risk appetite);

◆ the operation of the relevant controls and control processes and their effectiveness and relative costs;

◆ the effect on risk of the values and culture of the company and the way that teams and individuals are incentivised on the effectiveness of the systems of control; and

◆ the changes in the nature, likelihood and impact of principal risks, and the company's ability to respond to changes in its business and the external environment.

4.6 Agreeing how the principal risks should be managed or mitigated

The board should agree how the principal risks should be managed or mitigated and which controls put in place. In agreeing the controls, the board should determine what would constitute a significant control failing. The board should understand the residual exposure to risks after the risks have been managed or mitigated.

4.7   Monitoring and reviewing the risk management and internal control systems

Having ensured that suitable risk management and internal control systems have been implemented, it is necessary to monitor and review them to ensure they are functioning effectively and that corrective action is being taken where necessary. This should occur throughout the year. Additionally, an annual review of the effectiveness of the risk management and internal control systems should be carried out to ensure that it has considered all significant aspects for the company for the year. The annual review should define the processes to be adopted, including drawing on the results of the board's ongoing process such that it will obtain sound, appropriately documented, evidence to support its statement in the company's annual report and accounts.

The board should form its own view on effectiveness of internal control and risk management, based on the evidence it obtains. The annual review of effectiveness should consider all the matters covered under the board's six main risk-related responsibilities headings above.

4.8   Ensuring sound internal and external information and communication processes on risk management and internal control

The board should take responsibility for ensuring sound internal and external information and communication processes and external communication on risk management and internal control. It should specify the nature, source, format and frequency of the information that it requires and ensure the assumptions and models underlying this information are clear so that they can be understood and if necessary challenged. The board should monitor the quality of the information it receives and ensure that it is of a sufficient quality to allow effective decision-making and consider the company's whistle-blowing procedures.

They should determine whether to adopt the going concern basis of accounting and whether disclosures of material uncertainties in the financial statements are required.

In addition to the Code requirements in the section on Audit, Risk and Internal Control (in 4.1) the board should include the following in its annual report.

◆   A summary of the process for reviewing the effectiveness of the system of risk management and internal control and explain what actions have been or are being taken to remedy any significant failings or weaknesses.

◆   A description of the main features of the company's risk management and internal control system in relation to the financial reporting process, as required under the Disclosure and Transparency Rules.

CA2006 requires a description of principal risks and uncertainties (required in C.2) in the strategic report, which also requires a description of a company's strategy, objectives and business model. In addition, the 2014 FRC guidance on the strategic report requires an explanation of the main trends and factors affecting the entity; a description of its principal risks and uncertainties; an analysis of the development and performance of the business; and an analysis using key performance indicators.

There is no expectation to disclose information which would be prejudicial to a company's interests. Companies can choose where to position their reporting on risk, risk management and internal control systems and should cross reference if material is in different places. Boards should consider whether and how to link this to the information on principal risks in the strategic report and material uncertainties relating to the going concern basis of accounting in the financial statements. The FRC is trying to encourage 'joined-up' reporting on risk and related areas. This will require joined-up thinking on the part of company secretaries whose job it is to prepare the annual report.

Test yourself 10.3

Can you list the reporting requirements on risk-related issues?

The responsibilities set out above are onerous. They may be too much for most but the largest companies with access to a considerable amount of technical support. Smaller organisations should endeavour to apply the spirit of the Guidance in the most appropriate way they can. Appendix C of the Guidance is a list of 17 questions for boards to consider and discuss with management, internal audit and their advisors.

Stop and think 10.1

In 2008 the bank HBOS had a liquidity problem and needed government support. The UK Parliamentary Commission on Banking Standards report (2013)[11] into its failure found that it was not just one or two things which caused it to fail. It had losses in four divisions, any one of which would have required the bank to be refinanced. In 2004 the Chief Executive Officer fired the Head of Group Regulatory Risk following his warnings to the board about HBOS's risky sales strategies.

The report by the Financial Conduct Authority and the Prudential Regulation Authority[12] (2015) found the failure was explained by a combination of factors:

◆   **The board failed to instil a culture that balanced risk and return, and lacked sufficient experience and knowledge of banking**

---

11   Ibid.

12   Ibid.

resulting in a flawed strategy and a business model with vulnerabilities arising from excessive focus on market share, asset growth and short-term profitability.

◆ Executive management pursued rapid and uncontrolled growth, leading to over-exposure, increased leverage, and reliance on wholesale funding. The risks involved were either not identified or not fully understood.

◆ The board and control functions failed to challenge executive management effectively or ensure adequate mitigating actions.

As discussed in Chapter 9, the Commission interviewed many members of the board who spoke positively about their experience. The Commission concluded: 'We are shocked and surprised that, even after the ship has run aground, so many of those who were on the bridge still seem so keen to congratulate themselves on their collective navigational skills.'

Risk management was felt, wrongly, by the board to be sound. How could the board have felt it was doing a good job, even with the benefit of hindsight?

Stop and think 10.2

The FRC Guidance lists 28 responsibilities of directors on risk and risk management. Can you recall them? Rather than trying to learn each one, consider how they should apply in an organisation you know well. Are there any which seem more important than others? Do any seem irrelevant to you?

4.9 Audit committees

Provisions 24 to 26 of the Code refer to audit committees. The provisions set their high level duties (summarised in Chapter 5). In many organisations the board will delegate as much as possible to its audit committee. The FRC first published guidance on audit committees in 2003 in what was known as the Smith Report[13]. This was superseded in 2016 by 'Guidance on Audit Committees'[14], which addresses their establishment and effectiveness, their roles and responsibilities and how they should communicate with shareholders. The guidance on roles and responsibilities is consistent with that in 'Guidance on Risk Management, Internal Control and Related Financial and Business Reporting'. The distinction is that some of the board's responsibilities can be

---

13   FRC 2003 Audit committees combined code guidance. A report and proposed guidance by an FRC-appointed group chaired by Sir Robert Smith, Financial Reporting Council, London, www.ecgi.org/codes/documents/ac_report.pdf

14   FRC (2016) Guidance on Audit Committees, The Financial Reporting Council, www.frc.org.uk/getattachment/6b0ace1d-1d70-4678-9c41-0b44a62f0a0d/Guidance-on-Audit-Committees-April-2016.pdf

allocated to audit committees and those responsibilities are only covered in the Audit Committee Guidance. These include external audit and internal audit processes, where it says audit committees should regularly review the need for establishing an internal audit function.

4.10 Board oversight of risk in other organisations

The guidance above should be applicable to most types of organisation including unlisted companies and public and third sector bodies. Arguably, however, the time commitment which can be expected from governing bodies comprising volunteers or members paid a relatively small amount of remuneration is less than should be expected of highly paid executive directors and NEDs in FTSE100 companies. Fortunately perhaps, this has still to be tested in a law court and theoretically at least the obligations of a director in a small company and a large company are the same. A considerable amount of guidance and instruction has been published for public sector bodies by, e.g. HM Treasury, the Department of Health, Hefce, the Chartered Institute of Public Finance and Accountancy (CIPFA), Office of Government Commerce and Solace (the Society of Local Authority Chief Executives).

The Financial Reporting Council (2016) issued guidance in 'Going Concern Basis of Accounting and Reporting on Solvency and Liquidity Risks Guidance for Directors of Companies That Do Not Apply the UK Corporate Governance Code'[15]. This is intended to be a simplification which summarises the legal requirements, articulates best practice principles, suggests key focus areas and gives practical examples.

Skills CFA (a standard setting organisation for business skills and apprenticeship issuing authority in the UK) in 2013 produced a suite of National Occupational Standards for Governance of Risk[16]. They describe performance criteria and what governing bodies should know and understand but do not describe how to do anything. They are worth looking at as they include some important things not covered in the FRC Guidance. For example, Standard CFAGOR3 'Establish and maintain transparent and formal structures and policies in relation to risk and internal controls' includes a performance criterion 'adopt the most appropriate schedule of matters reserved to the governing body and the scheme of delegation of governing body responsibilities to its structures and individuals'. This is an important internal control.

The BS and ISO standards on risk management are also intended to be applicable to any type of organisation. They are only available through official bodies; a copy of BS31100 costs £190 for its 48 pages. Limited content of the ISO standards, however, can be previewed free of charge online. The price and availability may have limited both the extent to which they are commonly known and their adoption. These standards take a more holistic

---

15   FRC (2016) Going Concern Basis of Accounting and Reporting on Solvency and Liquidity Risks Guidance for Directors of Companies That Do Not Apply the UK Corporate Governance Code, The Financial Reporting Council, https://www.frc.org.uk/news/april-2016/guidance-on-the-going-concern-basis-of-accounting

16   Skills CFA (2013) produced National Occupational Standards for Governance of Risk.

view of risk management than the FRC and are based on the principle that risk management should be integral to all organisational processes and decision making. The International Federation of Accountants (IFAC) in 2015 published 'From Bolt-On To Built-In: Managing Risk as an Integral Part of Managing an Organization'[17]. This paper attempts to correct what many feel to be an unfortunate situation which has developed where risk management has become divorced from everyday management and is done by risk managers rather than by other managers. ISO has also published standards on Business Continuity Management Systems.

Making it work 10.3

The disclosures in Carillion's Annual Report 2016 suggested that Carillion's risk management practices and disclosures complied with best practice. The problem is that they gave the impression that Carillion knew what its risks were and had them under control. Furthermore the report says the audit committee had robustly tested whether the company would remain viable and concluded that it would for at least three years. What is not known yet was whether the risk management practices failed to alert management and the board to the reality of its problems or whether the disclosures omitted key information.

4.11 Board oversight of risk outside the UK

Several important sources of guidance on risk from outside the UK have already been referred to; this section provides some background to them. One of the most influential bodies in terms of risk management thought leadership and guidance is the US Committee of Sponsoring Organizations of the Treadway Commission (known as COSO). It published a seminal Integrated Framework on Internal Control in 1992 and heavily influenced approaches to assessing internal control and the guidance in the 1999 UK Turnbull Report. The Canadian CoCo control framework was also influential and was preferred by many risk practitioners as it was easier to use, more intuitive and more holistic. In implementing Sarbanes-Oxley rule 404, the US Securities and Exchange Commission decreed that three internal control frameworks could be used – namely the COSO Integrated Framework, the CoCo Framework or the guidance in the Turnbull Report. The Turnbull Report did not contain a formal framework for assessing control in the way that COSO and CoCo did but did include an appendix of control questions derived from COSO.

COSO followed the 1992 Framework in 2004 with 'Enterprise Risk Management – Integrated Framework'[18], which has since developed into a suite of

---

17   The International Federation of Accountants (2015) From Bolt-On To Built-In Managing Risk as an Integral Part of Managing an Organization.

18   COSO (2004) COSO Enterprise Risk Management Integrated Framework, Committee of Sponsoring Organisations AICPA, New Jersey.

publications including on risk assessment, risk appetite, key risk indicators and the role of the board of directors.

The OECD Principles of Corporate Governance (covered in Chapters 1 and 3), in common with the UK Code, also refer to risk, risk management and control and the 2015 version of the principles has expanded coverage on this. It goes into slightly more detail than the UK Code but considerably less than the FRC guidance.

The FSB has issued frameworks and a considerable amount of guidance for banks and other systemically important financial institutions (SIFIs) on risk and related matters such as market risk, risk culture and risk appetite.

Chapter summary

◆ The board is responsible for ensuring the organisation has an effective risk management and internal control system in place and for ensuring the principle risks facing the organisation have been identified and assessed.

◆ The word 'risk' can have more than one meaning.

◆ Key risk terms such as internal control and risk appetite are explained.

◆ The chapter outlines the requirements and guidelines on risk management in the UK Code of Corporate Governance and other documents issued by the FRC which is responsible for the Code.

◆ The FRC guidance should be relevant to most other types of organisation which have a board.

◆ Finally, the chapter summarises the main non-UK risk and internal control frameworks, sources of influential guidance and requirement.

Chapter eleven
Sources of risk

CONTENTS

1. Introduction
2. Categories of risk
3. Learning from the 2008 financial crisis and corporate failures
4. Boards as a source of risk

1. Introduction

This chapter looks at sources of risk for organisations and types and categories of risk in more detail. It considers some of the lessons for organisations which can be learned from the financial crisis and finally considers how boards themselves can be a source of risk.

2. Categories of risk

Organisations face all kinds of risk. Organisations find that different types of risk can be more conveniently identified, assessed and managed if they are slotted into various categories. The word cloud below shows some examples of the categories used. The list is by no means exhaustive and 'risk' can become a suffix to almost any label that could be applied to an organisation and what it does. So there is no single correct categorisation to use.

governance   production
liquidity   information
operational   strategic   legal   environmental
investment   people   reporting
health and safety   managerial

Figure 11.1: Risk types

Categorisation is a way of looking at risk. If a sphere represents the universe of risk for an organisation, categorisation is like taking a cross section of that sphere. The best categorisation for an organisation will depend, among other things, on what the organisation does, its sector, strategy, size and how it is funded. The board, senior executives and risk professionals should select a categorisation which works for the organisation at the time it is being used. Complex organisations may need to use more than one categorisation – like multiple cross sections of a sphere.

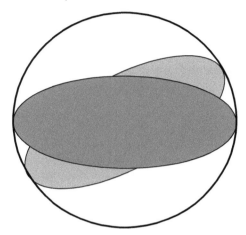

Figure 11.2: Categorisation within a universe of risk

The COSO Enterprise Risk Management Integrated Framework (2004) uses four high level categories: strategic, operations, reporting and compliance. This categorisation reflects the composition of the COSO, which included four accounting and finance bodies and the Institute of Internal Auditors and is relevant to the Sarbanes-Oxley Rule 404 requirement for companies to report on the effectiveness of internal control over financial reporting. Any other type of risk could theoretically fit into one of these four classifications.

For financial institutions, such as banks and insurance companies, taking and exploiting risk is a key part of the business model so they look at risk slightly differently. For them key risk categories are credit risk, customer risk, investment, solvency risk, liquidity risk, funding risk, currency risk and of course compliance risk. Compliance is such a big issue for banks that they may have subcategories of compliance risk such as money laundering and terrorist financing. A heavy engineering company would have production and health and safety among its key risks.

Organisations may choose to use two basic categories: external and internal risks. Internal risks are risks arising within the organisation and can usually be managed within the organisation such as production, people, managerial, compliance, operating and safety. External risks arise outside an organisation and can be harder for an organisation to manage. They could include the PESTLE factors (political, economic, social, technological, legal, environmental), customer, market, foreign currency exchange and competition. Not all risks fall neatly into external and internal categories, for example pricing, marketing, funding and environmental risks where the risk for an organisation depends both on what the organisation is doing and what is happening outside the organisation. Pricing risk, for example, would arise from a decision to fix a price and the willingness of the market to accept a price so has internal and external aspects.

Test yourself 11.1

Which categories of risk are used by the COSO Enterprise Risk Management Integrated Framework 2004?

Stop and think 11.1

Eastman Kodak was an iconic US company established in 1888 whose name was synonymous with cameras and photography dominating US consumer markets for cameras and photographic film until around 2000. It was an innovative company which held patents and developed the first digital cameras in the 1970s but did not develop the technology as it could threaten its existing film market. Kodak did develop digital technology in the 1990s but did not anticipate the pace of development and the threat to its existing business model. It was only in 2001 that sales of film dropped and Kodak wrongly, but understandably, thought this was a result of the terrorist attack on the New York World Trade Center on September 11.

Kodak began manufacture of digital cameras and by 2005 was the top seller in the US. Kodak manufactured in the US but could not make cameras cheaply enough to compete with Asian manufacturers so gradually lost market share while losing money on the cameras it sold. Kodak moved into manufacture of printers to make up for declining film sales but was running out of money. Kodak's strategy of charging a high price for the printer but a low price for ink turned out to be the wrong one as customers preferred to buy cheap printers and pay a higher price for ink. Kodak ran out of cash and filed for bankruptcy in early 2012. The company was then reorganised, assets including patents were sold and 18 months later emerged from bankruptcy protection to focus on commercial rather than retail customers.

As is the case in many corporate failures there were multiple reasons for failure rather than just one. List the risks that Kodak faced and rank them in order of seriousness.

Strategic risk can be any risk that could affect the achievement of an organisation's strategy. It can also be the risk to an organisation of having the wrong strategy. Marconi, discussed in Chapter 10, is an example of strategic risk causing a company to fail. The latter type of risk could also be called a governance risk. Strategic risks could fit many of the categories referred to above and could have an internal or an external origin. For obvious reasons they are risks which should be of interest to boards.

Business continuity risks should also be of particular interest to boards as these are the risks which could threaten the ability of an organisation to survive. These can be external such as the revolution in digital camera technology which affected Kodak or they can be internal. The use of cheating software in VW engines was an internally generated risk which at one point looked as if it could threaten VW's existence. See also the discussion of VW on page 136.

Making it work 11.1

The experience of the Swiss watch industry makes an interesting contrast with Kodak. The Swiss have for centuries made clocks and watches which enjoyed a strong reputation for workmanship. Like optical cameras, watches using spring-driven mechanical movements looked as though they would become obsolete. The first electronic movement watches using quartz were expensive but their cost fell dramatically as solid state technology was introduced in the 1970s and 80s. Swiss watch makers, like Kodak, were slow to embrace the new technology and around 1,000 of the 1,600 manufacturers closed down. They could not compete with Asian digital watches and the number of people employed in the Swiss watch industry fell by two thirds.

However, a few Swiss manufacturers, such as Rolex which only use mechanical movements, survived by rebranding themselves from manufacturers of watches for telling the time to producers of desirable items of jewellery, beautiful to look at and touch, which few people could afford. The cheapest Rolex watches retail for £4,500 to £5,000 with some models over £50,000. Twenty-year-old second-hand Rolex watches fetch around half the current new price and rarer watches are highly sought after.

In 1983 Swatch was formed after two of the major traditional Swiss watch manufacturers had failed and were merged by their creditors. The company succeeded against Asian manufacturers and is now the world's leading watch maker thanks to marketing of stylish digital watches emphasising the watches' Swissness. Asian watches, while technically excellent, lacked a certain style which consumers prized and were willing to pay for. Swatch took full advantage. Today the Swiss watch industry employs similar numbers of staff to in its pre-crisis days.

Kodak and the Swiss watch industry highlight how technological change can damage an organisation's business model. As discussed in the next chapter, risk management should consider risks to the continuing serviceability of the business model.

Reputational risk is another form of risk which will concern boards. Unlike most other risks, a risk to the reputation of the organisation or people within it is most likely to come from impropriety or misconduct or poor quality of product or service. Trust takes a long time to build but can be lost very quickly. Few commercial organisations are put out of business by damaged reputation. Arthur Andersen, discussed in Chapters 1 and 2, was a rare example of an organisation killed after reputational damage although its actual demise may have owed more to the firm losing its licence to audit. Ratners is another example of an otherwise thriving company almost fatally wounded by a self-inflicted loss to its reputation.

Stop and think 11.2

Gerald Ratner was chief executive of the successful high street jewellery chain Ratners. Its products were aimed at the mass market. Ratner, in a speech in 1991, described a sherry decanter set sold in his shops as 'total crap' and made derogatory remarks about a set of earrings. His remarks were widely reported and customers stayed away in sufficient numbers to threaten the chain's survival. Although the company survived, the name did not – the chain was rebranded Signet Group in 1993.

Can you think of any companies which did not survive a reputation crisis?

Another important category of risk that is now receiving much greater attention is people risk or cultural risk. Most things which can go wrong for organisations involve people so people are a source of risk. While it often makes more sense to consider many risks in terms of their function (e.g. production risk, credit, compliance health and safety risk) people risks can apply across many categories causing risk. People can also be contributors to, or causes of, other risks.

Test yourself 11.2

What types of risk are likely to be of most concern to boards?

2.1   Cause or effect

Risks can be thought of as causes and effects. For example, a fire can be considered as an effect caused by an electrical fault. It can also be a cause of damage to a building. So an effect can also be the cause of something else. The damage to the building caused a loss of production which lost sales and the loss of a valuable long-term contract with a long-established customer. The electrical fault which caused the fire which caused the damage to a building might have been caused by a worker not fitting an electrical appliance properly. The cause of that could have been the lackadaisical attitude of the worker caused by an argument with his boss.

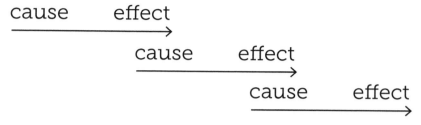

Figure 11.3 Risks can be both causes and effects

It makes sense then to consider risks as both causes and effects and consider the chain of causation working back to the root cause. Just like in medicine where it is better to treat the cause of an illness, in risk management it makes sense to treat the cause and where practicable treat the root cause. Often the root cause will be something to do with people, which is why it is so important for organisations to have a healthy culture.

3. Learning from the 2008 financial crisis and corporate failures

What started as a credit crunch in the summer of 2007 as banks became nervous about lending to each other, triggering the failure of Northern Rock, led in early 2008 to the collapse of investment bank Bear Sterns and then Lehman Brothers one year after Northern Rock. Lehman's failure created such collateral damage that the financial system in the US and UK would have collapsed without public rescue.

Chapter 2 discusses the implication for governance of the financial crisis. Here we consider what the crisis can teach us about risk. Banks and other financial institutions (BOFIs) are different from other companies, particularly in the importance of risk. The Walker Review (see Chapter 2) included this distinction:

'Probably the most helpful way of viewing the business of a BOFI is as a successful arbitrage among financial risks. In contrast to most other businesses, risk management in a BOFI is a core strategic aspiration of the business...

Monitoring and management of risk in a BOFI is not only a set of controls aimed at the mitigation of financial risk, as normally in non-financial business, but relates to the core strategic objectives of the entity. Principal risks in a non-financial business relate to its core product or service offering, the condition of relevant markets and sources of supply and the continuing effectiveness of its operations, for example in respect of health and safety, with financial risks as important but subordinate. By contrast, financial risks are the principal risks of any BOFI business... success is predicated on the effective use of a degree of leverage that is unique to the sector and not typically matched in any other business.

From the perspective of the BOFI board, determination of the strategy for the entity is, to a large extent, identifying the large franchise and other risks to the business, deciding on risk appetite for the entity in relation to those risks and then ensuring that the agreed risk strategy is implemented within a framework of effective controls.'

In other words, according to this view, a BOFI's core strength and purpose is making money by taking and managing risk. In other organisations taking and managing risk is something they have to do as part of their core product or service offering. As outlined in Chapter 10, Lehman prided itself in its risk management. For some time after the bank collapsed the Lehman website ironically continued to say 'the effective management of risk is one of the core strengths that has made Lehman so successful.

Test yourself 11.3

How is risk viewed differently by banks and insurance companies compared with most other types of organisation?

3.1   Perfect models and imperfect worlds

Banks developed sophisticated risk models: both they and banking regulators thought they understood risk. The risk models predicted the likelihood of events. Modelling involved assumptions about the expected distribution of data and events. For example, many models assumed a normal (also called Gaussian) distribution where the variability above or below an average is random.

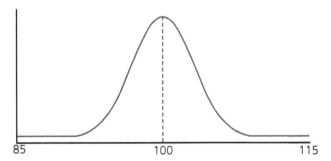

85	100	115

Figure 11.4 Normal distribution curve

standard distribution
A statistical term used to measure or describe the variation or dispersion above and below the mean (average) in a set of data. 68.2% of a random population will fall within one standard distribution of the mean, 95.4% will fall within two standard deviations and 99.6% will fall within three standard deviations.

Figure 11.4 shows a simple example of a normal distribution of data where the average is 100 and the **standard distribution** is 3. The vertical axis shows frequency and the horizontal axis shows a measurement such as length. In this case the curve could, for example, show the estimates of a large group of people for the length of an object 100cm long. The average estimate, which was also the most popular, was 100cm but estimates ranged between 85 and 115cm. A standard deviation (SD) of 3 means that 68.2% estimated the length to be between 97cm and 103cm. The shaded area under the curve shows the proportion who estimated a length of less than 106cm (two SDs from the mean). The area is 97.7%.

When banks modelled risk events it was often assumed that events which models said had a remote (say less than 0.5% chance of happening in a year) would not happen. The risk models worked well under normal conditions but not during abnormal conditions. The assumptions which would hold good during normal conditions were not valid when conditions changed. At the height of the financial crisis what had been thought of as extremely rare events were happening daily. Banks had put their faith in the models and the numbers and, in a form of groupthink, few sought to question the results of the models, the models themselves or the assumptions behind them. As is common in situations involving complexity or where specialised knowledge seems to be needed, people put their faith in experts. Many non-specialist people would not have attempted to understand the models.

The key learning point is that it is perfectly proper, and may be highly desirable, for lay people such as non-executive directors to question matters that might seem too difficult to understand. They should keep pushing for an answer until they get one they can understand and which makes sense.

3.2 Flawed paradigms

A paradigm is a worldview or way most people have of thinking about something. Examples in the financial crisis were beliefs that:

- US house prices could only go up;
- banks could always access funds in the market to support their borrowing needs;
- risk can be spread around many markets which are not correlated with each other;
- markets will naturally correct themselves, meaning minimal regulation is required;
- an asset's price in a market reflects everything that is known in the market; and
- this time things will be different.

Each of these views was proved to be wrong. US house prices went down, precipitating massive losses for many financial institutions; Northern Rock found it could no longer borrow in the short-term money market and collapsed; financial markets, rather than correcting themselves, demonstrated a feedback mechanism where a drop in market prices led to further falls in price rather than self-correcting; and markets which had been thought to be uncorrelated moved in the same direction. Efficient market theory, which essentially says an asset's price in a market reflects everything that is known in the market, was also found to be flawed as emotion and fear took over pricing in markets.

The curious thing is that these worldviews came to exist. It was well known that house prices can go down, that different markets can rise and fall at the same time, that markets do not always correct themselves, which is why regulation was put in place and that mania can grip markets leading to booms and busts. One reason people believed these things is that they believed that 'this time was different'. As shown time and again, history repeats itself. As the Italian philosopher George Santayana said, 'those who cannot remember the past are condemned to repeat it'.

The lesson, once again for organisations, and particularly their boards, is to consider what assumptions the continuing success of the organisation depends on and then question of whether those assumptions could be wrong.

Stop and think 1.1

Long-term Capital Management (LTCM) was a US hedge fund founded in 1993 which used the Economics Nobel Prize winning formula for pricing derivatives devised by two of its directors, Myron Scholes and Robert Merton. The pricing strategy, which used a Gaussian model, enabled the fund to generate returns of 21%, 43% and 41% in its first three years. The next year the fund lost $4.6 billion in four months, which was more money than it could afford to lose. LTCM collapsed and because of fears that the collapse would trigger a chain reaction of further failures on Wall Street the US Federal Reserve Bank organised a $3.6 billion bailout by its creditors.

The ostensible reasons for LTCM's failure were the Asian financial crisis in 1997 and the Russian default on its loans in 1998. These reasons however are almost irrelevant as the underlying reason was a misplaced faith in models and an erroneous understanding of how markets worked. The problem with Gaussian based models is that they did not properly predict what might happen at the tail end of the distribution.

Why do you think that in the early 2000s banks repeated the mistakes of LTCM in the 1990s?

3.3   Incentivising the wrong thing

Another lesson from the crisis was that banks incentivised their staff to do things which were not in the bank's interest.

Making it work 1.1

UBS (formerly Union Bank of Switzerland) suffered net losses of $18.7 billion on its exposure to US residential mortgages in 2007. Its report[1] to shareholders explaining the losses explained that two thirds of UBS'

---

1   UBS (2008) Shareholder Report on UBS's Write-Downs, http://maths-fi.com/ubs-shareholder-report.pdf UBS (2008) Shareholder Report on UBS's Write-Downs, http://maths-fi.com/ubs-shareholder-report.pdf

losses were attributable to the CDO (collateralised debt obligation) desk within the bank's fixed income business. The CDO desk essentially bought US subprime residential mortgaged backed securities (MBS) and repackaged them into new securities called CDOs which it sold but retained parts of the original securities because they yielded a higher rate of return than the internal rate at which they could borrow within the bank.

The fixed income desk earned fees from the sale of CDOs to third party investors and a portion of interest which was the difference between the income from holding mortgage-backed assets and the internal rate at which they could borrow within the bank. The difference is called the carry rate. Individual traders earned bonuses based on the profits they generated. The way to earn a large bonus was to buy a very large amount of MBS. Holding part of the securities to earn the carry rate of interest proved an expensive mistake as the price of those securities plunged during the crisis.

Two related mistakes the bank made were:

1.   allowing traders access to bank funds and not charging them according to the risk they were taking; and

2.   incentivising traders to do deals without taking account of the potential risk of those deals.

Organisations and their boards should ensure that incentive arrangements encourage people to do things which are in the organisation's long-term interest rather than the other way around.

3.4   Insufficient regard for the risk and compliance functions

Anecdotal evidence suggests that many bank staff working in the risk management and compliance areas were aware of the risks the organisations were running. Unfortunately they lacked sufficient status for their voices to be heard and given proper consideration. Why should a busy executive whose department is making huge profits for itself and its staff listen to relatively lowly paid staff who are widely regarded as naysayers and doom mongers? Chapter 12 discusses the case of head of group regulatory risk at HBOS being fired after he raised concerns.

3.5   The bigger picture and duty to society and stakeholders

The financial crisis revealed a financial system where banks made super profits and individuals they employed could earn enormous amounts of money with seemingly no personal risk. The risk was borne by taxpayers at whose expense governments refinanced banks, other businesses and society as many businesses failed and economies went into recession. Although banks enjoy a guarantee in the form of state protection for depositors and have a licence from society to operate, they seemed oblivious of the effect their actions might have. It also seemed that banks did not appreciate their duty to ensure the stability of the financial system. There seems widespread concern that the underlying problems which caused the crisis have not been fixed and could happen again.

As already outlined in earlier chapters, the Companies (Miscellaneous Reporting) Regulations 2018 requires boards to set out how they discharge their CA 2006 s.172 duties, which include having regard for stakeholders' interests. Such disclosure should force boards to be more sensitive to the interests of the various groups of stakeholder. ICSA published guidance in 2017, 'The stakeholder voice in board decision making'[2] to help boards consider how they ensure they understand and weigh up the interests of their key stakeholders when taking strategic decisions.

4. Boards as a source of risk

We have seen that boards can be a source of risk if they make bad decisions or fail to make decisions or take action which they should have taken. In summary, the risks are:

◆   risk blindness;
◆   not asking questions;
◆   turning a problem into a crisis;
◆   failing to hold executives to account;
◆   flawed business model;
◆   flawed strategy;
◆   flawed monitoring; and
◆   poor tone at the top.

4.1   Risk blindness

Being blind to the risks was a feature of the boards of failed banks such as HBOS. They failed to appreciate the risks that arose as a consequence of their bank's strategies and they failed to appreciate the interconnection between the inherent business risks and remuneration incentives. They were not aware how remuneration structures and bonuses encouraged short-termism, which neither supported prudent risk management nor worked in the interests of shareholders. The FCA and PRA report into the failure of HBOS lists 10 competencies, headed 'HBOS DNA', that it used to appraise executives. One of these was optimism, which said:

'Optimism – believes the unbelievable and conveys to all around a real sense of heroic optimism.'

With hindsight this was not so much a competency as foolhardy or reckless.

---

2   ICSA (2017) The Stakeholder Voice in Board Decision Making, www.icsa.org.uk/assets/files/free-guidance-notes/the-stakeholder-voice-in-Board-Decision-Making-09-2017.pdf

4.2 Not asking questions

A common cry when governance scandals unfold is 'where were the non-executive directors? How could they have let it happen?' One of the main duties of NEDs is to challenge constructively issues to do with strategy, assumptions about what drives the business model and what is ethically and socially acceptable. Failure to challenge means that flawed strategies are more likely to be approved by the board, weaknesses in the business model go unnoticed and the organisation does things which society finds unacceptable. All directors, executive and non-executive alike, have a common duty to challenge where they think appropriate but it could take a brave executive director to challenge proposals from the chief executive.

4.3 Failure to hold executives to account

The BHS example discussed in Chapter 2 is one of many instances of where boards failed to reign in executives and hold them to account.

4.4 Turning a problem into a crisis

A board can turn a management problem into a crisis if it reacts badly to news.

Making it work 11.3

Charity trustees should report serious incidents to the Charity Commission as soon as they suspect them. An employee of youth charity, LiftOff, was caught stealing petty cash from the charity and the charity director reported the matter to the trustees. The trustees decided to discipline the employee but chose not to inform either the police or the Charity Commission fearing it would expose the charity to scrutiny and reveal inadequate financial controls.

Unfortunately for the trustees and the charity a staff member told a journalist about the theft. A grant maker withdrew support and the Charity Commission investigated LiftOff because of serious concerns about financial management. The negative publicity was far worse than would have been the case had the trustees properly reported the incident when they first knew about it.

4.5 Flawed business model and/or strategy

The business model and its resilience are the responsibility of the board and senior management. Flaws or latent defects in the model could prove costly to an organisation and sometimes fatal. The flaw in Northern Rock's business model was that the bank depended on the money markets for much of its finance. When this market dried up the bank ran out of money very quickly.

Marconi's new strategy after selling its former activities was to enter the market for telecoms equipment, which had been particularly buoyant in 1999 as a result of the internet boom. Marconi paid inflated prices for its new businesses.

The flaw was that Marconi was buying into a bubble. Its directors had bet the company on telecoms and telecoms had disappointed.

The directors of new businesses may find they have no choice but to pursue high-risk strategies. Established companies may also find themselves in the same position but should, if they can, avoid placing themselves into a situation where they have to bet the company.

Making it work 1.1

Boeing bet its future on successfully recouping the investment needed to develop the Boeing 747 Jumbo jet. It was introduced in 1970 and proved extremely profitable for Boeing. At around the same time Rolls Royce found it had also bet its future on the development of a revolutionary new engine, the RB211, for the new Lockheed Tri-Star. Development costs proved more than expected and Rolls Royce became insolvent which also threatened the solvency of Lockheed. The Conservative government at the time nationalised Rolls Royce and allowed the engine to be completed.

4.6   Flawed monitoring

The board is the final internal monitor of an organisation's conduct. As already discussed it is impossible for boards of large and complex organisations to know everything that is going on but they must ensure, as far as possible, they know what is important.

Stop and think 11.4

As noted in Chapter 8, BP used the policy governance system. One of the four sets of policies is the set of limitations policies which limit the freedom of action for the chief executive. The board should receive reports on how the chief executive has complied with these limitations policies. These reports could come from executive management and from functions such as compliance, risk management and internal audit. In 2005, a process accident at the BP Texas City refinery resulted in 15 deaths and more than 170 injuries.

The independent Baker Report[3] of the BP U.S. Refineries Independent Safety Review Panel on the investigation reported in 2007 that the BP:

'board exercises "judgement in carrying out its work in policy-making, in monitoring executive action and in its active consideration of group strategy." The Board does not manage BP's affairs. The Board delegates this management function to the Group Chief Executive. The delegation

---

3   Baker Report (2007) The Report of the BP U.S. Refineries Independent Safety Review Panel, www.csb.gov/assets/1/19/Baker_panel_report1.pdf

is made subject to limitations set forth in the Board's executive limitations policy, which defines the boundaries of executive action. Within those boundaries, the Board monitors and gains assurance that the boundaries of delegated management authority are observed. The EEAC (Ethics and Environmental Assurance Committee) primarily serves this monitoring function for process safety. Two executive limitations relate to safety:

"The CEO will not cause or permit anything to be done without taking into account the effect on long-term shareholder value of the health, safety and environmental consequences of the actions . . . ."

"The CEO will not cause or permit employees or other parties doing work for the Group to be subject to undignified, inequitable, unfair, or unsafe treatment or conditions."

The BP board would have monitored whether or not the chief executive fulfilled these limitations policies. The Review Panel noted that 'the Board has been monitoring process safety performance of BP's US operations, as BP executive and corporate management have presented that performance to the Board. Management has made reports to the Board and proposed various actions to address perceived shortcomings in the implementation of BP's HSSE (Health, Safety, Security and Environment) management system.'

What more, if anything, could a board have done do to ensure such an incident could not happen?

4.7   Poor tone at the top

There have been numerous instances of poor tone at the top in companies. These include the FSA's letter in 2012[4] to the chairman of Barclays describing what it saw as behaviour at: 'the aggressive end of interpretation of the relevant rules and regulations' and about the bank's 'tendency to seek advantage from complex structures or favourable regulatory interpretations'.

Another example is the former Daily Mirror boss Robert Maxwell, who the DTI said in 1970 was 'not a person who can be relied upon to exercise proper stewardship of a publicly quoted company'.[5]

Surveys suggest that having a good tone at the top is the most important influence on good ethics in an organisation. Poor tone at the top is a big influence on bad behaviour.

---

4   House of Commons Treasury Committee (2013) Fixing LIBOR: some preliminary findings Second Report of Session 2012–13, https://publications.parliament.uk/pa/cm201213/cmselect/cmtreasy/481/481.pdf [CH 1 and Ch 11].

5   National Archives (2006) Mirror Group Newspapers plc Investigations under Sections 432(2) and 442 of the Companies Act 1985 Report by The Honourable Sir Roger John Laugharne Thomas and Raymond Thomas Turner FCA, 14 February 2006, http://webarchive.nationalarchives.gov.uk/+/http://www.dti.gov.uk/cld/mirrorgroup/summary.htm

Chapter summary

◆ It is a good idea to categorise risk but there are many ways of doing so.

◆ The COSO Enterprise Risk Management Integrated Framework uses four high level categories: strategic, operations, reporting and compliance.

◆ Risks can be thought of as causes and effects.

◆ For banks and insurance companies, a key part of their business models is taking and successfully exploiting risk. For most other types of organisation risk is a necessary consequence of doing business which needs to be managed.

◆ Banks invested considerable resource in risk management which, before the financial crisis, was seen as a source of competitive advantage.

◆ With the benefit of hindsight it turned out that their risk management practices were themselves a source of risk.

◆ Banks used complex mathematical models to predict risk but they proved problematic when market conditions changed.

◆ Such models wrongly assumed that events are essentially random and could be modelled using a normal (or Gaussian) distribution curve.

◆ Bank's remuneration practices incentivised individuals to take risks not in the bank's interest.

◆ Boards are responsible for effective risk management but can be a source of risk, they can come from:

    – risk blindness;

    – not asking questions;

    – flawed business model;

    – flawed strategy;

    – flawed monitoring;

    – poor tone at the top;

    – turning a problem into a crisis; and

    – failing to hold executives to account.

Chapter twelve
Practical issues in the management of risk

CONTENTS

1. Introduction
2. Managing risk
3. Dealing with malpractice
4. Assurance on risk management

1. Introduction

This final chapter builds on the previous two chapters by looking in more detail at some of the practical issues for managing risk. This includes considering conventional approaches to risk management and the shortcomings of these approaches and how to overcome them. It also looks at arrangements which can be put in place for preventing and detecting malpractice by staff. Finally, boards need to be able to assure themselves that all significant risks have been identified and assessed and that the organisations are only exposed to risks which are within their risk tolerance. The final section therefore considers how boards can obtain that assurance.

2. Managing risk

2.1 Conventional approaches to managing risk

As explained in Chapter 10, risk management involves three essential elements:

- risk identification;
- risk assessment and evaluation; and
- a decision to take, treat, avoid or transfer a risk (or a combination of these actions).

Risk identification and assessment in many organisations is done by managers and their staff, risk managers and internal audit. It is preferable for managers and their staff to do this as they understand the operations best and should know better than anyone how to manage the risks they identify. The role of risk managers should be to facilitate the formal process and provide professional guidance. Internal auditors should provide objective assurance on the whole process and may identify for themselves the most significant risks to which the organisation is exposed. Organisations are keen to embed risk management and an aim should be for managers and staff to consider the risk of something each time they make a decision. This seldom happens in practice. The varied reasons include:

◆ they think risk management is someone else's job, such as risk managers and internal audit;

◆ they have not been asked to and have received no training in how to do it; and

◆ they are too busy doing their jobs to think about risk.

Instead they are more likely to think about risk when they are specifically asked to as part of a risk management initiative. This initiative might take the form of a risk workshop or it might be a paper, computer or spreadsheet exercise they do individually. In any case people will typically be asked to think about their work objectives then consider and document the risks which could affect their achievement. Thinking about objectives gives important context to considering risk but people may be asked by risk managers simply to think about risks without reference to their objectives.

Stop and think 12.1

In many organisations the approach to dealing with risk is similar to how a cricketer would deal with the balls being bowled. The cricketer would assess the approaching ball and decide what to do. The cricketer may play it (which is like taking a risk), block it (which is like managing or transferring the risk), or leave the ball (which is like avoiding the risk). Whether a cricketer plays the ball would depend on the difficulty of the ball, the possibility of getting runs from hitting it and what else is going on in the match.

Can you see any flaws in dealing with risk in this way?

Having identified risks the next step is usually to consider their impact if they happen and their likelihood of happening (see Figures 10.1 and 10.2) and express this numerically. The risks and their expected impact and likelihood will be entered into a risk register which may be a spreadsheet, a database or part of dedicated risk management software. Other information often included would be:

◆ a reference number for each risk;

◆ the objective to which the risk relates;

◆ the date the risk was identified;

◆ an overall grading of the risk based on a combination of impact and likelihood;

◆ the controls in operation which may mitigate the risk;

◆ the action(s) to be taken to manage the risk;

◆ risk management action taken with dates;

◆ the residual risk after risk mitigation and management;

◆ the name of the person responsible for the risk and its management; and

◆ any further comments.

The top risks in terms of impact and likelihood in the risk register will be consolidated into a report for the next highest management layer and further consolidated for layers above that. The board or audit committee (if it is within its terms of reference) will receive information about what those below them decide are the most serious risks. They will be told what action is being taken to manage those risks and monitor new risks and any changes in the risk assessment.

This approach is widespread but has a number of shortcomings:

◆ The quantitative evaluation of impact and likelihood implies more accuracy than may be sensible.

◆ Many risks, like earthquakes, cannot usefully be predicted with a single distinct impact and likelihood but could be predicted with a range of impacts and likelihoods.

◆ Risks are considered and evaluated one by one, like in cricket, whereas in practice a number of risks may hit in succession. Several risks occurring at once are more dangerous. When companies fail there is rarely a single cause but a combination of circumstances.

◆ Risks are usually thought of as particular events, rather than as potential causes, which could give rise to a variety of unwanted effects. As in medicine, it makes sense to treat the causes not just the symptoms. As noted in Chapter 11 there is likely to be a chain of causes and effects. The root causes of risk should be identified and addressed.

◆ Risks are identified, assessed and dealt with in a serial or linear fashion but almost every risk arises from a combination of factors and cannot easily be predicted. Helpful analogies for risk in business could be:

  – risks are like London buses which arrive several in a bunch rather than evenly spaced out over time;

  – risks are like waves washing up on a beach; they are not all of equal amplitude and every few waves one is much bigger than the others.

◆ Risks are often considered in isolation and not related to organisational objectives or the benefits which can accrue from taking the risk. So risks should be balanced against the potential rewards.

◆ A risk register can give a spurious accuracy, and the impression that all risks are known and are under control.

◆ A one-off process in which risks are identified and assessed may soon be forgotten and have no effect in how people do their jobs.

◆ Once completed, the risk register is often largely ignored.

◆ People may be unaware of or fail to identify the biggest risks.

An added danger is that the process can seem like a compliance exercise with no practical benefit and if people participate with that belief it is likely to come true. Some risk experts think risk registers are themselves a source of risk and best not used.

Making it work 12.1

An earthquake could have a devastating impact or a milder one. The likelihood of a serious earthquake in any particular place cannot be estimated reliably and really can only be guessed at. It is known however that devastating earthquakes occur less often than milder ones. Long-term records of earthquakes in a region are known however so predictions can be made for a larger area and the predictions would involve a range of impacts and a range of likelihoods.

Organisations should weigh risk against reward. A risk may be worth taking if the expectation of a reward is greater than the expectation of a loss, in other words where the expected value (E (Gain)) of the gain multiplied by the probability (P (Gain)) of that gain is greater than the expected impact of a loss (E (Loss)) multiplied by the probability of that loss (P (Loss)). The simple formula is:

$$E \text{ (Gain)} \times P \text{ (Gain)} > E \text{ (Loss)} \times P \text{ (Loss)}$$

The approach could be used for considering single issues such as a project. In practice, when taking a decision, there may be more than one gain and more than one loss, so whether or not the sum of the expected values of gains exceed the sum of expected values of losses should be considered:

$$\sum(E \text{ (Gain)} \times P \text{ (Gain)}) > \sum(E \text{ (Loss)} \times P \text{ (Loss)})$$

The weighing up of reward against risk should be with reference to the rewards and risks to the organisation. Such judgement in practice is likely to be clouded by personal interest. People in a position to take risks where the organisation or a third party bears most of the risk but they benefit personally have a motive not to act in the organisation's interest. It is important therefore to ensure that such temptations do not occur.

It should also be understood that not all risks can be identified, while some can be predicted with reasonable accuracy, such as:

◆ a bus company can reliably estimate how many road traffic accidents its buses are likely to be involved in during a year based on its past experience; and

◆ a hospital can estimate how many patients will acquire an infection and how many of those will die, again based on past experience.

Other identified risks such as in the examples below are harder to evaluate and their impact and likelihood only guessed at.

Stop and think 12.2

The risk to an aircraft or airline company of a volcanic eruption is hard to quantify as not enough is known. In 2010, the Eyjafjallajökull volcano in Iceland erupted, sending a plume of fine-grained dust into the air to altitudes in which commercial aircraft fly. Concerns about the effect of the dust on jet engines led to most European air travel being grounded. The disruption caused losses estimated to be over $2 billion for airlines and collateral damage to related activities such as tourism. A risk such as this could easily have been dismissed either because it was considered too unlikely to take seriously, or because the scale of the effect may have been underestimated.

A few aircraft flew through the cloud and experienced no problems, suggesting the risk had been overestimated. Aviation authorities felt justified in their action as passenger safety is paramount. The airline industry enjoys an excellent safety record because it takes risk so seriously.

Before the turn of the century in the late 1990s computer experts and businesses feared that clocks in computers which recorded the year 1999 as 99 would record 2000 as 00 so might misinterpret 2000 as 1900. It was known as the Y2K problem or the Millennium Bug. It was thought that computers and any electrical device with an electronic clock might malfunction or cease to function. Governments encouraged businesses to protect themselves, leading to huge demand for anyone with software expertise. Estimates of the cost suggest several hundred billion US dollars was spent worldwide in preparation. In spite of the work done, there was widespread concern at the end of 1999 that the work would be ineffective and chaos would ensue on 1 January 2000. When January came nothing much seemed to happen and there was widespread criticism that there had been a collective delusion and the money spent was unnecessary. Some said that the pre-emptive work was justified as it prevented large-scale problems, while others pointed out few problems occurred in organisations where no pre-emptive work had been done.

These examples highlight the difficulty in assessing risk. Can you think of other examples?

Test yourself 12.1

Before taking or accepting a risk, what should you consider?

Workshops for considering risk can have the advantages that risk identification and assessment of risk is a team exercise and those present can come to a shared consensus about which risks are most important. Sadly a workshop based on the approach above is unlikely to have much value, no matter how good its facilitator or people involved. A good workshop needs a different approach (see the Stop and think below) and a good facilitator, preferably independent (not part of the team) but sufficiently well prepared to understand the organisation and what the workshop team is doing.

Stop and think 12.3

A workshop approach, which could be for a work team or participants drawn from several teams to consider a common objective or process, which avoids the shortcomings described above will include or involve most of:

◆ **Agreement that what is discussed in the workshop is confidential and those involved will have the opportunity to see any report of it before it goes to more senior management.**

◆ **Facilitation techniques which ensure that everyone has the chance to contribute including doing so in a way which is effectively anonymous, e.g. by using electronic polling systems and/or post-it notes. This is necessary to encourage people to express matters which they may otherwise feel inhibited from doing. It makes it easier for the real risks and problems to emerge.**

◆ **Consideration of how risks have causes and effects and are interrelated.**

◆ **Consideration of risk impact and likelihood in terms of a range of possibilities (see also Chapter 10, Figure 10.2).**

◆ **Consideration of what might happen if multiple risks happen at once.**

◆ **Acceptance that not all risks can be known so the team or organisation should aim to be resilient to unknown and unidentified catastrophic risks.**

◆ **Brainstorming techniques to encourage new thinking and reduce risk blindness.**

◆ **Allows any relevant cultural or people issues to surface, including groupthink and cognitive biases.**

◆ **Is related to organisational objectives and strategy and/or team or process objectives.**

◆ **Looks at risk in relation to the rewards which can accrue from taking the risk.**

- ◆ Includes an assessment using a control framework such as COSO, CoCo or a quality framework.

- ◆ Relates risks and issues identified to risk appetite and tolerance.

- ◆ Has an effective follow-up process which includes escalation to higher management of issues which the people in the workshop do not have authority to address on their own.

Can you improve on the list above? What about considering whether the reward and incentive systems create risks?

The above approach is likely to involve some simple scenario planning where people consider the ranges of impacts and likelihoods and how risks can combine to have a dramatically higher impact. Separate workshops intended specifically to consider and create scenarios can also be a very valuable risk management tool. There is no need for a scenario to anticipate correctly what will actually happen in practice. The value is in the interactive approach where people see how different futures could unfold and how they should respond. This helps people prepare for unexpected events when they happen. It can also help people be more aware that there are many uncertainties and things that cannot be known and be more comfortable with the fact.

Making it work 12.2

One specific scenario for a board or executive team to consider before embarking on a new project or strategy would be to imagine a situation at some point in the future, say in two years' time, where the project or strategy had turned out to be a complete disaster. The group then consider among themselves how it (could have) happened. This process would be a powerful antidote to groupthink and optimism and confirmation biases. People also enjoy doing it.

Another way of using scenarios would be to select two or more risks such as by spinning a top. The workshop would then construct a scenario where these risks, e.g. a criminal action, a natural event and a reputational impact, occur together.

There is another set of risks which cannot practicably be identified beforehand which could be termed unknown and unknowable. For obvious reasons it is difficult to give an example. An external event such as a meteor strike could perhaps come into this category as could an internal event such as the one described below, although a claim it was unknowable is open to question after the event. Scenario planning workshops can help to illuminate risks of which otherwise people would have been unaware.

Stop and think 12.4

Ryanair's 195-page 2017 Annual Report includes 13 pages of disclosure on risk factors. The report, with over 10,000 words, lists and discusses numerous risks from internal and external sources. Although labour relations is identified as a risk there is no disclosure of the risk that flights could be cancelled as a result of staff being unavailable. On the contrary the company creates the impression everything is under control.

'Ryanair has concluded 5-year pay and conditions deals with all 86 bases for pilots and cabin crew. Ryanair's senior management meets regularly with the different ERCs to consult and discuss all aspects of the business and those issues that specifically relate to each relevant employee group and to negotiate with these collective bargaining units. Ryanair's pilots and cabin crew operate under industry leading rosters and return home to their base at the end of every working day which is the most family friendly crew roster in aviation and offers personnel a good work/life balance.'

and:

'implemented industry leading fixed 5/4 rosters which consists of 5 days on, followed by 4 days off for pilots and 5/3 for Cabin Crew, 5 days on followed by 3 days off which provides an excellent work life balance.'

In autumn 2017, however, Ryanair cancelled thousands of flights, affecting hundreds of thousands of customers, as a result of what was described as a mess-up in how the company schedules time off for pilots. A further blow to Ryanair came when the Civil Aviation Authority launched enforcement action against the company for persistently misleading passengers about their rights.

The absence of anything about holiday rosters in the statement of risk does not mean that the risk had not been identified. However, it seems likely it had not been. It is a risk for which the organisation only has itself to blame. Can you think of any risks which could cause a major threat to your organisation which are not known about by management of the board?

2.2 The Three Lines of Defence model

The Three Lines of Defence is a concept used by auditors and risk managers to understand and discuss with management and boards how risks are managed and to clarify and help coordinate responsibilities. The first line of defence is operational management, the second line are the risk management (and if they exist compliance, health and safety and quality) functions and the third line of defence are the independent assurance functions such as internal audit. There is some variation in the interpretation of the model with some saying that the first line of defence involves all people involved in operations not just management, that the second line of defence would include a board risk committee and that the third line of defence includes, in addition to internal audit, the board, audit committee and external audit and, in a small organisation, its owners and, in a highly regulated organisation, the regulators.

Some organisations interpret the model based on the departments people work in rather than the functions they perform, while other organisations may use the model according to the nature of the activities rather than functions performed. So, for example, first line activities could include training, checking and authorisation, the second line activities such as budgetary control and quality inspection with the third line providing assurance on the activities in the first and second lines. The first line of defence could be regarded as being about the ownership and taking of considered risk, the second about control and compliance and the third about giving assurance.

The model can help to ensure that more people in an organisation take more responsibility for risk management. In particular, it can help ensure operational management exercise more responsibility for being aware of risks that they run or are exposed to and managing them than might otherwise be the case. The model is not without its detractors however. One is criticism is that the philosophy behind the model presumes that risk is something to be feared and that the second line is about stopping the first line taking risk and the third line is about getting assurance that this has been done. This may be appropriate in some organisations but in others it would be better to think of risk in terms of things to seek and exploit as well as things to fear.

2.3 Internal control

Internal control was introduced in Chapter 10. At its simplest, it is the means by which an organisation achieves its objectives. This section looks at some of the most important and common types of control, many of which have already been discussed.

The most important internal control is the board. The board controls an organisation through its policies and decisions. High-level policies include the schedule of matters specifically reserved to the board and the scheme of delegation, approving strategy, monitoring performance, ensuring the organisation has the necessary resources and setting its values and standards. A whistleblowing policy is also an internal control.

The next most important internal control is the executive team, who will have more detailed policies and arrangements for managing the organisation, covering, for example, staff issues and financial controls. The company secretary also provides internal control.

There are many different ways of thinking about and categorising controls. Generally they will be categorised according to the risks they try to manage and are often broadly categorised as operational, compliance, strategic and financial. Controls could be detective, detecting a risk or control failure that has happened or preventative, preventing a risk from happening. Such classification of control is not meant to be mutually exclusive; often controls, such as training, can be used to mitigate several types of risk.

Operational controls are controls over operations to prevent or manage operational risks. Operational risks include any risk which might affect the effectiveness of an organisation's operations and could be both external or internal to the organisation in origin.

Types of operational controls include:

◆ over people: controls to prevent fraud, bribery and corruption, breaches of employment law, unauthorised activity, loss or lack of key personnel, mistake (training), inadequate supervision;

◆ over processes: controls to prevent payment errors, documentation which is not fit for purpose, errors in processes, data loss or contamination, project management failures and controls over internal/external reporting;

◆ over systems: controls to prevent failures during the development and systems implementation process, as well as failures of the system itself; controls to ensure adequate resources; and

◆ over external sources of risk: controls to prevent external crime, outsourcing problems, natural and other disasters, regulatory risk, political risk, utilities failures; and over competition.

Operational controls can include: operating policies and procedures, training, separation of duties, skills tests, supervision, authorisation, signage, log books and controls built into IT systems and technology and employment checks.

Compliance controls are controls to detect or prevent non-compliance with the myriad of compliance requirements which some organisations have. These include compliance with various pieces of legislation, regulation, e.g. banking regulations, voluntary internal/external requirements such as to conform with a quality or other international standard or British standard, and internal policies. Compliance controls include policies and procedures including a code of conduct, compliance staff, training, authorisation, staff communication and enforcement.

Strategic risk is the risk that the organisation's strategy will not work and damages the organisation. This may be because of a strategy which was faulty at the outset or one which becomes faulty as a result of internal or external events, such as new technology destroying the need for a product. As strategy is a board issue the main control over strategic risk is an effective board supported by good executive capability.

Financial controls are high-level controls such as:

◆ periodic management accounts;

◆ a budgetary control system where budgets are set for expected income and expenditure and comparison made with actual financial performance as shown in the management accounts; and

◆ reviewing journal adjustments to accounting entries including any write downs of assets.

Lower level financial controls are likely to include:

◆ financial approval limits for expenditure and ordering;

◆ controls over ordering and payment for goods and services;

◆ separating duties so that two or more people are involved in an ordering or payment process in order to reduce the scope for theft and fraud; and

◆ additional checks such as requiring two signatures to authorise payments.

Matters such as training, recruitment and induction procedures and other formal policies and procedures are also forms of internal control as is having a responsible and ethical culture.

3. Dealing with malpractice

This section considers malpractice, meaning behaviour which is illegal, dishonest or immoral, by organisations and people working in them. It looks at what can be learned about the extent of malpractice and policies and practices which organisations can have in place to prevent it.

3.1 The prevalence of misconduct in the workplace

KPMG periodically publish an Integrity Survey of workers in the United States in different sectors. The most recent, in 2013[1], included responses from over 3,500 employees. Among other things, they tracked observations of misconduct in the employees' workplaces. Overall, 73% reported that they had observed misconduct in the past year and 56% reported observing serious misconduct that could cause 'a significant loss of public trust if discovered'. Looking at the business sectors involved, the highest prevalence of observed misconduct was 82% in 'consumer markets', followed by 79% in 'government and public sector'. The prevalence of serious misconduct in these sectors was 56% and 62% respectively. The highest prevalence of serious misconduct was 63% in 'electronics, software and services'. The percentage responses for 'banking and finance' was 71% for misconduct and 57% for serious misconduct.

KPMG found that the propensity to report misconduct to an ethics hotline had increased but, paradoxically, employees seemed more willing either to look the other way and do nothing or to report misconduct outside the organisation rather than internally.

In the UK, observation of misconduct would seem to be lower. The Institute of Business Ethics periodically commissions MORI to survey employees. The 2015 survey[2] of 674 UK workers showed 20% had been aware of conduct by colleagues or the employer that violated either the law or the organisation's ethical standards. This percentage has changed little since the question was first asked in 2005. Across continental Europe, 33% responded affirmatively to the

1   KPMG (2013) Integrity Survey 2013.

2   Johnson, D. (2016) Ethics at Work 2015 Survey of employees: Britain, Institute of Business Ethics, www.ibe.org.uk/userassets/publicationdownloads/ibe_survey_eaw15_main.pdf

same question in a similar survey of 3,000 workers.

Further information on the prevalence of misconduct comes from various surveys by accounting and law firms. A 2015 survey by IPOS for EY[3] covering Europe, Middle East, India and Africa revealed that more than half of the 3,800 respondents agreed that bribery and corruption was widespread in their countries. Within their own companies in the previous 12 months: 28% of senior management had heard of negotiating retrospective rebates, bonuses or discounts from suppliers; 23% had heard of revenues being recorded before they should to meet short-term targets; and 22% had heard of underreporting costs incurred to meet short-term financing budgets.

Making it work 12.3

Law firm Labaton Sucharow surveyed financial services professionals at the turn of 2014 and 2015[4]. There were 1,223 respondents: 925 in the US and 298 in the UK. 47% of respondents thought it likely that their competitors had engaged in 'unethical or illegal activity in order to gain an edge in the market'. This figure jumped to 51% of individuals earning $500,000 or more per year, whilst 34% of the same demographic said they had witnessed or had first-hand knowledge of wrongdoing in the workplace. 23% of respondents believed it likely that fellow employees had engaged in illegal or unethical activity in order to 'gain an edge'. 25% of all respondents said they would likely use non-public information to make a guaranteed $10 million if there was no chance of getting arrested for insider trading. The figure increased to 32% for UK respondents.

15% of all respondents (18% in UK) believed company leaders would ignore suspicions that a top performer was earning large profits from insider trading and look the other way. This rose to 21% for respondents earning $500,000 or more per year. 17% thought it unlikely that company leaders would report misconduct to law enforcement if company leaders learned a top performer had engaged in insider trading. The survey did not report whether the other respondents thought that leaders would take appropriate action.

The survey also revealed how difficult it could be to do the ethical right thing. 28% of respondents earning $500,000 or more per year (16% for all respondents) said their company's confidentiality policies and procedures barred the reporting of potential illegal or unethical activities directly to law enforcement or regulatory authorities. The problem seemed worse in the UK where 21% of all employees said this. 25% of all respondents earning $500,000 or more annually had signed or been asked to sign a confidentiality agreement that would prohibit reporting illegal or unethical activities to the authorities. 19% of all

3   EY (2015) Fraud and corruption – the easy option for growth?

4   Labaton Sucharow (2015) The Street, The Bull and The Crisis: A Survey of the US & UK Financial Services Industry.

respondents said it likely that their employer would retaliate if they were to report wrongdoing in the workplace. Again the UK situation seemed worse where 24% reported this.

Looking just at corruption, the costs worldwide would seem to be so high they are hard to comprehend. The OECD reports[5] 'corruption is one of the main obstacles to sustainable economic, political and social development, for developing, emerging and developed economies alike'. It says 'estimates show that the cost of corruption equals more than 5% of global GDP (US$ 2.6 trillion, World Economic Forum) with over US$1 trillion paid in bribes each year (World Bank)'. In addition to its financial costs, corruption has many victims. Corruption may in some situations be regarded as part of the cost of doing business but is never acceptable.

3.2 Policies, procedures and practices to prevent malpractice

The policies, procedures and practices which should be in place include:

Hiring procedures and pre-employment checks.
These may identify a previous criminal record but will not identify whether a person is going to be honest or ethical. Psychometric tests can give an indication of a person's ethical traits but should not be relied upon. Recruiters may want to avoid employing individuals with psychopathic tendencies but studies of samples of executives have suggested a higher proportion, between 3 and 20%, of senior executives fit the profile of a psychopath compared with 1% for the population as a whole. There are aspects of a psychopath's profile which are valued in business which include charisma, charm, confidence, coolness under pressure and the ability to create the impression of high performance. A psychopath would probably also know how to cheat any test aimed at identifying a propensity for immoral behaviour.

A code of ethics or code of conduct
The Institute of Business Ethics (IBE) found in 2003[6] that a sample of UK companies with a code of ethics had over 1997–2001 performed better in terms of three leading measures of financial performance (Price Earnings [P/E] ratio, Economic Value Added [EVA] and Market Value Added [MVA]) than a similar sized group which did not have a code.

As noted in Chapter 4 most organisations now have a code of ethics, code of conduct or document with a different name but having the same purpose such as 'The Way We Work Around Here', or 'The ABC plc Way'. It will set out the organisation's policy on ethics and will often also articulate its espoused values and standards such as fairness, honesty, integrity, openness, respect and trust.

The IBE says that the main purpose of a code is to give guidance for staff by translating the organisation's values, and its commitments to stakeholders, into

---

5   OECD (2014) The rationale for fighting corruption. Paris 2014, www.oecd.org/cleangovbiz/49693613.pdf

6   Institute of Business Ethics (2003) Does business ethics pay? www.ibe.org.uk/userfiles/doesbusethicpaysumm.pdf

how the organisation should operate. It will set out what behaviour is expected from people working in the organisation and provide guidance on how to respond to ethical dilemmas and challenges and issues that are important to the organisation.

ACCA research[7] of its members throughout the world on culture and ethics conducted in 2014 by the author found that ethical codes were not the most effective way of ensuring an ethical culture. Participants were asked 'how effective are the following in fostering ethical behaviour in your organisation?' and scored on a five-part scale where the top scores were 'effective' or 'very effective'.

How effective are the following in fostering ethical behaviour in your organisation?	Rank	Percentage 'effective' or 'very effective'
Creating an environment where people can comfortably discuss any concerns	1	74%
Informing people about what is ethical behaviour	2	70%
Actively encouraging teams to discuss ethical dilemmas in a safe environment	3	65%
Ensuring an effective and safe whistleblowing procedure	4	63%
Punishing unethical behaviour	5	58%
Rewarding ethical behaviour	6	55%
The organisation's Code of Ethics (or conduct)	7	52%

Table 12.1: Results of ACCA research

Out of the seven choices for ways of fostering an ethical culture, the nearly 2,000 people who responded ranked the code of ethics last. Perversely, perhaps, they ranked 'informing people about what is ethical behaviour' second – because a code of ethics would normally include what the employer considers ethical behaviour. The fact that 'creating an environment where people can comfortably discuss any concerns' and 'actively encouraging teams to discuss ethical dilemmas in a safe environment' were ranked first and third is perhaps surprising. It shows the importance of having an enabling corporate culture. It also suggests that organisations should make time for such discussion.

Test yourself 12.2

In the ACCA survey about culture and ethics it would seem that respondents did not equate 'informing people about what is ethical behaviour' with a code of ethics. Why might this be?

---

7   Moxey, P. and Schu, P. (2014) Culture and channelling corporate behaviour: summary of findings, ACCA, London.

3.3 Corruption

The World Bank and Transparency International (TI) define corruption as 'the abuse of entrusted power for private gain[8]. This is a broad definition which encompasses unethical behaviour which could be either illegal or legal. Corruption includes bribery, which according to the Ministry of Justice is 'giving someone a financial or other advantage to encourage that person to perform their functions or activities improperly or to reward that person for having already done so'. The Foreign Corrupt Practices Act 1977 in the US and the Bribery Act 2010[9] in the UK make it illegal for companies and their supervisors to influence foreign officials with any personal payments or rewards. Under the Bribery Act, not preventing bribery can also be an offence[10]. Organisations, particularly those dealing with or having operations in foreign countries should have procedures in place to prevent bribery and corruption and ensure they are complied with.

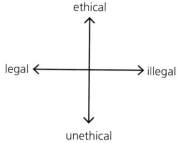

Figure 12.1: legal and ethical matrix.

Corrupt acts can be unethical but legal and both unethical and illegal (see Figure 12.1).

In a paper by the author[11], TI identifies that corporate incentive systems can inadvertently encourage unethical and sometimes illegal behaviour. It suggests 14 principles for good practice:

Ensuring strong culture and values

1.   Ensure the organisation's culture supports and encourages ethical, sustainable business practices.

---

8   The abuse of entrusted power for private gain. Corruption can be classified as grand, petty or political, depending on the amounts of money lost and the sector where it occurs. www.transparency.org/glossary/term/corruption
     And www1.worldbank.org/publicsector/anticorrupt/corruptn/cor02.htm

9   HM Government (2010) The Bribery Act, www.legislation.gov.uk/ukpga/2010/23/contents

10   For an introduction to the Bribery Act see Ministry of Justice (2010) The Bribery Act 2010 – Quick start guide, www.justice.gov.uk/downloads/legislation/bribery-act-2010-quick-start-guide.pdf

11   Moxey, P. (2016) Incentivising Ethics: Managing incentives to encourage good and deter bad behaviour, Transparency International, London, www.transparency.org.uk/publications/incentivising-ethics-managing-incentives-to-encourage-good-and-deter-bad-behaviour/

2. Establish a strong tone at the top and set clear values that resonate with staff.

3. Demonstrate commitment to ethical business conduct through actions that are consistent with the tone at the top.

Risk assessment

4. Identify and assess the risks created by existing incentive structures.

5. Take a cross-functional approach to risk identification and management, including HR, ethics and compliance and the risk function, and integrate the assessment of incentives into existing risk assessment processes.

Designing ethical incentives

6. Ensure the overall approach to incentives is aligned with and does not inadvertently undermine the company's values and culture.

7. Set targets which are achievable without resorting to illegal, unethical or negligent behaviour.

8. Set ethical targets or use ethical thresholds for rewards to distinguish outcomes from the means used to achieve them.

9. Avoid paying staff for performance based purely on output measures, and instead encourage the pursuit of intrinsic reward.

10. Ensure that staff are not promoted or rewarded if they have breached the company's principles, even if they have met or exceeded their targets.

Embedding ethical incentives

11. Use training and communication to reinforce the primacy of ethical behaviour over achieving targets.

12. Listen to staff and create opportunities for them to consider their work and actions from an ethical perspective.

Monitoring and evaluation

13. Ensure that internal functions (e.g. HR, ethics and compliance, risk, internal audit, finance and sales) are monitoring for signals that staff may be incentivised to contravene the company's code of ethics.

14. Record all breaches of the code of ethics and make adjustments to incentive structures as appropriate.

Practices to avoid include:

◆ management not walking the talk by not doing themselves what they tell others to do;

◆ shooting a messenger of bad news or otherwise discouraging staff from raising concerns on ethical issues;

◆ stifling innovation, creativity and common sense through too many rules and controls;

◆ paying bonuses for achievement of targets and ignoring how they were achieved;

◆ introducing measures and targets without considering if there are unintended consequences;

◆   not thinking about whether the company has the right culture;

◆   turning a blind eye to wrong doing; and

◆   telling people, rather than finding out, what their values are.

3.4 Whistleblowing or speak-up policy

Whistleblowing is where a person raises a concern about a wrongdoing, danger or other serious risk in his/her workplace. A concern might be about suspected illegality, unethical conduct or poor safety. More unusually it might be about corporate strategy, as was the case at HBOS where the head of group regulatory risk warned in the early 2000s that the bank was too strongly motivated by sales. The UK Code of Corporate Governance in Principle E provides that 'the workforce should be able to raise any matters of concern'. Provision 6 provides 'there should be a means for the workforce to raise concerns in confidence and – if they wish – anonymously. The board should routinely review this and the reports arising from its operation. It should ensure that arrangements are in place for the proportionate and independent investigation of such matters and for follow-up action'.

whistleblowing
Where a person who raises a concern about a wrongdoing in their workplace. Also called 'speak up'.

In the past it was more common for organisations discourage staff from raising concerns. Reasons for this included that it was 'not the way we do things here', the belief it is disloyal and the belief that it would encourage staff to tell tales on others or cause trouble. Whistleblowers are rarely popular. Colleagues willing to tolerate, or who were actually engaged in, inappropriate behaviour resent them and senior managers are unlikely to want to employ a known whistleblower they consider may be a trouble maker.

Being a whistleblower is therefore often a career-limiting choice. The HBOS whistleblower was fired in 2004. In another high-profile case an auditor in the European Commission was fired after drawing attention in 1998 to irregularities, fraud and mismanagement within the Commission. People who lose their jobs find it difficult to work again.

The Wells Fargo example discussed in Chapter 9 provides another instance where staff who raised concerns were forced to leave. They were not fired for speaking up but ways were found to get rid of them, such as if they failed to meet their performance objectives.

In the UK employees are legally protected by Employment Rights Act 1996 (as amended by the Public Interest Disclosure Act 1998) if they make a qualifying disclosure in the public interest, which means the concern must affect others, e.g. the general public. Qualifying disclosures include disclosure about:

◆   criminal offence;

◆   breach of a legal obligation;

◆   miscarriage of justice;

◆   danger to the health and safety of any individual;

◆   damage to the environment; and

◆   deliberate attempt to conceal any of the above.

Disclosures should be to the employer or to one of a number of prescribed bodies such as the FCA, FRC and HMRC. The former Department for Business, Innovation and Skills published a guide for employers and Code of Practice[12] in 2015.

The law, however, has been strongly criticised as inadequate by Blueprint for Free Speech[13] in a detailed analysis published in 2016.

In May 2018 it was reported[14] that Jes Staley, Barclays' chief executive, had been fined a total of £642,430, representing just 14% of his total compensation, by the UK's financial regulators for trying to uncover the identity of an anonymous whistleblower. Barclays will avoid any sanction by the Financial Conduct Authority and the Bank of England's Prudential Regulation Authority, but will have to tighten its whistleblowing systems and annually report back to the watchdog. Cases of whistleblowing rarely become public. Often an employee who raises concerns and then leaves the organisation will be bound by a confidentiality clause prohibiting them from saying anything about what happened. The HBOS whistleblowing only became known after the whistleblower used Parliamentary privilege in giving evidence to an inquiry into the bank's failure. He was reported later to have regretted blowing the whistle after the stress it created.

Although some organisations still do not welcome whistleblowing, most now accept it is important to have arrangements in place for staff to report concerns, even if that is because it has become a requirement of a governance code or government policy in the public sector. Some recognise that encouraging whistleblowing is actually a good management internal control as it provides a means for senior management of the board to learn about problems that need to be addressed. They also recognise it is better for someone to raise their concern within the organisation than for them to make it public.

The term 'whistleblowing' has a stigma attached to it so many organisations use the term 'speak up' or 'speaking up' instead. Employers emphasise their commitment that no one who raises reasonably held concerns will face any form of retaliation such as threat, intimidation, exclusion or humiliation.

Many staff nevertheless remain reluctant to raise concerns. Some organisations recognise that staff should have a variety of means for raising concerns and that blowing the whistle is a last resort. Staff are therefore encouraged to talk to colleagues or their line manager, another manager, or someone from a function such as HR, compliance or internal audit, before using a formal whistleblowing

---

12   Department for Business, Innovation and Skills published a guide for employers and Code of Practice in 2015: www.gov.uk/government/uploads/system/uploads/attachment_data/file/415175/bis-15-200-whistleblowing-guidance-for-employers-and-code-of-practice.pdf

13   Blueprint for Free Speech (2016) Protecting whistleblowers in the UK: a new blueprint Blueprint for Free Speech and the Thomson Reuters Foundation, https://blueprintforfreespeech.net/wp-content/uploads/2016/05/Report-Protecting-Whistleblowers-In-The-UK.pdf

14   Barclays chief Staley fined £640,000 over whistleblowing scandal. Financial Times 11 May 2018 www.ft.com/content/8a172758-550e-11e8-b3ee-41e0209208ec

or speak-up line. Some organisations nominate their internal auditor as the person to whom to direct concerns through the whistleblowing or speak-up process. Although more objective and independent than management, internal auditors have management responsibility to executive management even if they report professionally to an audit committee. Many organisations therefore use one of a number of independent agencies to whom concerns can be expressed in complete confidence.

Chapters 2 and 10 discuss the requirement for audit committees to review arrangements for whistleblowing.

Test yourself 12.3

What is another name for whistleblowing?

4. Assurance on risk management

Chapter 10 sets out the board's role in relation to risk management. In summary, boards should:

◆   monitor and review risk management arrangements throughout the year to ensure they are functioning effectively, taking corrective action where necessary;

◆   annually review the effectiveness of risk management and internal control systems considering all significant aspects for the year and up to the date of approval of the annual report;

◆   ensure risk taken is within the risk tolerance it is prepared to take in achieving strategic objectives; and

◆   determine whether the going concern basis of accounting can be used and whether disclosures of material uncertainties in the financial statements are required.

To do so the board needs to obtain assurance, which is sufficient evidence, to reach a view on these matters. The board is likely to receive most of this information from management, the internal auditor and the external auditor. It may also obtain information from other functions within the organisation such as risk management, compliance, HR, quality and legal and externally from consultants and other professional advisors.

Much of the work involved will fall to the audit committee. Responsibility remains with the board so this section talks about boards rather than audit committees and boards for brevity.

Key challenges for a board are knowing what evidence is available and what is missing, whether evidence is understandable, relevant, reliable, objective and unbiased, and when it has enough information to reach its conclusions. Boards receive a massive amount of information and data. What they are given is somewhat like pieces of a jigsaw puzzle which they have to piece together.

Unfortunately the board does not have the picture of the complete jigsaw. Nor does it know how many pieces there should be or whether all the pieces they have are part of the same puzzle or come from other puzzles.

Further problems for boards in evaluating the evidence are:

◆ the temptation, referred in Chapter 8, for managers to sanitise information to make sure that information prepared for boards does not raise difficult questions. This could mean boards get false assurance; and

◆ managers' and executives' natural optimism which could mean boards receive a rosier view than justified by reality.

4.1 Internal audit

According to the Institute of Internal Auditors (IIA)[15] the role of internal audit is to 'provide independent assurance that an organisation's risk management, governance and internal control processes are operating effectively'. To be effective, internal audit must have qualified, skilled and experienced people who can work in accordance with the IIA Code of Ethics and their International Standards contained within their International Professional Practices Framework.

Internal audit in most organisations is not just about financial and related arrangements, they will also look at economy, efficiency and effectiveness of operations. Some of the larger public sector internal audit organisations employ a multidisciplinary team including accountants, specialists in IT and counter-fraud, nurses (in the NHS) as well as qualified internal auditors.

Large private sector organisations may employ few career auditors and instead rotate staff between internal audit and other management functions as a way to give staff wider experience. An internal auditor's primary skill is understanding systems, how they should work and actually work, and how one system may be related to another system. That skill can usefully be applied in many ways.

The UK Code in provision 25 specifies that one of the audit committee's responsibilities is 'monitoring and reviewing the effectiveness of the company's internal audit function or, where there is not one, considering annually whether there is a need for one and making a recommendation to the board'. Provision 26 provides that the annual report should describe the work of the audit committee, including 'where there is no internal audit function, an explanation for the absence, how internal assurance is achieved, and how this affects the work of external audit'.

Most public sector organisations are required to have an internal audit function.

The function may be provided by staff employed by the organisation or contracted out to a third party such as an accounting firm or to semi-autonomous specialist internal audit consortia or agencies which is common in the public sector. Sometimes an organisation will employ a chief internal auditor but the internal audit service is provided externally and sometimes an organisation will employ a small internal audit team which will buy in additional

---

15   Chartered Institute of Internal Auditors (2017) What is internal audit? www.iia.org.uk/about-us/what-is-internal-audit/

specialist services, such as IT audit, as required.

Normally both the head of internal audit and the external auditor attend audit committee meetings including meeting the audit committee members at least once a year without any executive management present. The internal auditor will normally report professionally to the chairman of the audit committee.

Internal audit, working with the audit committee, will prepare an internal audit plan for the year ahead, or some other period if appropriate, based on consideration of the key risks facing the organisation. That consideration will be informed by the internal auditor's own work, external audit work, and any other relevant work such as by the risk management, compliance and quality functions. It will also be informed by the work of any external regulators. The internal auditor and audit committee will aim to ensure all key risk areas are covered, aligned and coordinated, leaving no significant gaps and avoiding unnecessary duplication. The internal auditor can help the audit committee by acting as an overall evaluator of all the sources of assurance and evidence from them. In this way they can help the audit committee make sense of the jigsaw pieces and decide if all the pieces of the assurance jigsaw puzzle are in place and what picture they make.

The internal auditor will make regular reports to the audit committee which have normally been discussed beforehand with relevant management. These will include recommendations for improvement and any agreements on action to be taken. Progress on implementation will be monitored at least annually and the auditor will normally provide an annual report summarising their work, the recommendations, action taken and any matters which are outstanding. The reports will also include the internal auditor's opinions on the effectiveness of control which will be a primary source of assurance for the audit committee.

Test yourself 12.4

What sources of assurance on the effectiveness of risk management are available to the audit committee and the board? Which sources are likely to be of most use?

4.2 External audit

External audits are provided by firms of professional accountants such as the big four firms, Deloitte, EY, PwC and KPMG, which according to Statista[16] (an online statistics portal) employ around 900,000 people worldwide in 2017. Apart from audit all these firms provide a growing range of other professional services. The external auditor's primary role, as already discussed, is to express an opinion to shareholders on the financial statements and on limited other matters such as on part of the corporate governance disclosures and on disclosure of directors' pay. They are also required to state whether there are any disclosures in the

---

16   Statista (2016) Number of employees of the Big Four accounting / audit firms worldwide in 2016, www.statista.com/statistics/250503/big-four-accounting-firms-number-of-employees/

annual report which are inconsistent with their knowledge of the organisation gained from their other work. In doing this the external auditor will have to look at systems, carry out tests, review many documents and talk to people.

External auditors can never be 100% sure that all relevant information has been disclosed to them so, before signing an audit report, will require a management representation letter from management confirming inter alia:

- management acknowledging its responsibility for the system of financial controls and the financial statements;
- all financial records have been made available;
- board minutes are complete for all board meetings;
- all letters from regulatory agencies regarding non-compliance have been made available;
- there are no other transactions which should have been recorded in the accounts;
- all related party transactions, contingent liabilities and claims have been disclosed; and
- the net effect of all uncorrected misstatements is immaterial.

It is important that the external auditor is objective and the audit is of satisfactory quality. It is normally the audit committee's job to evaluate the objectiveness and independence of the external auditor and the quality of their work. The audit committee, on behalf of the board, will make recommendations to the board for the appointment of the auditor including negotiating the fee and scope of the audit, and for their eventual removal. Matters which can influence a view of their independence and objectivity would include how long the audit firm has had the audit contract, how long the audit partner has had the assignment, any relationships between the audit and management and whether the firm provides other non-audit services to their client.

Non-audit services are services provided by the external audit firm which are not actually part of the audit. These could potentially include tax compliance and consulting, consulting support on information technology, board evaluation and corporate finance. The Institute of Chartered Accountants of England and Wales identifies[17] three categories of non-audit service:

1. Services required by legislation or contract to be undertaken by the auditors of the business.
2. Services that it is most efficient for the auditors to provide because of their existing knowledge of the business, or because the information required is a by-product of the audit process. This could include assistance with tax compliance.
3. Services that could be provided by a number of firms where the fact that the firm is the auditor is incidental. Examples of such services include: management consultancy, tax advice and human resources consultancy.

---

17 Institute of Chartered Accountants in England and Wales The provision of non-audit services to audit clients, www. icaew.com/technical/ethics/auditor-independence/provision-of-non-audit-services-to-audit-clients

It is the last category which was considered highly contentious after the Enron scandal as it was felt that a firm's desire to sell more lucrative consulting services posed a conflict of interest which would cause an audit to be less objective or thorough than it should have been. It used to be common for the fees for non-audit services charged to large companies to exceed the audit fee.

The matter was addressed for UK listed companies by requiring audit committees to review auditor independence and objectivity, audit quality and have a policy on the provision of non-audit services as set out in Provision 25 of the UK Code and fuller guidance in the FRC Guidance on Audit Committees.[18]

Evaluating audit quality is actually very difficult for an audit committee. While there are procedures which an audit committee can satisfy itself are in place, ultimately it is not possible for an audit committee to be sure that the audit has been thorough.

In addition to an external auditor's report to shareholders (Chapter 7) the external auditor will also make a report to 'those charged with governance', which generally means the board. The format is highly regimented and for the UK is laid out in International Standard on Auditing (UK) 260, Communication With Those Charged With Governance. It was revised in June 2016[19]. The report will include:

◆ the auditor's responsibility in relation to the audit of the financial statements;

◆ the planned scope and timing of the audit;

◆ significant findings arising from the audit including for companies for which the Corporate Governance applies comments on:

   – significant risks,

   – accounting policies,

   – management valuations,

   – the robustness of the board's assessment of the principle risks,

   – the company's prospects, and

   – going concern; and

◆ a statement on auditor independence.

---

18   Financial Reporting Council (2016) Guidance on Audit Committees. www.frc.org.uk/getattachment/6b0ace1d-1d70-4678-9c41-0b44a62f0a0d/Guidance-on-Audit-Committees-April-2016.pdf

19   Financial Reporting Council (2017)International Standard on Auditing (UK) 260 Communication With Those Charged With Governance, www.frc.org.uk/getattachment/e5b17b63-d1c7-4fe6-9d9b-e75a318b5422/ISA-(UK)-260_Revised-June-2016_Updated-July-2017.pdf

Chapter summary

◆ The role of risk managers should be to facilitate the formal process of managing risk and provide professional guidance to operational managers.

◆ For many organisations, the main component of their risk management system is a risk register but the way in which they are compiled is problematic and their usefulness is questionable.

◆ The risk of doing something should be weighed against the expected benefit of doing it.

◆ Risks do not usually present themselves one by one; often several will combine to cause a bigger problem than anticipated.

◆ Not all identified risks can be quantified and not all risks are capable of being known.

◆ Scenario planning can help organisations be aware of risks which might otherwise have been missed and help people to ensure the organisation is more resilient to catastrophic risks which have not been identified.

◆ When identifying and assessing risk it is important that people involved feel comfortable that they can raise issues freely without any concerns about retribution.

◆ Internal controls range from low level controls such as two signatures to approve payments to the most important control which is the board itself.

◆ Surveys suggest wrongdoing is common in organisations.

◆ Corruption is estimated by the World Bank to equate to 5% of global GDP.

◆ Ways of preventing wrong doing include recruitment checks, a code of ethics, whistleblowing and ensuring the organisation does not unintentionally incentivise such behaviour.

◆ Boards need to assess the effectiveness of risk management and internal control.
   – to do so they need to be able to assure themselves;
   – this requires obtaining and assessing evidence from management, internal audit, external audit and other sources;
   – it is like piecing together a jigsaw puzzle.

◆ Internal audit should provide independent assurance that an organisation's risk management, governance and internal control processes are operating effectively.

◆ In addition to reporting to shareholders external audit will prepare a report to 'those charged with governance' on the results of the audit and findings made.

Test yourself answers

Chapter 1

Test yourself 1.1

What do the definitions of corporate governance and views on its purpose have in common? Do you see any contradictions?
The BSI definition of governance is very similar to the original Cadbury definition and adds 'accountability'. The Cadbury Report makes it very clear that 'accountability' is important to good governance so the two definitions are consistent in this respect. The BSI definition also adds 'core purpose over the long term'. The Cadbury Report does not discuss the purpose of corporations or time horizons but does make it clear that part of the board's governance role is setting strategic aims. The G20/OECD Principles do not address the purpose of corporations but do refer to objectives and emphasise relationships, including with other stakeholders, whereas the Cadbury Report is concerned with relations within the board and with shareholders. King IV does not contradict the other definitions but has a very different emphasis on ethics and legitimacy.

The current UK Code's statement on the purpose of corporate governance is consistent with the Cadbury, BSI and G20/OECD definitions of governance but largely misses King's concern with ethics and legitimacy. The purpose given in the Finnish Code seems overly concerned with procedure to miss the key benefits of good governance.

Test yourself 1.2

What would you include in a board governance index?
The researchers included the following factors in their board governance index:

◆ separate chairman and chief executive;

◆ majority of independent NEDs;

◆ presence of deputy chair and/or senior NED;

◆ presence of remuneration committee;

◆ independent NED chairing remuneration committee;

◆ remuneration committee composed entirely of independent NEDs;

◆ presence of audit committee;

◆   independent NED chairing audit committee;

◆   at least half of audit committee members are independent;

◆   presence of nomination committee;

◆   NED or board chair is chairing nomination committee; and

◆   majority of nomination committee members are NEDs.

These are all derived from the UK Code of Corporate Governance. Is there anything you would add?

Test yourself 1.3

How would you evaluate corporate governance in an organisation?
The starting point would be to consider the organisation's governance practice with the prescribed governance code (if there is one) e.g. the UK Code of Corporate Governance if the organisation is a listed company with a primary listing on the UK Stock Exchange. If there is no prescribed code consider the relevance of leading codes. King IV™ is intended to be applicable to any organisation and most of the main and supporting principles in the UK Code are relevant to most organisations. It is not sufficient to consider only stated compliance with code provisions; it is important to consider how well an organisation has applied the principles based on what the organisation says it has done and taking into account anything else you know or should know about the organisation. Harder to evaluate is the quality of leadership and the oversight by the board. Information can come from public documents issued by the organisation, media news and personal interaction with the organisation. Such information may reveal inconsistencies, suggesting the picture presented by an organisation may not fit reality. Obviously it is important to be suitably sceptical about the reliability of information.

Chapter 2

Test yourself 2.1

What is a business model?
There are many definitions and some controversy but in essence a business model is a description or representation of how a business makes its money and/or creates value.

Test yourself 2.2

1.   *When was the requirement to have independent NEDs make up at least 50% of the board introduced?*

2003

2.   *When was the Stewardship Code introduced?*
2010

3.   *When was a requirement for companies to disclose their*

business model introduced?

2010

4.   *When was a provision requiring disclosure of the board's policy on diversity introduced?*

2012

Test yourself 2.3

What is the Senior Managers' Regime?

The Senior Managers' Regime potentially makes individual directors and executives performing 'senior management functions' personally responsible for matters under their control. The FCA and PRA list functional responsibilities of institutions which must be allocated to named individual managers. Financial institutions must list key activities, business areas and functions and allocate responsibility for them to one or more senior manager. The senior managers concerned will be accountable and will be required to take reasonable steps to prevent regulatory breach in their area.

Test yourself 2.4

How is governance enforced in NHS foundation trusts?

Foundation trust boards theoretically report to a council of governors appointed by its members who are patients and members of the public who volunteer for the role. They were accountable to NHS Monitor and now to NHS Improvement.

Chapter 3

Test yourself 3.1

Where can you find a resource giving access to most of the world's corporate governance codes?

A list of most of the codes around the world can be found on the European Corporate Governance Institute website: www.ecgi.org/codes.

Test yourself 3.2

Who is the intended audience of the G20/OECD Principles of corporate governance?

The Principles are written for national policy makers rather than individual companies.

Test yourself 3.3

How can corporate governance be enforced?

In the UK and other countries with widely held shares and engaged investors the corporate governance system largely relies on institutional shareholders to apply pressure on companies. In many countries there are not such active investors and one approach is for external auditors to be asked to assess compliance with a code. Another approach is to include governance requirements in law or regulation and introduce a formal system of supervision or enforcement.

Test yourself 3.4

Most countries have a corporate governance code and many have several. Does the US have a corporate governance code?
The United States has a number of corporate governance codes but unlike most countries no single code which applies to listed companies.

Chapter 4

Test yourself 4.1

What is the estimate of fines in 2016 for banks involved in foreign exchange manipulation, Libor-rigging and mis-selling?
£53 billion in the UK and £190 billion worldwide.

Test yourself 4.2

Why is short-termism a problem?
Short-termism is a problem because it leads companies to focus on short-term financial performance which may lead to poorer long-term performance and failure to consider properly factors which are important to the longer term such as relationships with staff, suppliers and customers.

Test yourself 4.3

Why is there an ambiguity around s. 172 of the Companies Act?
The ambiguity is whether the interest of the company or the interests of shareholders is preeminent.

Test yourself 4.4

What are the three main ethical theories?
Utilitarianism or consequentialism, duty and virtue.

Test yourself 4.5

Who argued that the social responsibility of business is to increase its profits?
Milton Friedman.

Chapter 5

Test yourself 5.1

Does the UK Companies Act 2006 set out the role of the board?
No, it sets out the role of directors but makes no mention of boards.

Test yourself 5.2

Why have a balanced board?
So that the board has a range of complementary, skills, knowledge, experience and perspectives to provide effective leadership and oversight of the organisation. It should also ensure that no individual or group can dominate board-decision taking.

Test yourself 5.3

How should a board determine whether a NED is independent?
This is covered in the UK Code Provision 10. It is up to the board, with the advice of the nomination committee, to decide but in making its judgement it should consider if the director:

◆ has been an employee within the last five years;

◆ has or has had a material business relationship with the company;

◆ has remuneration from the company apart from a director's fee;

◆ has close family ties with any of the company's advisers, directors or senior employees;

◆ holds cross-directorships or has significant links with other directors;

◆ represents a significant shareholder; or

◆ has served on the board for more than nine years from the date of their first election.

Chapter 6

Test yourself 6.1

In what circumstances may a shareholder not be allowed to ask questions in a general meeting?
Shareholders normally have a right to ask questions and receive an answer unless it would:

◆ interfere unduly with the preparation for the meeting, or involve the disclosure of confidential information; or

◆ if the answer has already been given on a website in the form of an answer to a question; or

◆ it is undesirable in the interests of the company or the good order of the meeting (s. 319A CA2006).

Test yourself 6.2

Summarise the rights of shareholders.
These are set out in a company's articles of association and in company law. Shareholders have the following rights:

◆ A reserve power to direct the directors to take or refrain from a particular action.

◆ To call a general meeting.

◆ To propose a resolution to be voted on at a general meeting.

◆ To vote at a general meeting.

◆ To appoint a director and remove a director.

◆ To appoint a proxy to vote on the shareholder's behalf.

Test yourself 6.3

Summarise the responsibility of shareholders

Shareholders do not have any obligations under the Companies Acts other than to pay in full for their shares. Institutional shareholders have a fiduciary responsibility exercise their voting rights and have an obligation to appoint the directors and the auditors and satisfy themselves that the company is well governed and take steps to improve governance where needed. The UK Stewardship Code includes seven principles for shareholders. They should:

◆ publicly disclose their policy on how they will discharge their stewardship responsibilities;

◆ have a robust policy on managing conflicts of interest in relation to stewardship which should be publicly disclosed;

◆ monitor their investee companies;

◆ establish clear guidelines on when and how they will escalate their stewardship activities;

◆ be willing to act collectively with other investors where appropriate;

◆ have a clear policy on voting and disclosure of voting activity; and

◆ report periodically on their stewardship and voting activities.

Many would say that institutional shareholders also have a responsibility to ensure that companies are responsible with regard to society and the environment.

Test yourself 6.4

Who are institutional investors?

Institutional investors include:

◆ occupational pension funds;

◆ insurance companies;

◆ pooled investment vehicles such as unit trusts, open-ended investment companies (OEICS);

◆ investment trusts; and

◆ other financial institutions such as charities, endowments and educational institutions.

Hedge funds and investment banks may also be regarded as institutional investors.

Chapter 7

Test yourself 7.1

For what type of company was the audit requirement first introduced in company law?
Joint-stock companies. The requirement for limited companies was introduced in 1900.

Test yourself 7.2

What is required by the Companies Act 2006 Part 15 Accounts for the contents of a company's annual report?
The requirement is for a:

◆ balance sheet as at the last day of the financial year which must give a true and fair view of the state of affairs of the company as at the end of the financial year;

◆ profit and loss account which must give a true and fair view of the profit or loss of the company for the financial year;

◆ strategic report (ss. 414A to D not required for smaller companies);

◆ directors' report (ss. 415 to 419A not required for smaller companies);

◆ directors' remuneration report including report on remuneration policy (ss. 420 to 422A required only for quoted companies);

◆ governance statement (s. 419A required for companies with a primary London Stock Market listing).

Part 16 requires:

◆ an auditor's report on the financial statements, the strategic report, directors' report and parts of the remuneration report and governance statement (ss. 495 to 497A).

Chapter 8

Test yourself 8.1

What are the two most important board policy documents?
A schedule of matters and powers reserved to the board and a scheme of delegation from the board to its committees and executives.

Test yourself 8.2

What is an appropriate notice period for calling a board meeting?
Nothing is prescribed by company law. Seven days' notice should be sufficient.

Chapter 9

Test yourself 9.1

Which legislation removed the requirement for private companies to have a company secretary?
Companies Act 2006 (s. 270).

Test yourself 9.2

Which documents must be files at Companies House?
Information to be filed at Companies House includes:

- the company's financial statements once approved;
- an annual confirmation statement (this replaced the Annual Return in 2016);
- certain company resolutions (passed by the members);
- changes in directors or the secretary;
- changes in share capital or the rights of shares;
- changes to the articles of association or a new memorandum and articles; and
- change of company name or registered address; and changes in mortgages or charges.

Test yourself 9.3

Who introduced the requirement for UK listed companies to have a board effectiveness evaluation?
Sir Derek Higgs in 2003 in his Review of the Role and Effectiveness of Non-Executive Directors.

Test yourself 9.4

List two of the examples of dysfunctional group dynamics and culture in the study of board evaluation of 187 North American public and private companies by Rock Center for Corporate Governance at Stanford University and The Miles Group.
The study highlighted six examples:

- 46% believed that a subset of directors has an outsized influence on board decisions.
- 74% said directors allow personal or past experience to dominate their perspective.
- 53% did not express their honest opinions in the presence of management.
- 47% said directors are too quick to come to consensus.
- 44% said directors do not understand the boundary between oversight and actively trying to manage the company.
- 39% said fellow board members derail the conversation by introducing issues that are off-topic.

Chapter 10

Test yourself 10.1

How would you define internal control?

There is no single universally agreed definition. Views differ from a broad 'it is the means by which an organisation achieves its objectives' through to the COSO definition 'internal control is a process effected by an entity's board of directors, management, and other personnel, designed to provide reasonable assurance regarding the achievement of objectives relating to operations, reporting, and compliance' through to the meaning given by Sox which looks at control only over financial reporting.

Test yourself 10.2

How would you evaluate different risks?

There is no single right way but most risk managers start by evaluating them in terms of their likelihood and impact. Such an approach on its own, however, is too simplistic. The possibility of several risks happening at the same time should also be considered together the quality of information which led to the evaluation of likelihood and impact.

Test yourself 10.3

Can you list the reporting requirements on risk-related issues?

The reporting requirements are:

◆ A fair review of the principal risks and uncertainties facing the company and how they are managed or mitigated (required by the Companies Act 2006 and the Code).

◆ Confirm that it has carried out a robust assessment of the principal risks and that the board should describe those risks (required by the Code).

◆ Whether the directors have a reasonable expectation that the company will be able to continue in operation and meet its liabilities as they fall due (required by the Code).

◆ Whether the going concern basis of accounting can be used (required by accounting standards and the Code).

◆ Review of the risk management and internal control system (required by the Code), as a minimum, the board should acknowledge that it is responsible for those systems and for reviewing their effectiveness and disclose:

◆ that there is an ongoing process for identifying, evaluating and managing the principal risks faced by the company;

◆ that the systems have been in place for the year under review and up to the date of approval of the annual report and accounts;

◆ that they are regularly reviewed by the board; and

◆ the extent to which the systems accord with the guidance in this document the main features of the company's risk management and internal control system in relation to the financial reporting process (required under the UK Listing Authority's Disclosure and Transparency Rules).

Chapter 11

Test yourself 11.1

Which categories of risk are used by the COSO Enterprise Risk Management Integrated Framework 2004?
The COSO uses four high level categories: strategic, operations, reporting and compliance.

Test yourself 11.2

What types of risk are likely to be of most concern to boards?
Risks relating to strategy which could either affect the achievement of strategy or mean the strategy is flawed. The other risks which should most interest the board are those which could threaten the organisation's survival. These could be termed business continuity risks or business model risks. The other risk which will concern boards is reputational risk but a reputational risk will always be a consequence of another risk occurring.

Test yourself 11.3

How is risk viewed differently by banks and insurance companies compared with most other types of organisation?
The business model for banks and insurance companies is taking and successfully exploiting risk. For most other types of organisation the business model is about making a product and or providing a service which involves being exposed to and taking risk. Risk is a necessary consequence of doing business which organisations need to avoid, manage or transfer.

Chapter 12

Test yourself 12.1

Before taking or accepting a risk, what should you consider?
Whether the expected gain is worth the expected cost if the risk happens or if the expected gains are worth the expected costs if things go wrong. This is a good general rule although it may not be suitable for every occasion. Sometimes an organisation may have no choice but to take a risk but in such a case the expected gain could be the survival or the organisation. Judgements should of course be by reference to the gains and risks for the organisation and not the individuals involved.

Test yourself 12.2

In the ACCA survey about culture and ethics it would seem that respondents did not equate 'informing people about what is ethical behaviour' with a code of ethics. Why might this be?
We do not know for sure but it is likely that people felt something was missing from the code of ethics. It may be that people associated a code of ethics or conduct with a set of rules and required conduct of shoulds and should-nots whereas they would have appreciated more philosophical guidance on deciding what is ethical and empowerment to make their own decisions.

Test yourself 12.3

What is another name for whistleblowing?
Speaking up.

Test yourself 12.4

What sources of assurance on the effectiveness of risk management are available to the audit committee and the board? Which sources are likely to be most useful?
The main sources of assurance are management, internal audit and external audit. Other sources include the compliance, risk management, HR, quality teams and third party professionals. External audit and internal audit should provide independent and objective assurance which should therefore be the most reliable. In addition, internal audit may help boards to piece together and make sense of the different sources of assurance so the audit committee or board can make a decision on whether risk management is effective.

Glossary

Accountability – The quality or state of being accountable meaning an obligation or willingness to accept responsibility and to give account for actions and omissions.

Accountable Officer – A term used in the public sector for the head of an organisation accountable to the next higher level in the bureaucracy and ultimately to a Secretary of State and then Parliament. Under the Public Finance and Accountability (Scotland) Act 2000 accountable officers have a personal responsibility for the propriety and regularity of the public finances for the body for which they are answerable and ensuring that the resources of the body are used economically, efficiently and effectively.

Accounts – See financial statements. The term accounts may also be used for financial statements used within an organisation for management and control purposes.

Board – The governing body of a company and many other organisations whose members are directors.

BS (British Standards) 31100 Risk Management – The British Standards Institute was established in 1901 and has 76 offices worldwide and over 36,000 current British standards including BS31100 on risk management.

Business model – A description or representation of how a business makes its money and/or creates value.

Cadbury Committee – The Committee on the Financial Aspects of Corporate Governance.

Cadbury Report – The 1992 Report of The Committee on the Financial Aspects of Corporate Governance.

Combined Code – The 1998 predecessor of the UK Corporate Governance Code issued by the FRC.

Chief executive The most senior executive or manager in an organisation and usually a executive director. S/he will normally have delegated authority from the board for running the organisation.

Code – Guidance, principles and provisions which are not legally binding but which nevertheless have recognition and some authority setting out how e.g. corporate governance should be practised.

Companies Act 2006 – An Act of Parliament which consolidated and updated previous companies acts. It is the primary source of company law in the UK and the longest piece of legislation in the history of Parliament.

Company law – The set of laws that control how businesses are formed, controlled and wound up.

Corporate and social responsibility – There are various definitions which include the concept of a company as a corporate citizen fulfilling its obligations to society and the environment, the efforts of a company that go beyond what is required in law to preserve the environment and be a good employer, supplier and customer and a company being ethical particularly as far as employees, society and the environment is involved.

Corporate culture – A combination of the values, attitudes and behaviours manifested by a company in its operations and relations with its stakeholders (FRC definition).

Corporate governance – One authoritative definition is 'the system by which organisations are directed and controlled'.

Director – A formally appointed member of a board.

Disclosure and Transparency Rules – These are rules of the Financial Conduct Authority (FCA) to implement the EU Transparency Directive and to make other rules to ensure there is adequate transparency of and access to information in the UK financial markets. The Rules apply to companies whose shares have a Premium Listing on the London Stock Exchange.

Ethics – Moral principles that govern a person's or an organisation's behaviour or conduct.

European Bank for Reconstruction and Development – Established to help build market-oriented economies and promote private and entrepreneurial initiative in Central and Eastern Europe in 1991. It has since expanded and is owned by 66 countries from five continents, as well as the European Union and the European Investment Bank.

European Corporate Governance Institute (ECGI) – A European based international scientific non-profit association that provides a forum for debate and dialogue between academics, legislators and practitioners, focusing on major corporate governance issues and best practice. Its primary role is to undertake, commission and disseminate leading research on corporate governance.

Executive – A senior manager with delegated authority and accountability for one or more functions who may also be a director.

Financial statements – A financial report by an organisation prepared for an external audience complying with applicable law and standards setting out its financial position at a particular date, its income and expenditure and movements of funds for a particular period.

Fiduciary duty – Where one person or group is in a position of trust and has a legal or ethical obligation to act for the benefit or best interests of another person or group.

General purpose financial reports – A financial report intended to meet the information needs common to users who are unable to command the preparation of reports tailored so as to satisfy, specifically, all of their information needs.

Going concern – The accounting basis used for all organisations expecting to remain in business. The alternative basis is to value assets at what price they could fetch if the organisation was being broken up. In the general sense it means an organisation is viable, is able to meet its financial obligations and will remain in business over the medium to long term.

Groupthink – Occurs when a group of people with a desire for harmony or conformity in the group does not question or challenge leading to dysfunctional decision making.

Institutional shareholders (or investors) – A collective term for pension funds, insurance companies, unit trusts and other owners or managers of shares.

Internal control – Internal control is a process effected by an entity's board of directors, management, and other personnel, designed to provide reasonable assurance regarding the achievement of objectives relating to operations, reporting, and compliance (COSO) or simply the means by which an organisation achieves its objectives.

International Finance Corporation (IFC) – A member of the World Bank Group, the IFC is the largest global development institution focused on the private sector in developing countries. It assists in areas such as finance, infrastructure, employee skills, and regulatory environment.

ISO (International Standards Organisation) 31000 Risk Management Principles and guidelines – ISO is an independent, non-governmental international organisation based in Switzerland whose members are the 162 national standards bodies. ISO has published over 21,000 standards including 31,000 on risk management.

Listed companies – Companies listed on a recognised stock exchange.

Listing Rules – These are the obligations issued by the FCA that companies with a listing on the London Stock Exchange have to meet and are based on the minimum EU directive standards.

Management – The planning, execution and monitoring of the activities of an organisation in order to achieve objectives.

Materiality – In an audit context materiality refers to misstatements, including omissions, that are considered to be material if they, individually or in the aggregate, could reasonably be expected to influence the economic decisions of users taken on the basis of the financial statements (ISA 320).

Non-governmental organisation – A non-profit voluntary citizens' group organised on a local, national or international level, usually active in furthering a social or environmental purpose.

Organisations – Companies, public sector bodies, charities with a separate legal status having a group of people working in it and a hierarchy of control.

Organisation for Economic Co-operation and Development (OECD) – The OECD is an international organisation based in Paris with 35 member countries. OECD helps governments foster prosperity and fight poverty through economic growth and financial stability. It also helps to ensure governments take into account environmental implications of economic and social development.

Premium listing – The Listing Rules allow for three types of listing on the London stock Exchange Main Market: Premium, Standard and High Growth Segment. The rules for a Standard listing comply with EU requirements. The rules for a Premium listing are higher than required by the EU. Most UK companies with a listing have a Premium listing for their ordinary shares. The UK Code of Corporate Governance applies to these companies.

Principles – The fundamental and foundational high level elements of a code or other guidance.

Provisions – More prescriptive elements of a code, other guidance, law or regulation requiring adherence.

Prudence – The prudence concept, as the term implies is about making prudent judgements about assets, liabilities, income and expenditure. So, for example, under the prudence concept, income is not recognised until it has been earned and will be paid for, profits are only recognised when they have been realised and provision is made for all anticipated future expenses and losses.

Regulation – A rule or directive made and maintained by the government or other authority.

Risk – The 'effect of uncertainty on objectives' or something which might happen which would have a dangerous, unpleasant or costly outcome or doing, or exposing someone to, something which might have a dangerous, unpleasant or costly outcome.

Risk appetite – The level of risk the board of an organisation is willing to take or 'the aggregate level and types of risk a financial institution is willing to take'.

Risk management – Coordinated activities to direct and control an organization with regard to risk or simply managing risks.

Risk tolerance – Organization's or stakeholder's readiness to bear the risk after risk treatment in order to achieve its objectives.

ROA, ROE and ROIC – Financial performance ratios – return on assets, return on equity and return on invested capital.

Sarbanes-Oxley Act 2002 (Sox) – An Act passed by US Congress to protect investors from fraudulent accounting by companies, improve disclosure and controls, including accountability over corporate reporting. It was a response to accounting scandals such as at Enron, WorldCom and Tyco.

Shareholders – Real and legal persons who are holders of shares in a company, and generally whose names would appear on the company share register.

Standard distribution – A statistical term used to measure or describe the variation or dispersion above and below the mean (average) in a set of data. 68.2% of a random population will fall within one standard distribution of the mean, 95.4% will fall within two standard deviations and 99.6% will fall within three standard deviations.

Stewardship – Acting as a good steward looking after another person's, group of people's or an organisation's assets.

Sustainable value – Value which is created which is sustainable, and unlikely to be eroded, over many years.

True and fair – This is a simple term which broadly means a set of financial statements are reasonably accurate, balanced and not misleading. There is no statutory definition however and pages of legal opinion have been given on what is an extremely complex subject.

Turnbull Report 1999 – Guidance issued by the Institute of Chartered Accountants in England and Wales on internal control and risk management.

Value – In a governance context something which is created or lost by organisations which is important or beneficial, not necessarily only in a monetary context but including social and environmental value.

Values – A person, team or organisation's judgement of what is important in work and/or in life.

Whistleblowing – Where a person who raises a concern about a wrongdoing in their workplace. Also called 'speak up'.

Zero hours contract – A contract between an employer and a worker where the employer is not obliged to provide any minimum working hours and the worker is not obliged to accept any work offered.

Index

A

Accountability   11
  nature of   4
Accounting origins   117
Accounting records   120–121
Accounts
  meaning   31
  purpose   118–120
Agency theory   20
AIM Rules   43
Annual report   122–128
  challenges when
    producing   129
  contents   122–128
  financial statements   123–124
  strategic report   –125
Audit   121
Audit committees   93
  risk management, and
    180–181
Audit report   126–127

B

Barclays
  Serious Fraud Office
    investigations   59
Behaviour   67–71
BHS   58
Board   83–99
balance   86–87
  composition   86–92
  corporate governance codes,
    and   84–86
  meaning   3
  role of   83–86
  size   86–87
  structure   –92
  worker representation on
    63–64
Board committees   92–93

Board diversity   65–67
  2018 Code   67
  Davies review   66
  FRC Guidance   67
  Hampton-Alexander
    review   66
  Parker review   66
Boardroom effectiveness
  49–164
  asking good questions   158
  conflicts of interest   162–163
  dominant CEO or chair   160
  problem areas   159–163
  evaluation   153–159
  group dynamics issues   160
  HBOS   155–156
  Higgs Report   154
  illegal or unethical conduct
    161–162
  knowing what is going on
    160–161
  maintaining independence and
    objectivity   161
  methods of evaluation
    158–159
  personality issues   160
  US statistics 2016   156–157
  Wells Fargo   162
Boards as source of risk   194–197
  Boeing   196
  BP   196–197
  failure to hold executives to
    account   195
  flawed business model and/or
    strategy   195–196
  flawed monitoring   196
  Lift Off   195
  not asking questions   195
  poor tone at the top   197

  risk blindness   194
  turning problem into
    crisis   195
BS 31100 Risk Management   168
Business model   31

C

Cadbury
  committee   4
  report   4, 26–27
  shares   114
Calling meetings   144
Chair
  role   88
  separation of role from Chief
    Executive   87–88
Charities   39–40
Chief Executive
  role   88–89
  separation of role from Chair
    87–88
Codes   15–19
Codes of ethics   70
Combined Code   28
Combined Code 2003   29
Companies Act 2006   7
Companies (Miscellaneous
  Reporting) Regulations
  2018   42–43
Company law   8–11
Company secretary   149–152
  code requirement   149–150
  legal requirement   149–150
  responsibilities   150–152
  role   150–152
Concepts of value   74–75
Consequentialism   69–70
Corporate governance
  consequences of failure   13

corporate performance, and 13–14
definitions 3–5
evolving regulatory background 7–11
importance to global economy 13
issues 58–67
management distinguished 6
meaning 3
origins 3
regulatory responses 6–7
scandals 6–7
Corporate governance development for UK listed companies 24–34
Corporate governance theories 20–22
Corporate reporting 117–130
accounting records 120–121
audit 121
origins 117
purpose 118–120
requirements 120–122
team effort 128–129
Corporate social responsibility 75–80
EU Directives 77
reporting initiatives 77–78
Corruption 213–215
definition 213
legal and ethical matrix 213
practices to avoid 214–215
principles for good practice 213–214
Culture 67–71

D
Deontology 70
different, roles of 86–92
liability 84
meaning 6
responsibility 83–84
Directors' and officers' insurance 143
Directors' duties 61–62
Directors' remuneration 94–99
2018 Code 98
consultants 95
legislation 96
make-up 94
performance-related 95

policy 97
UK government response 97
UK legislative and Code requirements 96–99
Directors' remuneration report 126
Directors' report 125
Disclosure and transparency rules 8
Dodd-Frank Act 51, 56

E
Enlightened shareholder theory 21–22
Enron 52–55
Ethics 11–12, 67–71
consequentialism 69–70
deontology 70
Kantian 70
theories in practice 70–71
understanding 69–70
utilitarianism 69–70
virtue 69
Eumedion 48
European approach 47–49
European Bank for Reconstruction and Development CGF 49
European Corporate Governance Institute 45
Evaluating governance 22
Executive 6
Executive pay 64–65
LTIPS 65
disclosure 64–65
External audit
risk management, and 219–221

F
Fiduciary duty 21
Financial Conduct Authority 35
Financial crisis 2008 189–194
duty to society and stakeholders 193–194
flawed paradigms 191–192
incentivising wrong thing 192–193
Insufficient regard for risk and compliance functions 193
learning from 189–194
Walker Review, and 30

Financial sector regulation 35
Financial statements 123–124
meaning 3
Finnish Code of Corporate Governance 5
Flawed paradigms 191–192
FRC (Financial Reporting Council)
Corporate culture and the role of boards 68
Friedman, Milton business, on 71–72

G
General meeting 101–102
General purpose financial report 119
Glossary 234–237
Going concern 32, 169
Good governance
difficulties of recognising 14–15
Good meeting practice 133–148
board charter 141–142
board policies 141
clear aim 134
company law requirements 139
constructive challenge, need for 135–138
Co-operative Bank 136
directors' and officers' insurance 143
effective time management 134–135
financial crisis, and 135
good chairing 134
good practice matters 140
groupthink 137
ICSA Guidance note 140
key documents to be made available 138–143
new directors 135
policy governance 142–143
powers reserved to board 138–139
scheme of delegation 140–141
Silent Sloan 137
specific matters to be dealt with 139–140

Governance statement 126
Greed 58–59
Greenbury Report
    executive pay, and 27–28
Groupthink 137

H
Hampel Report 28
Hedge funds 106
Higgs Report 28–29
High-level Expert Group on
    Sustainable Finance 76

I
Inappropriate investor pressure
    111–112
Institutional investors 106
Integrated reporting 78–80
    value creation process 79
Internal audit
    risk management, and
    218–219
Internal control 169–170
International Finance
    Corporation 45
International Integrated Reporting
    Framework 78
Investment banks 106
Investor apathy 111
ISO 31000 168

J
Johnson & Johnson
    credo 72–73

K
Kantian ethics 70

L
Listing Rules 7, 173
LTIPS 6

M
Malpractice 209–212
    code of conduct 211–212
    code of ethics 211–212
    hiring procedures 211
    observed 209–210
    policies to prevent 211–212
    practices to prevent 211–212
    pre-employment checks 211
    procedures to prevent
    211–212

results of ACCA research 212
    statistics 209, 210–211
Management 6
Mason, Kenneth
    business, on 72
Materiality 127
Mauritian approach 50–51
McKinsey survey 16
Minute taking 147–148
Misconduct 58–59

N
Nomination committee 92–93
National Health Service 36–39
    bodies 37–38
    governance 36–39
    systemic failures 37
Netherlands
    corporate governance 48
NHS England 38
NHS foundational trusts 37–38
Nolan Principles 36–37
Non-executive director
    role 90–92
Non-governmental
    organisation 75
Not-for-profit sector 39–40

O
OECD 46
    principles of corporate
    governance 46

P
Panasonic company missions
    73–74
Parmalat 47
Policy governance 142–143
Premium living 8
Principle-based code 19
Principles 15–19
Principles for Responsible
    Investment 76
Provisions 15–19
Prudence 119
Purpose of commercial
    organisation 71–74

Q
Quakers 72

R
Regulation 7
Remuneration Committee 65
Reporting on corporate and social
    responsibility 127–128
Risk 167–183
    2018 Code 174–175
    board oversight in other
        organisations 181–182
    board oversight of risk outside
        UK 182–183
    boards as source 194–197
    BOFIs, and 189
    business continuity 187
    categories 184–188
    cause or effect 188–189
    COSO Enterprise Risk
        Management Integrated
        Framework 185
    cultural 188
    Eastman Kodak 186
    internal control 169–170
    Lehman 172
    LTCM 192
    Marconi 174–175
    meaning 168
    normal distribution curve 190
    people 188
    PESTLE factors 186
    reputational 188
    role of board in relation
        to 173–183
    sources 184–198
    strategic 187
    Swiss watch industry 187
    UBS 192
    UK Governance Code
        requirements 173–175
Risk appetite 171–172
    meaning 30
Risk assessment 169, 170–171
Risk evaluation 171
Risk management 170–171
    agreeing how principal risks
        should be managed or
        mitigated 177–178
    annual report, and 178–179
    assurance on 217–221
    audit committees 180–181
    board control 207
    Carillion 182

compliance controls   208
conventional approaches
   199–206
design of systems   176–177
determining principal risks
   faced   117
earthquakes   202
elements   170, 199
ensuring appropriate culture
   and reward systems   177
ensuring sound internal and
   external information and
   communication processes
   178–180
external audit   219–221
management representation
   letter   220
report   221
financial controls   208
FRC Guidance   175–176
HBOS   179–180
Iceland volcano   203
identification   200
implementation of systems
   176–177
internal audit   218–219
plan   219
report   219
internal control   207–209
lower level financial controls
   209
malpractice   209–212
meaning   170
monitoring systems   178
operational controls   208
practical issues   199–222
prediction   201, 202
reviewing systems   178
risks which organisation is
   willing to take   177
role of board   217–221
Ryanair   206
scenario planning   205
skills CFA   181
strategic risk   208
Three Lines of Defence
   model   206–207
Turnbull Report   175–176
workshop approach   204–205
Risk models   190–191
Risk tolerance   172

ROA   14
ROE   14
ROIC   14
Role of business in society   71–74
Royal Bank of Scotland   17
Running meetings   144–148
   agenda   144–145
   agenda planning   144–145
   board and sub-committee
      papers   145–146
   decision making   147
   governing not
      micromanaging   146
   minute taking   147–148
   quorum   145

S
Sarbanes-Oxley Act 2002   55–56
Senior non-executive director
   role   92
Shareholder responsibilities
   103–105
   Stewardship Code   104–105,
      107
Shareholder rights   102–103
Shareholders   100–116
   chain linking savers and
      pension scheme members
      with companies   108
   complex investor chain
      105–109
   complexity   113
   conflicts   112–113
   engaging with   100–192
   general meeting   101–102
   lack of accountability
      113–115
   lack of transparency   113
   meaning   3
   misalignment of interest
      112–113
   problem areas   109–115
   short-termism   110–111
Short-termism   60
   shareholders, and   110–111
Smaller companies   40–43
South Africa
   King IV Code   18, 50
South African approach   50
South Sea Bubble   25
Sports Direct   60–61
Stakeholder theory   21

Stakeholders   62–63
Standard distribution
   meaning   190
Stewardship   104
Stewardship theory   21
Strategic report   124–125
Sustainability   75–80
Sustainable value   6
Stewardship Code   104–105, 107

T
Test yourself answers   223–233
Three Lines of Defence
   model   206–207
Turnbull Report 1999   173

U
Uber   63
UK Corporate Governance Code 3
   recent developments   31–34
Unlisted companies   40–43
Unsuitable employment practices
   60–61
US approach   51–56
Utilitarianism   69–70

V
Value creation   71–75
   reporting on   75
Values   11–12, 67–71
Virtue ethics   69

W
Walker Review
   financial crisis, and   30
Welch, Jack
   profit, on   72
Whistleblowing   215–217
   career, and   215
   meaning   215
   qualifying disclosures   215
   stigma, as   216
Winter report   47
Worker representation   63–64